ROD STEWART

THE CLASSIC YEARS

SEAN EGAN

Backbeat
Books

Essex, Connecticut

An imprint of Globe Pequot, the trade division of
The Rowman & Littlefield Publishing Group, Inc.
4501 Forbes Blvd., Ste. 200
Lanham, MD 20706
www.rowman.com

Distributed by NATIONAL BOOK NETWORK

British Library Cataloguing in Publication Information available

Library of Congress Cataloging-in-Publication Data

Names: Egan, Sean, author.
Title: Rod Stewart : the classic years / Sean Egan.
Description: Essex, Connecticut : Backbeat Books, 2023. | Includes
  bibliographical references and index.
Identifiers: LCCN 2022054638 (print) | LCCN 2022054639 (ebook) | ISBN
  9781493068227 (cloth) | ISBN 9781493073481 (epub)
Subjects: LCSH: Stewart, Rod—Criticism and interpretation. | Rock music—
  1971–1980—History and criticism. | Rock music—1961–1970—History and
  criticism. | Faces (Musical group)
Classification: LCC ML420.S843 E53 2023 (print) | LCC ML420.S843 (ebook)
  | DDC 782.42166092—dc23/eng/20221109
LC record available at https://lccn.loc.gov/2022054638
LC ebook record available at https://lccn.loc.gov/2022054639

♾️™ The paper used in this publication meets the minimum requirements of American National Standard for Information Sciences—Permanence of Paper for Printed
Library Materials, ANSI/NISO Z39.48-1992

CONTENTS

INTRODUCTION

THE 1970S BELONGED TO ROD STEWART.

For the North London singer with the distinctive haystack haircut, and even more distinctive gravelly voice, the period in and around that decade was key in setting out the parameters of his abilities and establishing a market for them. His image during this time covered the gamut from working-class hero to jet-setting superstar. His musical output was of similar breadth.

The solo albums he made for the Mercury label between 1969 and 1974 were critically acclaimed, a unique synthesis of folk, blues, soul and rock underpinned by a winning proletarian humanitarianism. They include the 1971 album *Every Picture Tells a Story*, which some critics assert is literally the best album ever made by any artist. Said timeframe also saw Stewart front the group the Faces. Their records were likeable more often than they were classic, but this mattered little set against the fact that they were one of the most exciting live attractions in the world, their gigs imbued with an unmatched matey bonhomie. Journalist Paul Nelson said of Rod during this period, 'Stewart was considered the Bruce Springsteen of his time: our least-affected, most down-to-earth rock star'.

As his success increased, and as he graduated to working with new musicians, Stewart's music took on a different tone. That Nelson description certainly couldn't apply to Rod from 1975 onwards, when he, in rapid succession, switched to the bigger Warner Bros. label, became a tax exile, took up with exotic actress Britt Ekland, adopted makeup and began employing a bottom-wiggling stage schtick many found utterly mortifying. He also hired a backing band that exhibited virtuosity and flash more than it did rootsiness and emotion. Some of his old fans simply refused to listen to his new work. However, his sales went ever upwards and he continued to score artistic triumphs.

A *Night on the Town* (1976) was a fine album and might have been more widely recognised as such were it not for its cover depicting Stewart at a garden party in blazer and boater, imagery that came to serve as shorthand for the sentiment 'Why Punk Had to Happen'. 'The Killing of Georgie (Part I and II)' was not just a great song but a brave statement of affinity with gays at a time when homophobia was viciously rife. *Foot Loose & Fancy Free* (1977) featured Stewart compositions—'I Was Only Joking' and 'You're in My Heart (The Final Acclaim)'—that are quite simply among the greatest love songs of the twentieth century. Meanwhile, 'Da Ya Think I'm Sexy?' (1978) remains a thumpingly good record long after the disco boom that gave rise to it died a bloody death. And, as with his earlier work, all those records were graced with Stewart's unique rasp, one of the most expressive singing styles of all time.

Rod Stewart: The Classic Years addresses the most fecund and vital period in the life and career of one of popular music's most important artists. With the help of exclusive interviews with Stewart's friends, collaborators, colleagues and lovers, it describes how he moved from the status of folk-oriented street performer to globe-straddling purveyor of glossy stadium anthems, and how he realised commercial accomplishments on a scale the music industry had rarely seen while laying down songs that resonate with millions worldwide to this day.

1
FIRST STEPS

'HE'D NEVER GIVEN UP TRYING', observed Ian McLagan of Rod Stewart.

The keyboardist who would be Stewart's Faces colleague for over half a decade had by the turn of the 1970s known Stewart for a long time. So had a lot of successful musicians. Whereas Stewart, though, had often seemed on the cusp of becoming a star, he had never quite managed to make the jump from wannabe to big cheese that so many of his contemporaries had. McLagan is a case in point. In November 1965, he became keyboardist with pop-soulsters the Small Faces and proceeded to enjoy the life of a chart-topping teen idol at a juncture where Stewart—four months his senior—was still in the foothills of his singing career, occupying a berth in the underachieving Steampacket. When Stewart's and McLagan's careers later dovetailed, though, the latter would eventually find himself in a position of hanging on to Stewart's coattails.

Roderick David Stewart was born in the Archway Road, North London on 10 January 1945 to Scot Robert Stewart and Londoner Elsie Stewart. He was the youngest of a family of five. Some have posited Stewart as petit bourgeois rather than proletarian because his father, after retiring from the building trade, opened a newsagent (candy store in US parlance) when Rod was in his early teens. However, Dee Harrington—Stewart's romantic partner from 1971 to 1975—insists, 'His father was working class, his family was working class, Rod was working class. . . . That's where he got his down to earth [nature]'. She does, though, state of his upbringing, 'I don't think it was poverty stricken'.

As a child, Stewart had no interest in music, his hobby being model railways. He was therefore more than a little surprised when on his fourteenth birthday his father gifted him a Zenith acoustic guitar with the observation that there was money to be made from the instrument. The guitar initially sat gathering dust, but Stewart eventually began some desultory strumming which culminated in him learning his first song, 'It Takes a Worried Man to Sing a Worried Song'. He then underwent the rite of passage of so many of his generation in joining a skiffle band. Skiffle was a sort of cousin of American jug band music whose makeshift approach to instrumentation was rooted in the fact that the impoverished UK was still subject to the rationing that had begun in war time and would continue until 1954. He was a fan of not just rock 'n' roll idols like Bill Haley and Eddie Cochran but also melodramatic movie singer Al Jolson.

Not that Stewart began harboring any ambitions to be a recording artist. After leaving school at the age of fifteen, he set his sights on being a professional soccer player. West London's Brentford Football Club took him on as an apprentice. However, he found that he didn't have the dedication and discipline to pursue the long path from youth team to first team, and it was then that he switched his ambitions to music. Speckled in this trajectory is employment in his father's shop, a framery, a gravesite and a funeral parlor.

Stewart started his musical career on the very bottom rung of the profession's ladder by fulfilling the role of busker (street performer). Ultimately, strumming and warbling popular hits to the accompaniment of acoustic guitar became a two-man act in the company of his friend Raymond 'Wizz' Jones. Stewart turned his busking into an international proposition, graduating from London's grey streets to the boulevards of continental Europe. His musical tastes had, by this point, widened to take in folk.

Stewart started out his stage-performing career on the cusp of his twenties in Jimmy Powell and the Five Dimensions, although at this point by playing harmonica rather than singing. He picked up some tips on the instrument by observing Mick Jagger's technique when the Dimensions would play in the intervals of sets by the up-and-coming Rolling Stones. He then sang for Long John Baldry and the All Stars, also known as Hoochie Coochie Men, after a legendary encounter on a platform at

Twickenham railway station after Stewart had been to a Baldry gig and was idling the time before the arrival of his train home by intoxicatedly blowing harp and warbling. He was soon pulling in a healthy weekly wage of £35 (nudging £500 in today's money). 'I never really considered myself a blues singer', he told *Melody Maker* several years later. 'I still don't. I'm a folk singer if I'm anything. It was John who introduced me to Big Bill Broonzy and Joe Williams'. By this point, he'd abandoned his scruffy folkie image for short but immaculately coiffed hair and pristine, stylish suits—a look that garnered him the nickname 'Rod the Mod'. The latter image secured him a TV documentary of that title, broadcast in November 1965. More TV appearances were generated by his 1964 solo single, a version of the blues standard 'Good Morning Little School-girl'. There were three further unsuccessful singles scattered throughout the 1960s: 'The Day Will Come' (1965), 'Shake' (1966) and 'Little Miss Understood' (1968).

Steampacket was a talent-oozing aggregation, but never managed to get it together enough to release any records. Formed by Baldry, it featured organist Brian Auger, guitarist Vic Briggs and vocalist Julie Driscoll. All were virtuosos but none more than Stewart himself. It was clear that his rasping tone and impassioned delivery put him in the same bracket as Eric Burdon, Chris Farlowe, Steve Marriott and Stevie Winwood—that is, he had one of the best half-dozen blues voices in the country. For a long while, little good it seemed to be able to do him. Partly, this was because of a lack of stagecraft. Music journalist Keith Altham saw Stewart at various gigs during this period. 'I wouldn't have picked him out as a star', he says. 'He had a good voice, but he wasn't especially charismatic on stage'.

Stewart departed Steampacket in 1966 and briefly found a berth in Shotgun Express, who had a similar cross-gender and star-studded lineup and who were similarly unsuccessful, although they did at least manage to release the single 'I Could Feel the Whole World Turn Around'.

Stewart's recruitment in early 1967 by ex-Yardbird Jeff Beck for his new venture must have seemed the big break he had been aching for. Beck was part of a British holy trinity of guitar masters that also included Eric Clapton and Jimmy Page. Initially, Stewart's stagecraft didn't show signs of improvement in the band that styled itself the Jeff Beck Group, not least because they were playing gigs in the United States, a virtually mythical place to British musicians in an era before cheap air travel made it accessible to ordinary people. 'I was the only one who had been to the States before and the boys were all scared stiff', Beck told Chris Welch of *Melody Maker* about the band's first US tour. 'Rod hid behind the amplifiers when he was singing. The audience were amazed—they thought I was a ventriloquist'. Those imagining Beck was exaggerating are mistaken: Stewart has subsequently publicly admitted his petrified peekaboo act.

Despite such tribulations, and an initial churn of musicians, the Jeff Beck Group had settled down by early 1968 into a lineup that was—on paper—world-beating. As well as Stewart and Beck, the band boasted the talents of Ronnie 'Woody' Wood on bass, Nicky Hopkins on keyboards and Micky Waller on drums. If talent was all it took, this ensemble would have made the greatest records ever released. Rarely, though, has there been such a gap between ability and achievement.

To be fair, the band did rack up some musical accomplishments. For instance, they may very well have invented heavy metal. The resemblance between the sound heard on their 1968 debut album, *Truth* (an LP actually strangely credited just to Beck), and that on the first Led Zeppelin album is quite remarkable, right down to a mutual cover of Willie Dixon's 'You Shook Me'. Beck's effort was first by six months, but the style that would retroactively be given the designation 'cosmic blues' would be credited to, and more fully exploited by, Zeppelin, an ensemble led by his guitar rival and ex-Yardbirds colleague Jimmy Page.

'Jimmy Page was waiting in the wings', Stewart later observed to Rob Partridge of *Record Mirror*. 'As soon as we broke up, he was right in there'. The right group probably won the war. It's difficult to imagine the Jeff Beck Group parlaying their talents into transcendent classics like 'Stairway to Heaven': for all their gifts, they simply did not have prolific songwriters within their ranks. Moreover, while Led Zeppelin were known for a rock-solid in-camp solidarity, the Jeff Beck Group were riven by dispute, which is why, by July 1969, they were careening to a close.

Although under Jeff Beck's aegis Stewart had fulfilled every British musician's dream of touring America and securing a top-20 US album-chart placing, he was uninterested in continuing his musical journey within its ranks, not least because of what he claimed was the shabby treatment meted out to him and Wood by the dictatorial Beck. Neither, naturally, was Wood. 'Beck needed a singer and I was his singer; that was it', Stewart later told Bud Scoppa of *Circus*. 'Everything was geared to his own playing. He used all of us. That's why he's had so much trouble keeping a group together'. Altham—personally familiar with both Beck and Stewart through his journalism and later PR work—suspects that the reality was different to Stewart's claims. 'Rod was not what we would call a team player', he asserts. 'Rod believed he was a star and totally responsible for the success of whatever it was he was doing with anybody else. Right from the word go, his ambition was pretty avaricious. Most people who become stars have that in them. They have a kind of ruthlessness. If you get in the way of them, they just drive over you. In a way, you've got to expect it because they wouldn't become a star if they didn't have it. And you've got to expect that sometimes if you're working with them, for them, or whatever to find that that ruthlessness rebounds in some way on you. Otherwise, they wouldn't survive'. And what about the view that Beck is himself a difficult character? 'Jeff had a reputation for that. I think he just worked *with* difficult characters and maybe some of it got deflected on him. I always found him incredibly cooperative and a really nice bloke'.

Whatever the truth, Stewart and his remarkable talent were at a loose end once more. From today's vantage point, the fact that he was twenty-four and a half years of age might seem to suggest that he still had time on his side, but that was not the perspective of either him or others. 'He's been around for so long that he's almost a vintage rock singer', observed Rob Partridge of *Record Mirror* in 1970 of the overdressed youthful figure he remembered singing 'Good Morning Little Schoolgirl' on the by-then long-defunct TV show *Ready Steady Go!* The climate in the 1960s and 1970s for people who had been around the almost-famous block a few times was somewhat more unforgiving than it is now. In an era before the ascent of the notion of 'heritage artists', the only currency worth anything was 'New and Happening'. 'I had been knocking around for the best part of seven years', Stewart later reflected in his autobiography. 'The Beatles had come and, to all intents and purposes, gone in that time'. Consequently, when in October 1968 Mercury Records gave him a chance at a solo album, he adjudged it 'a last shot at the big time'. Perhaps he took some comfort from the fact that, at this juncture, the remnants of the once all-conquering Small Faces were at an even lower ebb than he.

The Small Faces had racked up nine top-twenty UK hits in three years. Although their success had never translated to America, they had won wide respect and admiration for the way they had evolved from teen idols to heavyweight recording artistes, exemplified by their majestic 1967 single, 'Tin Soldier', and the fact that on side two of their May 1968 *Ogdens' Nut Gone Flake* LP they helped pioneer the idea of the rock opera. Yet not much over six months after that latter lauded and chart-topping work, they had splintered. Lead singer Steve Marriott's reasons for departing were never quite clear—in many ways it would seem even to himself—but it left his ex-colleagues resentful, bewildered and anxious about a future in which it would seem they might inhabit that agonising situation of being simultaneously famous and broke.

Asked if it was a frightening period after Marriott left the Small Faces, McLagan says, 'Oh yeah. We didn't know what we were going to do'. (McLagan has passed away since speaking to the author, as have several interviewees for this book. For reasons of stylistic consistency and clear attribution, the present tense has been maintained when deploying their quotes.) McLagan (universally known as 'Mac'), drummer Kenney Jones and bassist Ronnie Lane stayed together almost out of desperation. 'To be honest, we were lost', says Jones. The three began disconsolately jamming at a rehearsal space owned by the Rolling Stones in Bermondsey, London.

Despite all this, though, when Stewart realised that the remnants of the Small Faces needed a front man, he would seem to have considered it far more of an opportunity than the fact that he now had a recording deal. 'Rod wasn't terribly interested in his solo career', says Billy Gaff, Stewart's manager from 1969 to 1982. Even after the release of his critically acclaimed second album, *Gasoline Alley* (1970), Stewart was telling *Record Mirror*'s Rob Partridge, 'The solo albums I've always regarded as sidelines'. In fact, the solo career that saw Stewart eventually become a superstar may only have been inaugurated by him as a piece of short-term financial opportunism. McLagan asserted that Stewart signed his Mercury deal for precisely the amount of money needed to buy a Marcos kit car, the automobile equivalent of IKEA's self-assembly furniture.

McLagan: 'The fastest thing for under a thousand pounds. Fiberglass piece of old rubbish'. Stewart insists the cost was £1,300 (and furthermore that he bought his ready-made). The modest sum involved can still be posited as an extraordinary expression of lack of faith in his own potential.

Stewart's lukewarm attitude to the idea of being a solo recording artist is understandable on one ground: he has never been a prolific songwriter. In 1970, Stewart was frank in discussing with *Rolling Stone*'s John Morthland how difficult he found the process. 'It takes me a long time to write a song', he said. 'I write lyrics best . . . I don't pretend to be a songwriter, really. I try really hard, but it takes me about three weeks to write a song'. 'I don't think he was frustrated by it', notes Dee Harrington. 'He's always had an open mind to recording songs of other people and not having to be the writer. He has got the ability to take a song that's really great for him that someone [else] wrote'.

Immediately post-Beatles, and for a long time thereafter, someone who could only write or co-write a handful of songs per year was not considered a heavyweight artist, no matter how great his singing voice. Stewart would help to change this perception simply by dint of managing to make albums that were clearly classics despite the fact that he had composed a relatively small proportion of them. Another feat that belied his absence of fecundity was writing a remarkably high quotient of *great* songs. That, though, was quite a way into the future.

Things began to seem a little less grim at Bermondsey when Lane turned up one day with Ronnie Wood in tow. Wood had progressed through the ranks not just of the Jeff Beck Group but also the Birds (British, 'y'-less version) and the Creation. He began livening up the atmosphere with his chirpy personality and his crow's-caw guitar sound.

The ex–Small Faces were now beginning to think in terms of a new group in which Wood would play a part. 'We didn't really want a singer', says McLagan. 'That was the whole plan of us rehearsing. We were actually rehearsing with some other guitarists and eventually we realised that the four of us was great. We thought, "Well, Ronnie Wood can sing a little bit, Ronnie Lane can sing, and Ian McLagan could sing a little bit". But Kenney realised that we didn't really have it together'. 'Ronnie Lane had a great voice [but] after Steve Marriott—that powerful voice—I didn't think it was strong enough', says Jones. There was someone knocking around, however, whose pipes had just the sort of gritty and larger-than-life qualities that Marriott's had, because Wood had taken to turning up with best mate Stewart. Humble Pie drummer Jerry Shirley perceives the benignly Machiavellian hand of Marriott—now ensconced with him in supergroup Humble Pie—at work. 'It was Steve that suggested Ronnie Wood in the first place as his replacement, and he wasn't stupid: he knew that if Ronnie came along, chances were Rod'd come with him', he says. 'Rod used to sit on the amps in Bermondsey waiting for us to finish and then we'd have a break and go up the pub', recalls Jones. 'We kept doing this for a few weeks, and I kept thinking, "This is nuts". We got into a situation where we had to get real. So when we went up the pub one time, I said to Rod, "Do you fancy joining the band?" He said, "Oh, do you think the others would be alright with that?" I said, "Yeah, no problem". Then I got a shock'.

Ian McLagan was well aware of Stewart's talents, not least because he had recently played on his debut solo LP, now awaiting release. 'Woody was working with him on that, so he got me in on it', notes McLagan. Stewart's abilities, though, seemed less relevant than the disquieting prospect of jumping from frying pan to fire. 'Ronnie and Mac just felt that they didn't really want to compromise things and have another Steve Marriott in the band who would just walk out', says Jones.

Lane and McLagan were gradually won over to the idea. 'They were still with the Beck Group because Woody had to do one more tour', says McLagan of Stewart and Wood. 'We went to see the Beck Group kind of like the dirty boyfriend: we were stealing their singer and bass player'. 'They replaced one massive ego with another massive ego', notes Altham of the Marriott-Stewart changeover. 'I thought that was extraordinary, really'. All these machinations came as news to the band's manager. 'I signed the Faces and basically they didn't have a singer and Woody called Rod and brought him in', says Gaff. 'Nothing to do with me'.

Stewart later said he was not that impressed by the music he heard in Bermondsey and admitted that making the decision to join was a plunge motivated by something other than logic or ambition. 'I was more impressed with them as people', he told *Rolling Stone* in 1970. 'I said, "What a nice bunch of guys—I'll join that band!"' Gaff suspects different. 'He joined really because he thought the Faces were going to be big', he says. 'I think everybody thought the same thing'. Although Gaff subsequently became Stewart's manager as well, when asked if he thought that the ex–Small Faces would be a bigger act than the solo Stewart, he says, 'Truthfully, yes I did'.

The group did not consider themselves in any meaningful way a continuation of the Small Faces. Jones insists that it was 'a brand-new band'. He says, 'It never crossed any of our minds to call it Small Faces or Faces, never in a million years. It was only when we went to do the record deal with Ian Ralfini, who was the boss of Warner Brothers in those days, he said, "Right, well you'll have to call yourself the Small Faces". We said, "No, we're not doing that". He said, "Well, you can't have the money then. We want you to be called the Small Faces because that's a well-known name"'. The band were not in much of a bargaining position. Desperation for the finance necessary to start a new life led them to cave in, although they did wring a concession. Jones: 'We said, "Okay, the first album we'll let go out as Small Faces, thereafter we'll call it the Faces"'. (The band were billed as 'Faces' on their output in their home country from the get-go. The situation being different Stateside is somewhat ironic in light of the fact that they had achieved no significant success and hence brand recognition in the US.) The new appellation also made sense for a different reason. The Small Faces had partly got their name because of the fact that they were all not much taller than five and a half feet. With Stewart and Wood being normal height, it no longer made much sense.

There was, incidentally, one signature absent from the contract. Slightly shockingly, McLagan notes of Rod, 'The Faces was only four people. He was never a member of the band because he had a solo deal. He couldn't sign the contract'.

The fact of Stewart joining the Faces served to create an overlap with his debut solo album, it being the case that the participation of Jones and McLagan meant that three-fifths of the new band were to be found on some tracks. This would be the usual situation over the next six years, with Stewart always employing his Faces colleagues on his own LPs in various configurations. Moreover, on one track on each album, he would simply use the Faces as a whole. Yet a conundrum much publicly discussed was the fact that his solo offerings never sounded like Faces' albums. 'It was because on his solo albums he got his own way and on the Faces albums he got no way', says Gaff. 'He wasn't allowed to dictate anything'. McLagan offers a more musicological reason: 'The thing is, he was a bit of a folkie and it had to come out'.

Stewart's album was produced, at least according to the credits, by Lou Reizner, the man who had arranged his solo deal. Stewart has always disputed this. McLagan claims he himself had a greater role in the album's recording than is suggested by his misspelled sleeve credit, 'Organ, Piano: Ian Maclagen', and the fact that—with the exception of 'Handbags and Gladrags', credited to its composer, Mike d'Abo—the album's sleeve notes attribute only Stewart with arrangements. McLagan says, 'He had a producer who didn't do very much, and in fact he asked me to arrange a couple of tracks'.

Stewart's entrée is in some ways pretty much what you would expect of a project that was entered into primarily to obtain a cheap car. In an era when it was beginning to be accepted that an album of anything less than forty minutes was paltry, its parsimonious running time of under thirty-three minutes was perilously close to 'rip-off' territory. It's slight in other ways, too. It feels cobbled together, its eight tracks encompassing a fatuous Rolling Stones cover, a folk tune one suspects was included primarily because its public-domain status enables the artist to cop the publishing royalties and a brace of tracks whose elastic structures give them the whiff of glorified jams.

Yet cheek-by-jowl with such quasi-filler are cuts evincing exquisite care and high-production values, ones foreshadowing greatness that is to come. Moreover, even those tracks that sound superficially like anyone-can-do-it offerings are nothing of the sort: there are few musicians in the world as talented as these. In addition to the adroit Wood and McLagan, contributors include Micky Waller on drums (which makes this as much a nigh-on Jeff Beck Group album as a nigh-on Faces album), the Nice's Keith Emerson on organ, and guitarists Martin Pugh and Martin Quittenton, both alumni of the accomplished Steamhammer, who released their debut album in 1969. (Pugh does not crop up much more in the Stewart story, but Quittenton would shortly be key to his superstardom.)

Micky Waller was a superb drummer, although it's a small miracle that he ever managed to achieve this status. 'Micky Waller had no drum kit at that point', recalls McLagan with amusement. 'I used to hire one for those sessions', explains Waller. 'I owned a snare drum, and I used to hire the rest from a friend of mine. Sometimes I own one and sometimes I don't. If I get a good offer, I'll sell it. I've never had to practice'. Stewart opting for Waller on his solo records in preference to Kenney Jones—whom he liked as a person and respected as a musician—can be viewed as a microcosm of the strict demarcation he maintained between his own output and Faces fare. McLagan: 'Micky is an old soul. He was a blues and jazz player. . . . That great drum sound is all because of the way he plays. It's like Charlie Watts: what you hear is Charlie, not the drums . . . Kenney was a rock 'n' roll player. Rod needed that feel, I think. It separated it, which was good'. 'The difference is he plays a lot lighter', says Jones. 'Rod thought Kenney was a better drummer than me on stage and I was better in the studio', says Waller. 'He said it in interviews'.

In addition to the talents of the sidemen, there were few singers around as impressive as Stewart. It's unclear precisely why a vocal style reminiscent of a man recovering from a tonsil operation should be so affecting—his voice originally took some getting used to, and some detest it to this day. 'The Golden Catarrh', Chris Salewicz of the *New Musical Express* once described Stewart's voice. 'Somebody who had tonsillitis singing in tune', offers Pete Sears, who would be a regular Stewart sideman in the first half of the 1970s. Sears adds, 'But he had a certain flair about the way he sang'. 'It wasn't just the gravelly voice', says Billy Gaff. 'That made him very distinctive, but I think it was his ability to sell a lyric. There aren't many can do it. When he did a ballad he got to me, and I think to everybody else'. Stewart himself said of his ambiguous gift to *Sounds*' Barbara Charone in June 1976, 'It's not a gravel voice. It's got much more warmth. I always feel my voice is like black velvet. A combination of black velvet on sandpaper'. Stewart's voice wasn't always as sandpapery as it famously became. In 1970, he reasoned to John Morthland of *Rolling Stone* that it had only begun assuming that quality after the release of 'Good Morning Little Schoolgirl' and had become incrementally hoarser as a consequence of 'belting my ass off for five years'. He also admitted, 'I learned a lot from Beck . . . I learned how to . . . be a lead vocalist, and fit in with the guitar . . . which now comes out so I can phrase well'.

To this day, Stewart cites Sam Cooke as the biggest influence on his vocal style. The black singer/songwriter nicknamed 'The Man Who Invented Soul' was responsible for hits like 'You Send Me', 'A Change Is Gonna Come', 'Cupid', 'Wonderful World', 'Chain Gang' and 'Bring It on Home to Me'. Stewart told Morthland, 'Sam Cooke was the only one that really influenced me. Over a period of about two years, that's all I listened to. . . . It had to do with the way I sounded; I didn't sound at all like anybody, Ray Charles or anybody, but I knew I sounded a bit like Sam Cooke, so I listened to Sam Cooke'.

For Jeff Beck, Stewart's best work vocally was under his aegis. Speaking to Steven Rosen of the *Los Angeles Free Press* in December 1973, Beck opined that a lack of formal training meant that Stewart's breathing and pitching were sometimes inadequate but that he'd been fearful he would quit the group if he'd told him he was out of key. 'His voice was just amazing in those days', he said. 'He had so much over-tone. . . . It was warm and it was raucous and it was everything rolled into one. When he sang a blues it just moved me; it was beautiful'.

The opening track of Stewart's first album is 'Street Fighting Man'. Written by Mick Jagger and Keith Richards, it was the Rolling Stones' response to the riots that broke out across the Western world in 1968, when bellicose youth took to streets and campus grounds to make demands relating to civil liberties denied them or others in what were then rather authoritarian societies. Like that same year's 'Revolution' by the Beatles, it articulated an ambivalence about the demands and/or tactics of the brick-hurlers and placard-wavers. Whereas John Lennon was scathing about those who presumed to criticise Western democracies while exalting a totalitarian like Chairman Mao, Jagger points out that civil unrest in his understated, overly polite, often deferential home country is destined to have a somewhat different tone to the conflagrations in Paris, Berlin or Chicago, summarised in the line, 'In sleepy London Town there's just no place for a street fighting man'. Such nuance was lost on the authorities in the United States, where the track's release as a single in August 1968 saw it subjected to radio bans. The notoriety and hence cachet of cool it consequently picked up blinded many to the track's faults, namely a staccato rhythm and a melody that borders on yowling tunelessness.

And where does Rod Stewart fit into all this? His decision to cover the song may have been an act of whimsy or a space-filling measure, or even an expression of the fact that, like so many of his generation, he adored the Stones. On some level, though, he probably thought that in some inchoate, almost reflexive way he was showing solidarity with the counterculture, for when he was a young man, Stewart was very much a man of the Left. At one point, he moved abode so that he would be closer to Highgate Cemetery, North London, wherein is located the grave of Karl Marx.

Musically, the recording is less fast and less dramatic than the Stones' original, with the cooing nature of Stewart's vocals coming almost as a shock. Wood's keening guitar and McLagan's jolly piano also seem to miss the edgy point. Things change on three and a quarter minutes when a respite is followed by a switch to a faster tempo and a more urgent vocal tone, which in turn is succeeded by a quite galvanising bass solo from Wood. Unfortunately, the sense of people not understanding the material they are covering, or even mocking it, rears its head again when McLagan takes the song into the fade with, apropos of nothing, the piano lick heard on the Stones' 1967 single 'We Love You'. Moreover, at over five minutes—outlasting the Stones' version by two minutes—the track is purposelessly elongated.

This befuddling entrée is followed by 'Man of Constant Sorrow'. Bob Dylan had a presence on all Stewart's long-playing Mercury output. In all other cases, this took the form of a cover of one of his songs. In this case, it constitutes a version of a song with which Dylan was associated. The sleeve lists the composition details of 'Man of Constant Sorrow' as 'Trad. Arr. R. Stewart'. A similar credit appeared on Dylan's eponymous debut album in 1962, with of course the difference that it was then Dylan who was claiming to have devised a new arrangement for a song so old as to be out of copyright. It was one of a clutch of songs on *Bob Dylan* in which the artist peculiarly chose to cover material constituting the narrative of a much older man with a lifetime of hardship behind him and a bleak future in front of him. Despite his tender years, the roughness of Dylan's voice made it work. Something similar applies with Stewart.

On the record's sleeve, Stewart proudly claims credit for the track's guitar playing, by which is presumably meant the acoustic stuff, which consists of gentle strumming and doomy picking. It's juxtaposed with flecks of electric guitar from Wood. In a lyric suffused with mythic self-pity, the narrator tells a lover who has done him wrong that he is set to rob a train and may die in the attempt but, if he survives, will be going back to Colorado, where he asserts he was 'probably raised'. The latter bizarre phrase is, like so much of the recording, copied exactly from Dylan's rendition. Stewart's version, though, is far superior. Although Dylan's voice has often been unfairly maligned, his recital of 'Man of Constant Sorrow' was caterwauling. Stewart puts in a passionate but understated performance which generates no little pathos, not least his poignant kiss-off, 'I'll see you on God's golden shore'. In contrast to the way the opener overstayed its welcome, 'Man of Constant Sorrow' makes its point by two and a half minutes and then judiciously departs the stage.

Three tracks in, we come to the set's first bona fide Stewart composition. The blues-rock 'Blind Prayer' feels—in its high drama, blues bent and interplay between vocals and instruments—very much like a song originally intended for the Jeff Beck Group. It's also the sort of agonised tale of woe for which Stewart was, at the time, attracting some ridicule. This is not because of his arguably lower-middle-class hinterland. Nor was it due to the phenomenon of a welfare-state white boy presuming to articulate the travails of American black people. While this had been a debating point for most of the 1960s, it hadn't been a particularly heated one: the combination of British musicians' evident love of and respect for the source material, compassion for the 'Negro' and surprising finesse in rendering the blues ensured that there was, at the time, nothing equivalent to denunciations of 'cultural appropriation'. What aroused people's ire is Stewart's overwrought style, or as esteemed rock critic Robert Christgau put it, 'his broken-down bluesman imitation'. 'Blind Prayer' is a typical example of Stewart's snicker-inducing propensity to take his tales of woe way too far.

Dark, echoey piano, keening guitar and a wail by Stewart provide an impressively dramatic opening. However, the first-person litany of misfortune Stewart proceeds to unfurl is parody level. We are solemnly informed that the protagonist lost both parents to a fire and was struck blind by the age of ten. Homeless for the next five years and friendless bar for his dog, he is bullied at school and at what passes for home. Entering the world of adulthood, he works his fingers to the bone, but his gainful-if-grinding employment is offset by the death of his faithful hound. He finds love but is left reflecting that he never knew it could hurt so much even as he begs God to never take it away from him.

All of this is depressing on an oh-Gawd-what-next level. A different issue is the fact that the objective striven for by the composer of every sad song—evoking empathy—is made impossible: nobody can relate to such a shaggy-dog story. An extra layer of risibility is created by Stewart's gauche phraseology and scene-setting. He comically undercuts the poverty tableaux by stating that he is the son of a lawyer; even if orphaned, it's difficult to imagine such a progeny would be left anything like destitute. Another example of inept mythmaking, as well as clumsy grammar, is Stewart's statement that his bereavement occurred when he was 'approximately the age of four—or perhaps five'. The final snort-worthy straw is the 'And that ain't all!' that he desperately delivers between tragic episodes. It's all rather a shame because the instrumentation has a dark, churning urgency. Graced with a more thought-through lyric, it could have made for a powerful track, either on this or the third Jeff Beck Group album that never happened.

From the ridiculous to the sublime. The flawlessly classy 'Handbags and Gladrags' is on a higher plane than anything else on the album. Mike d'Abo—who had written Stewart's 1968 single 'Little Miss Understood'—had a day job as lead singer of Manfred Mann, which he had inherited from Paul Jones in 1966. D'Abo, though, was more than a singer, being an accomplished pianist and a versatile songwriter. Both talents were deemed surplus to requirements in Manfred Mann: the keyboardist role was taken by the iconically bearded and bespectacled South African from whom the group took its name, while the band was so unreceptive to d'Abo's compositions that he had to farm out the likes of 'Build Me Up Buttercup' and 'Handbags and Gladrags' to more receptive parties like the Foundations and Chris Farlowe, who proceeded to have hits with them.

An oboe creates a mournful opening before d'Abo comes in with a sophisticated piano motif. This presages quite possibly the least fashionable type of song imaginable at that point in history. Since the mid-1950s, popular music had been associated with a rebellious and youth-oriented outlook. 'Handbags and Gladrags' is written from the point of view of the old and traditionally minded. Its narrator is a grandfather who is watching in distress as his beloved granddaughter spends the money he gives her on the latest fashions: the titular clothes and accessories that will be derided as last season's gear in five minute's time. The tone, though, is not hectoring or condemnatory but, instead, sad, if tinged with anger. It is also beautifully phrased, nowhere more so than when grandad laments, 'So what becomes of you, my love?'

Stewart's version of the song is less bluesy than Chris Farlowe's, which scraped the UK top 30 in January 1968. Both have a towering orchestral arrangement, but Stewart's is more dynamic, containing a thundering instrumental section with racing syncopated drums and horns. Throughout the track, Stewart weighs each word to optimum effect and resists showboating. At a time when such things were important, it was a great closer to the album's first vinyl side. It can now be seen as possessing greater long-term significance: the first classic of Stewart's recording career.

The first three tracks on this album's second side demonstrate a blossoming songwriting ability on Stewart's part, with them all bearing his name, even if only one of them could be termed substantial. That latter accolade belongs to 'An Old Raincoat Won't Ever Let You Down'. The track is also the first significant stirring of what will be a trait in Stewart's work over the next half decade: a warm-hearted, proletarian communality, the type that for several years conferred on him the status of Man of the People. In this particular poverty tableaux, the titular overcoat becomes metaphor and talisman, a means of protecting the protagonist—and the listeners, whom he addresses in the second person, a tactic always likely to engender solidarity—from adversity, whether it takes the form of the elements or financial hardships. The track seems rooted in personal experience but, as is his wont, Stewart exaggerates. No doubt he had indeed had his share of getting thrown off trains when discovered to be travelling without a valid ticket and slept rough with a copy of *The Times* newspaper covering his face, but that scuffling would have been less to do with lack of options than making the lifestyle choice to bum around Europe. Not that it really matters. The very act of taking an interest in the underprivileged feels like an act of compassion and broadmindedness, the poverty tableau is intrinsically interesting and the overarching spiritual warmth is affecting. Adding to the general likability is an imaginative melody line, a brisk tempo and some galvanising piano work.

'I Wouldn't Ever Change a Thing' displays to an even greater extent Stewart's ability to tug at the heartstrings, the song's very title epitomising the vulnerability, optimism and emotional frankness of his life-affirming modus operandi. Unfortunately, the song's assertion that the narrator would change nothing about his life even if he could start over is pretty much all the track amounts to. Its formlessness raises the suspicion of extemporisation. In lines that barely rhyme, Stewart reflects on people, places and situations he has known and wonders how things have changed. Behind him, Waller uncertainly taps cymbals and McLagan meanders on piano and Emerson on organ. The impression of scraping a song together from a mere sentiment is heightened by a bizarre middle section wherein Stewart and Reizner engage in spoken-word call-and-response that involves Stewart's producer disagreeing with the composition's it's-all-good philosophy.

The generically importuning 'Cindy's Lament' feels similarly cobbled together. Against a churning blues guitar riff and staccato rhythm, Stewart chides a woman for ignoring him, even though—gasp—he lent her his library book. In a twist ending, the narrator reveals that—unbeknownst to her disapproving mother and brother—he and Cindy have already spent a night together. When the instrumentation fades out and fades in again, it only confirms the directionlessness.

That Stewart is still groping his way towards songwriting competence and his own style—the classic growing up in public—is demonstrated by the closing track, 'Dirty Old Town', written by Ewan MacColl, a man most famous for his much-covered 'First Time Ever I Saw Your Face'. This bittersweet folk song has all the emotional tenderness and melodic nous that Stewart clearly desires for his own creations but of which he is currently only capable in patches. The landmarks in this tale of love among the lower orders are gasworks, canals, factory walls and docks, and—more to the point—they are speckled undemonstratively among the lyric in stark contrast to the way Stewart histrionically piles on the privations in 'Blind Prayer'. Moreover, the melody, though basic, is lovely. To be fair, Stewart delivers the lyric with a panache beyond its composer, who preferred a vocal style involving quasi-bizarre vowel elongation.

In his native UK, Stewart's solo debut appeared under the name *An Old Raincoat Won't Ever Let You Down*, although in the US was titled *The Rod Stewart Album*. 'The original title was *Thin*', says Gaff. 'They thought it was a stupid title'. McLagan: 'If you look very closely, you'll see it written very small at the bottom left corner, and in America it was written in white against yellow, so you really couldn't see it'. In Britain, the record came out in February 1970 on the Vertigo label, a progressive wing of the Philips company. It was housed in a gatefold sleeve depicting models posing as old people frolicking with young children in a park. The sleeve of the US release—issued three months earlier on the same umbrella company's Mercury label—was more prosaic on the outside, featuring only italicised lettering but carrying sleeve notes (albeit banal) and, on its inner sleeve, photos of the musicians and a picture of Stewart in what was already his classic pose: head thrown back at the microphone.

There were some good reviews: Richard Williams of British weekly *Melody Maker* adjudged Stewart's debut a 'fine, fine album', while the *Village Voice*'s Robert Christgau said, 'I'm still not quite convinced. But the music is excellent instrumentally, and Stewart's singing and composing mostly superb'. Greil Marcus of *Rolling Stone* adjudged it a 'superb album' and said 'this one is for keeps'. However, the album failed to chart in the UK and didn't make it to the top 150 of America's *Billboard* album chart.

There was one cast-iron classic on the album that might well have propelled the LP higher had it been a hit. Mercury lifted 'Handbags and Gladrags' for Stateside single release, but it wouldn't be until two years later—when Stewart was sufficiently big for people to be keen to check out his back catalogue—that it made the charts, and even then, it didn't crack the top 40. Billy Gaff is mystified. 'The song that made me love Rod Stewart and I realised that he was brilliant was when he did "Handbags and Gladrags"', he says. 'I could never understand, to this day, why that never took off'.

Still, Stewart was probably not that bothered. He now had his eggs in more than one basket.

ALTHOUGH HE HAD A PARALLEL SOLO CAREER, Stewart's commitment to the Faces in all other respects was total. Having thrown in his lot with them, he would never, during the Faces' lifetime, play a solo gig. Moreover, their concert billing was emphatically a collective one, something that remained the case even as his solo sales and fame pulled away from theirs. 'If the Faces were on tour, one of the conditions was you weren't allowed to mention Rod Stewart's name', says Gaff. 'That was the rule of the band. It was a band: it wasn't "Rod Stewart and the Faces"'.

This admirable loyalty on Stewart's part stemmed from the fact that, in the early days, the Faces' camp was characterised by a unique *esprit de corps*. This was one thing that the Faces had in common with the Small Faces: the group genuinely loved each other's company. They were a permanently cheery bunch, something assisted in no small measure by imbibing. 'We were half-drunk most of the time', admits Jones. 'We were having such a great time being with each other. We were great mates'. Yet though their infectious alcohol-fueled happiness—on stage and off—is part of the Faces' legend, Jones always felt that less time in the pub and more in the studio would have enhanced their legacy. The Faces had none of the Small Faces' work ethic. Whereas the Small Faces virtually lived in the studio, the Faces couldn't wait to get out of it to head for the nearest 'boozer'. Consequently, the Faces' sound would always be somewhat sloppy and scraggly, a far cry from the vital and sheened Small Faces hallmarks. This fact can be seen on the Faces' first album, recorded across December 1969 and January 1970.

The album—Ronnie Wood reading the guitar beginner's manual *First Step* was the only clue to its title on the LP's cover—starts oddly with 'Wicked Messenger', a song from Bob Dylan's musically understated but spiritually tormented 1968 album, *John Wesley Harding*. Detailing Dylan's disgust with himself for the way he was seduced by stardom, it simply doesn't lend itself to Stewart's dramatics and certainly not to his self-aggrandising whoops and hollers.

The rock-oriented nature of Faces' albums would always be leavened by a sprinkling of tracks of a more folkie flavor. Surprisingly, they tended to come not from the pen of Stewart but the increasingly acoustic-oriented Ronnie Lane. As with so many Lane songs, 'Devotion' possesses an admirable sensitivity. However, as would often be the case, it doesn't compensate for insubstantiality. Stewart, who shares vocals with Lane, strains to no avail before the song drifts away with no impression made.

'Shake, Shudder, Shiver' is a stuttering Lane/Wood collaboration that never lives up to its intriguing title, which was inspired by the teeth-chattering temperature in the bathroom in Wood's Shepherd's Bush flat where the Faces would sometimes rehearse. 'Stone' is a country-folk Lane composition. It possesses a pleasing groove, courtesy of mouth harp from Wood, banjo from Stewart and tinkling McLagan piano work. As with many Lane ventures into this kind of roots territory, the melody is slightly generic but catchy. Its pantheistic religiosity seems informed by his recent embrace of the teachings of Indian philosopher Meher Baba.

'Around the Plynth' is a reinvention of 'Plynth (Water Down the Drain)' from the second Jeff Beck Group album, *Beck-Ola* (1969), although now credited to Stewart/Wood, with Nicky Hopkins' contribution airbrushed from history. A cry of despair, it's melodically undistinguished, while the combination of Wood's nagging slide guitar work and Stewart's affected vocal create the impression of much ado about nothing. The *Beck-Ola* template is much sprightlier.

The album's vinyl side two opens with 'Flying', a collaboration by Lane, Stewart and Wood. Its lyric—concerning a man returning home after a five-year prison sentence incurred for being poor and hungry—has all the hallmarks of a Stewart poverty-claiming tall tale. A lovely background choral part aside, the indistinct music certainly doesn't live up to the melodrama.

'Pineapple and the Monkey', an instrumental written by Wood, is a meandering, featureless chug that is laughable when set against the memory of the galvanising instrumentals in which the Small Faces specialised, like 'Grow Your Own'. 'Nobody Knows' is a Lane/Wood composition sung jointly by Lane and Stewart. It has a lovely lilting melody but is also guilty of the cluttered boringness that would afflict so many Faces recordings. 'Looking Out the Window' has an unfortunate title: gazing through panes being associated with a lack of inspiration or wandering attention. The spikey guitar·work on this Jones/McLagan-composed instrumental makes it mildly more interesting than 'Pineapple and the Monkey', but that still means not particularly interesting at all.

With the closing track, we finally get a song of substance. 'Three Button Hand Me Down' is a McLagan/Stewart co-write. The keyboardist found in his collaborations with him that while Stewart was never prolific, he was enthusiastic and inventive. 'He was an incredible fast writer', says McLagan. 'He would just rip it out. I wrote two or three things with him and he would have a basic idea and then I'd just sort of flesh it out. He'd have the melody. He'd just sing it and you'd figure out the key he was in and go from there'. 'Three Button Hand Me Down' seems to owe something to Stewart's 'An Old Raincoat Won't Ever Let You Down' in the way it invests an item of clothing with class-based talismanic properties. In this case, adversity revolves largely around women who wish to separate the narrator from his father's heirloom and exchange it for something smarter. The setting is American, but some might suggest that this fabricated hinterland deals in not much more fiction than Stewart's habitual fetishisation of a British underclass he barely belonged to. The lyrics are smart, snappy and have a whip-crack rhyming scheme, and they ride on a midtempo melody possessed of a catchy chorus.

Unfortunately, a strong closer can never redeem a predominantly forgettable album. The *First Step* title is appropriate, but not in a good way. The LP is so tentative as to almost make a mockery of the vast experience and proven abilities of its participants. A record it curiously resembles is *Wild Life,* with which Paul McCartney would choose to introduce his new band, Wings, the following year. In both cases, it is both shocking that a group should make their entrée with such an underdeveloped product and difficult to believe that the quality of its music would have ever obtained the band a record deal had they been comprised of unknowns.

Glyn Johns, who had lately moved from status of studio engineer to producer, had been instrumental in getting the Faces a deal in the first place through a demo tape of six songs whose recording he had overseen at London's Olympic Studios. McLagan hadn't felt sufficiently grateful to agree to let Johns produce the debut that his efforts had made possible. The keyboardist baulked not at Johns' insistence on being credited as producer but, rather, at his request for a 2 per cent royalty. His veto was a considerable mistake. One wonders whether, had Johns been retained, he might have prevailed on the Faces to prune the tracks. The album is a quarter of an hour longer than Stewart's solo debut LP, but this hardly qualifies as generosity. Leaving aside the issue of the deterioration of sound quality on a vinyl album that exceeds forty minutes, the tracks are uniformly overlong, with all except one being four minutes or more, and four exceeding five minutes. It's bad enough that most of the songs are flimsy, but the fact of them also outstaying their welcome moves them from the territory of minor to boring.

The album provided another reason why the permanent retention of the group's former name would have been inappropriate. Whereas the Small Faces were pop-soulsters turned psychedelia merchants, the Faces' music adhered much more to the riffing rock template of the Rolling Stones, albeit a somewhat more rough-hewn variant. 'It's funny, looking back, because it's the same guys really', concedes McLagan. 'Woody and Steve played very similar too. The thing is, when we formed the Faces, we kind of were eager to not be a pop band anymore. You grow up a little bit. Also, it's hard to write pop songs as you get older. It's really a young person's medium'. There would also seem to be a certain element of deliberately distancing themselves from the old sound which went, to an extent, hand in hand with an image. 'Small Faces were forever try-ing to run away from our teenybopper image and that sort of thing and the "Itchycoo Parks"', says Jones. 'Even though they're great tracks, they didn't represent the band. When we got together with Rod and Woody, we had a chance to break free. The same with Marriott when he had a chance to break free with Humble Pie'.

This all meant that this band would be of little interest to old Small Faces fans. In order to make headway, they would have to generate their own following. This was illustrated by *First Step*'s chart action, or lack thereof. It made number 119 on *Billboard* and number 45 in the UK. This underwhelming performance was partly the result of poor choice of single. The infectious and likeable 'Three Button Hand Me Down' was overlooked in favour of 'Flying'. It provided Lane and Jones with the novel experience of releasing a single that wasn't a hit: not since the Small Faces' second disc back in 1965 (which preceded McLagan joining the group) had they failed to bother the chart compilers with an officially sanctioned release.

'*First Step* was quite good, I thought', says Jones. 'It was a step in the right direction and was a matter of discovering each other for the first time'. Reviewers, of course, had different priorities than whether it enabled the group to discover each other. The underwhelming notices must have been as much a dash of cold water as the low sales. As recently as two years before, the British weekly *New Musical Express* (*NME*) had voted the Small Faces' *Ogdens' Nut Gone Flake* 'Album of the Year'. The reception to what might be posited as *Ogdens'* follow-up was somewhat more muted, to say the least. *Melody Maker*'s Chris Welch seemed to be straining to find good things to say, the 'Back with a bang' with which he opened his review hardly lived up to by phrases like 'while it is rather patchy, there are some great moments', and 'occasionally they sound a little ragged, but there is drive and strong emotion to compensate'. Joel Selvin of *Rolling Stone* wrote, 'The basic weakness with the album is that although the music is original, it is also highly derivative. The final effect leaves one considerably less excited than the lineup promises'. Meanwhile, just when Robert Christgau had begun to be won round to Stewart by his solo debut album, he now found himself faced with a 'mystery', asserting that the singer had reinvented himself yet again but only as a 'leader of a mediocre white r&b band'.

The Faces at least rose to the challenge of carving out a live audience for themselves. They first played together at a Cambridge University ball in July 1969 under the name Quiet Melon. Even with their new, semi-famous name, they initially found achieving progress a grind: Stewart later averred that audiences at British gigs never topped a hundred during their first six months. The band was what you might term the opposite of a supergroup: an ensemble comprised of backline leftovers of once-famous bands. Being uncomfortably conscious of their rejects image was, for Stewart, what made them all turn to drink: the boozing that became so much part of their legend started out as a means to obtain Dutch courage. Yet the following that they began building up was at least a receptive, attentive one: society was changing and the screaming teenagers who had hitherto dismayed the Small Faces by drowning out concerts had matured into young adults who were prepared to listen.

The Faces played their first American dates in early 1970. Although Stewart and Wood had been Stateside with the Jeff Beck Group, at the time it was a big deal to the former Small Faces, who for various reasons had never played in the birthplace of rock 'n' roll. 'I think we went over there with the right attitude', says Jones. 'There were a few bands that were trying to hype their way into the American people's hearts.

Americans don't like hype. They want to adopt you. We went and played a few little clubs first and we always had time for everybody and we had a party and invited the whole bloody audience back to the hotel every night. It was in the Vietnam days, so [there were a lot of] GIs and people like that. We became a people's band. Word of mouth was unbelievable. We'd do one gig and, when we got to the next place, people were going nuts. Our reputation *was* preceding us. And everywhere we went we just a had a party, on stage and off'.

2
MY WAY OF
GIVING

JUST TWO AND A HALF MONTHS after *First Step*, Stewart's second solo album appeared. As before, it put Faces product to shame. Once again, this was slightly mystifying, as Stewart's impetus was again more mammon than great art.

Despite its flaws, *The Rod Stewart Album* had sold a healthy one hundred thousand copies in the States, leading to Irwin Steinberg, president of Mercury Records, to request from Lou Reizner a follow-up album. Reizner later told Stewart biographer George Tremlett that Stewart had responded, 'If you are my manager you have got to get me some more money'. This was not the first time Stewart had tried this trick. After signing his contract with Mercury, Stewart failed to begin work on his first album for a year. John Rowlands, who co-managed Stewart with Geoff Wright, told George Tremlett, 'He thought the advance that he had been paid was insufficient. . . . Eventually, in order to put the LP together Mercury agreed to pay him an extra 10,000 dollars—because Lou really had got great faith in him. And for an unknown singer to get that much money in those days was really very good indeed. In fact, it was practically unheard of'. Reizner (not, in fact, Stewart's manager) relayed the latest request to Steinberg. 'Steinberg said he would give me $12,000 to produce the album, and then whatever part of that I didn't spend Rod could have the difference', said Reizner. 'And it was then that his Scottish ancestry came out and he became very mean and frugal . . . and there were all sorts of scenes in the studio'. These were followed by scenes outside the studio. When Reizner returned to the UK after attending his brother's wedding in the US, he found Stewart refusing to hand over the finished album because his part of the advance hadn't yet arrived. As to how much that sum was, Reizner recalled, 'The cost of producing the LP turned out to be thirty-five hundred pounds'. This means that Stewart would have pocketed over $35k in today's coinage. 'He's cheap to a fault', says McLagan. 'Tight to a turn'. 'They did go fast, these recordings', confirms the album's studio engineer, Mike Bobak.

From such mercenaryism miraculously came magnificence. Stewart may have been hustling his sidemen to complete the recordings in as few takes as possible but judging by the results—ultimately released under the title *Gasoline Alley*—it made little or no difference to the quality of what was produced. Admittedly, this time around there were no extravaganzas like 'Handbags and Gladrags', but the LP was overall far stronger than the debut and contained some tracks that achieved just as much power and poignancy as that track with far fewer instruments and far fewer production flourishes.

Although Stewart had joined the Faces (at least nominally) since laying down his first solo outing, the instrumentation was largely supplied by the same cast heard on *Raincoat*. It, together with some additions, would populate Rod's solo work for the next few years.

'It's natural for a musician to use a different set of musicians for his solo career', reasons Pete Sears, from this album onwards, Stewart's solo-LP pianist. 'I don't think it was through any frustration with [the Faces'] ability to play in the studio or anything. Didn't Micky play on that first album? So he was already in the mix, so it's a natural thing for him to use those musicians again'. 'There may have been some kind of contractual thing there as well, though', says Ray Jackson. 'Because he had a contract with Warner Brothers and a contract with Mercury Records. One of the provisions was that the Faces couldn't record together on a Mercury album I believe, because it would negate the terms of their contract with Warner Brothers'. Jackson thinks he heard this from Mercury's artist liaison manager, Tony Powell.

Whereas the Faces were a band comprised of a bunch of mates, Stewart's solo band was a collection of individuals who would probably never have coalesced were it not for work purposes. 'It was an oddball, eccentric group of musicians and people', notes Sears. This ensemble never had a collective name and never played a gig together, but would be highly esteemed, to such an extent that it would be compared in terms of power to the bands that played on Bob Dylan's classic mid-1960s albums *Highway 61 Revisited* and *Blonde on Blonde*.

Sears was yet another Steamhammer graduate. 'I was playing in a band called Silver Metre with Leigh Stephens from Blue Cheer and with Micky Waller', says Sears. 'Micky, I guess, at some point introduced me to Rod. They were going to do *Gasoline Alley*. I actually met him the afternoon of the first recording'. Although Sears would primarily play piano on Stewart's records, he also occasionally assumed bassist duties. He has no preference. 'I've always played bass or piano or both in bands', he says. 'It's like apples and oranges. I enjoy both very much but they're entirely different'. Even so, 'They both influence each other in my playing'.

Dennis O'Flynn and Dick Powell are credited on *Gasoline Alley* with violin. Mandolin is attributed to Stanley Matthews. The latter would seem to be a joke by football-mad Stewart, as this musician's handle has never cropped up on any other recording and happens to be the name of one of the most iconic English soccer players of all time.

Of Stewart's retention of Powell, Sears recalls, 'We needed a violin player. He sent somebody around to the Italian restaurant around the corner to get the guy who played violin there in'. For Sears, this spur-of-the-moment expedience encapsulates the spirit of Mercury-era Stewart sessions. He says, 'I've been playing since 1964 with different bands, but those albums were some of the most enjoyable I was part of. . . . We'd go over to his house in the afternoon with all the band members that were going to play that night and he'd play the tune on an acoustic guitar. He usually had a piano there in his house. (He had a progression of houses, getting bigger and bigger, depending on each album.) He just played the song and sometimes it was an original song and sometimes it was a cover, and we just listened to him play and we'd play along with him and run over the track and come up quickly with a part and we'd pop over to the studio and pretty much it was all done in about one or two takes, two or three takes at the most'. 'Didn't use to play it before, used to do it straight away in the studio', says Waller. 'Some of them we rehearsed a few days before. 'Maggie May' was rehearsed in Rod's house with me and Martin and Rod. 'You Wear It Well' was done like that. But a lot of them, you just turned up at the studio and there was hardly ever any rehearsal before the recording sessions. I hate rehearsing anyway, so it actually suited me fine to do it like that'. Nor does Waller remember Stewart giving the musicians much in the way of instruction. 'He used to leave it to everyone to get on with what they wanted themselves'. 'He just appeared with all his musicians, started off, and then I had to get a balance and a sound pretty quick because they only ever wanted to do it once or twice', says Bobak. 'There wasn't a lot of time between seven and eleven'.

As to why Sears was retained when Stewart already had at his disposal an able keyboardist in McLagan, Sears offers, 'Ian was playing the B3 [Hammond organ] and I was playing the piano. . . . We had live piano and live B3, so he didn't have to have overdubs'. This was an important part of the sound. Although Sears says, 'Ron would overdub the bass usually . . . and he'd overdub some slide work perhaps', that was generally the extent of the *ex post facto* instrumentation. 'For some of those songs, there are two acoustic guitars', says Sears. 'Rod liked to have two acoustic guitars going, usually one lower and one higher. Ron and Martin would play it live on the basic, and the drums and bass and piano. I don't think I ever overdubbed the piano. . . . Most of the electric [guitar] on the basic track was always kept. . . . For better or worse, it was all done live'. For Sears' part, live was better. 'The feel of the track was very important, unlike later production styles, especially in the '80s, when precision perfect recordings or performances were required by engineers and tuning and all this business. We just went for the feel of a track'.

That live feel may also apply to some vocals. 'He usually sang a work vocal, which most people do, live with the band', says Sears of Stewart. 'These days, of course, it's all Pro-Tooled to death with taking this phrase from that track and this phrase from that, but back then quite often you'd realise that the work vocal—in spite of the leakage into the microphone from the band—was the best vocal, so there may be some live-with-the-band vocals used'.

Also important was not refining a song to death. Sears: 'It was a party-like atmosphere going on really. Just do it, just play. There are probably parts I could have done better, but the whole thing just came together. I've produced people myself here and there, and having done a lot of session work, quite often they go back to the first take. You do, like, twenty takes and you end up with the first take because there's something about that first or second take that just feels right, even though there may be mistakes'. Bobak agrees: 'There was a certain amount of keep doing it and it sounds worse and worse. That's why I had to be really quick getting a balance and a sound'. By this post–*Sgt. Pepper* point in rock history, such ad hoc methods, Bobak notes, were 'really unusual'. He elaborates, 'With Cat Stevens, they used to spend, like, three days doing one mix. I used to think, "If I hear this song once again I'm going to go mad". It was the start of that era, which was awful'.

Although Sears says, 'Everything was so fluid and just worked out on the spot', he does admit that there was some sort of plan, or even formula, involved. 'There were certain song structures that seemed to recur, or patterns within a song, and that would be starting off almost acoustic, with very little drums in the beginning of the song, maybe even until halfway through, and then the drums would come in and it would give this lift into a more rock vein. So that song structure would go from a folkie feeling to a really rowdy kind of rock feeling. Always a fantastic feeling'.

It was on this album that the Mercury Rod Stewart–LP blueprint was set for several years, both in terms of track components (cover versions juxtaposed with three-to-four compositions by Stewart, with and without collaborators, one Dylan song, and one jam on an oldie) and musical elements (the previous album's concoction is completed by lashings of fiddle and/or mandolin manipulatively introduced at junctures of extreme emotion). It was also set in terms of genetic musical makeup, although the overall style was a synthesis of so many influences that it can be difficult to define. Sears: 'He was very influenced by Sam Cooke and Bob Dylan—I could tell that in his playing—but he also had that sort of Stonesy feel with Micky Waller drumming because Micky had that same backbeat and he hit the drums in that same sweet-spot that Charlie Watts [did]. It wasn't really pure folk but there was that definite folk, slightly Celtic feel, so it became its own thing. It was folk-rock with a soul influence'. Stewart's old busking partner, 'Wizz' Jones, marveled to Stewart biographers Tim Ewbank and Stafford Hildred, 'He had done what we had all been trying to do. Rod had been inspired by raw acoustic folk music and he had taken it, put it into a rock form, and come up with something new'.

Production is now jointly credited to Stewart and Reizner. 'He was there on all the sessions for *Gasoline Alley* that I was part of', says Sears of Reizner. However, Bobak says of Reizner, 'He never did anything. He just came along and sat there'. This doesn't mean, though, that the artist was truly in control or at the controls. It would have been impossible for either Stewart or Reizner to have been able to produce a professional sound without the aid of someone conversant with mixing desks. Enter Bobak. 'I was an engineer at Morgan Studios and was allocated to that particular session', he recalls. As well as Cat Stevens, Bobak had worked with the likes of Donovan and the Kinks. There was an instant chemistry with his new client. 'He obviously liked what I did and we kept going for another five or six albums', Bobak—who also worked on Faces fare—reflects. Sears speaks of his contribution in less understated terms: 'Mike Bobak was just a brilliant engineer. Great ear and ability for mic placement and a very patient fellow'. As for how he felt about his new client, Bobak says of Stewart, 'He was one of the lads. Not big headed or anything like that'.

The fact that *Gasoline Alley*'s opening, title track is bereft of bass, drums and keyboards might give rise to the suspicion that it evinces signs of the parsimoniousness that Stewart assiduously practiced during this album's gestation. Perhaps so, but it in no way sounds bare. This is by dint of the fact that it departs from the usual live-in-studio approach, boasting a veritable orchestra of guitar parts, all courtesy of the repeatedly-overdubbed Ronnie Wood, who co-wrote the song with Stewart. A lovely strummed acoustic fanfare is quickly augmented by electric guitars whose alternately keening and cooing tones are perfectly in keeping with a tale of homesickness shot through with, if not class consciousness, then an acknowledgement of status-seeking pretension ('Better swallow up my silly country pride').

Amusingly, John Morthland of *Rolling Stone* assumed that Gasoline Alley was some sort of British slang for a Bowery equivalent (he being presumably unaware that 'gasoline' is not a word in common usage in the UK, where the liquid that powers motor cars is known as 'petrol'). Perhaps just as amusingly, Stewart had assumed that it was a real place in San Francisco rather than a US metaphor for insalubrious environs. Stewart's ears pricked up when a female fan told him backstage at concert venue the Fillmore that she'd better get home in case her mother thought she'd ventured into Gasoline Alley. (English songwriters Roger Cook, Roger Greenaway and Tony Macaulay seemed better informed of the meaning of the phrase in 'Gasoline Alley Bred', another song about a man realising he has ideas above his station, which by an interesting confluence was a UK hit for the Hollies in October 1970, four months after Stewart's song first appeared.) The way in which Stewart co-opts the phrase doesn't quite make sense—'Gasoline Alley' is urban, not rural—but the fact that he filed it away for future use proves that his writing instincts were becoming enhanced, as does the very fact that he helped craft an affecting modern folk song from it.

Bobby and Shirley Womack's 'It's All Over Now' was originally recorded by the Valentinos, but was most familiar to Stewart's compatriots from the 1964 chart-topping single by the Rolling Stones, which was also a top-30 US hit. Once the Jagger/Richards songwriting axis had kicked into gear, the Stones' reinvention of the Valentinos' chugging original retroactively came to sound like a quintessential Stones anthem. Stewart reinvents the song again, indulging in what is clearly a penchant for stretching out a familiar, much-loved but previously concise creation, but doing so far more successfully than he did on the previous record's risible take on 'Street Fighting Man'. This agreeable recording's playful mood is illustrated by a section in which respites enable different instruments to each play a phrase (one of which happens to be the central riff of 'Gasoline Alley'). McLagan's piano runs are rollickingly enjoyable and Wood—who plays bass on the album with the exception of a couple of tracks Sears handles—provides a throbbing bottom end. The only flaw is that, before the end of its six-and-a-half-minute playing time, it begins to approach tediousness, especially in Stewart's multiple repetitions of the title phrase.

'Only a Hobo' is the perfect intersection of Stewart's triple penchant for poverty tableaux, aching compassion and Bob Dylan songs. It also inaugurates a pattern. Long before he did lazy covers of the likes of 'Just Like a Woman', Stewart habitually recorded Dylan songs that the composer himself had not released versions of. These unused songs were in no way substandard. Such had been Dylan's prolificness since his recording career began eight years before—helped by the fact that it was only in the mid-1960s that he began writing truly original melodies instead of adapting old folk tunes—that oodles of his creations never ended up on his records.

Stewart's keenness to record Dylan songs, and specifically lesser-known ones, made it logical to assume that he was a serious devotee of the man who had transformed popular music by bringing the literacy and social conscience of folk to the musically exciting but lyrically juvenile world of rock. Stewart had certainly been knocked out by Dylan's first album (rather oddly, as it is atypical of his records in being chiefly comprised of covers). However, Stewart seems to have heard it at a key point of personal and musical development, loving its Americana and learning to play guitar and harmonica in the wake of being exposed to it. That is the extent of his Dylan fandom. As to how Stewart seemed to have an aficionado's knowledge of the byways of Dylan's back pages, McLagan explains, 'There was some guy from Mercury and he would give him cassettes of demos of his stuff'. That Mercury employee was Paul Nelson, who later became a journalist. It was he who introduced Stewart to 'Only a Hobo'. 'I'd never heard it before until he played it to me', said Stewart to Nelson's biographer Kevin Avery. 'He was such a Dylanologist . . . and he would turn me on to such obscure Bob Dylan songs'.

'Only a Hobo'—recorded for Dylan's 1964 album, *The Times They Are a-Changin'*, before ending up on the cutting-room floor—is a thematic precursor to Phil Collins' 'Another Day in Paradise'. It finds a narrator noting a hobo (not a word in common usage in Stewart's homeland then or now, where 'tramp' tends to be employed to describe the long-term homeless) who has passed away in the street overnight. He sadly reflects that nobody will be left to mourn someone so clearly lacking social attachments. Folkie Hamilton Camp recorded the song on his 1964 album, *Paths of Glory*. Stewart's version knocks both his and Dylan's (finally released in 1991) into a cocked hat. To be fair, a full-band rendition will often confer an advantage on versions involving merely voice, acoustic guitar and harmonica, and that's certainly the case here. Its opening sees Stewart, Wood and Quittenton provide a lilting acoustic guitar chorus that tugs at the heartstrings without a word having been sung. Stewart then proceeds to take the song to a whole new level of pathos. With a tempo that's slower than the previous interpretations, the mood is exquisitely tender, providing the perfect entrée for Stewart, who, with understated but tear-jerking compassion, poses the question of how any human being can come to 'lie in the gutter and die with no name'.

Interspersed instrumental passages of a faster tempo find Wood deploying bottleneck, O'Flynn violin bass and Powell violin in one of the best Dylan covers ever recorded.

On 'My Way of Giving', the Small Faces meet the Faces. A Marriott/Lane composition that had appeared on the Small Faces' eponymous second album (1967), Jones, Lane and McLagan are able to have another crack at the song in the company of their new colleagues, Stewart and Wood. It's perhaps the first out-and-out pop song Stewart ever recorded. However, it's far more of an adult love song than most 1960s pop numbers, expressing romantic affection in nuanced and poetic ways, the narrator vouchsafing doubts about love even as he articulates a desperation for it. Musically, the song alternates stately verses with marching choruses. There's not much to choose in terms of the quality of the singing of Marriott and Stewart (or indeed Chris Farlowe, who released it on single in 1967), but the *Gasoline Alley* band play the song in a more funky manner than it has previously been treated to, while Jones' blazing performance trumps his more sedate drumming on the Small Faces' version.

In October 1970 (January 1971 in the US), Elton John released a most peculiar album called *Tumbleweed Connection*. His third studio LP, it is one of the lesser-known (though certainly not one of the lesser-purchased) concept albums, comprising a collection of songs by him and lyricist Bernie Taupin with pronounced Wild West and Americana settings and flavourings. 'Country Comfort' is a typical example of its almost contradictory olde-worlde aura (i.e. a harkening back to the 'ancient' times of what is actually a very new country). Its verses find deacons preparing sermons, grandmothers asking their able-bodied grandsons to lend a hand on the farm and craftsmen lamenting the encroachment of industrialisation, while its choruses give thanks for the prospect of returning to such environs. (One suspects it had more than a little influence on 'Take Me Home, Country Roads', a John Denver co-write released the following year.)

Elton John's version was one of no fewer than five to appear in 1970. English band Silver Metre included it (and another *Tumbleweed Connection* song) on their eponymous album in April 1970. John and Stewart are of course famously good friends, but the personnel on the Silver Metre records may explain how Stewart came to be cognisant of the song: it not only included Micky Waller and Pete Sears but also Leigh Stephens, who had briefly rehearsed with the nascent Faces.

Either Silver Metre and Stewart were working from the same publisher's demo or Stewart's version is simply a cover of the Silver Metre recording, as like theirs—and unlike the other 1970 versions, which also included renditions by Orange Bicycle and the Chanter Sisters—it replaces 'deacon' with 'parson' and talks of a 'road', not a 'truck', taking the narrator home. (John's own version additionally has a longer lyric.) 'Rod . . . got the words wrong', John lamented to Charles Shaar Murray of the *NME* in March 1975. 'Apparently he'd got the words off Silver Metre. . . . I've had that out with him since then'. Incorrect his reading may be, but Stewart's version is the best of them all. Displaying his impeccable feel for mood, he ensures that his colleagues take the tempo right down and that they don't make a nonsense of a rustic and antediluvian vista with an overly electric soundscape. (Only Wood's echo-treated electric guitar solo contradicts the pastoralism, although it's enjoyably gnarly in itself.) When the misty-eyed narrator says of his granny, 'Poor old girl she needs a man down on the farm', we believe completely in the bucolic picture being painted. 'It was much better than mine', John had to admit to Murray. 'Rod's version is so much more natural and laid-back'.

'Cut Across Shorty', written by Marijohn Wilkin and Wayne P. Walker, is a creation cleaving to country music's story-song tradition. It concerns the romantic intrigues among country boy Shorty, city dweller Dan and one Miss Lucy, whom both Shorty and Dan are keen to wed. This mundane triangle takes a turn for the bizarre when it's agreed among them that the competing affections will be decided by a race, the winner of which will become Lucy's groom. Although Dan is monied and handsome, Lucy wishes Shorty—who possess some quality 'that can't be found in books'—to be her life partner. Accordingly, she fixes the outcome by advising Shorty of a short cut.

The song was first recorded by Eddie Cochran, and indeed was the last thing he ever laid down. His rendition, with backing from the Crickets, appeared as the B-side of the final single of his lifetime, 'Three Steps to Heaven', in April 1960. Although it failed to chart in his native US, it benefitted in the UK from the British populace's inclination to sentimentally propel the latest release of a recently deceased pop star to the top of the charts, not least because Cochran's tragic death at the age of twenty-one in a car crash occurred in England. In the US it could be the case that Cochran's version is less well known than that of country artist Carl Smith, who issued it on single in November 1960. Smith's version boasts an exquisite splashing piano solo but lacks the punch and speed of Cochran's original.

Stewart was presumably attracted to the song because of its celebration of the unprivileged and the underdog. As was his wont, he takes his recording into completely unexpected and even illogical areas, perhaps inevitably when his version is over three times longer than Cochran's sub-two-minute template. The instrumentation is incongruously gothic, the most prominent factor in which is Powell's sinister violin. A feeling of menace is completed by downstrokes on acoustic guitar and a midtempo pace that sounds not so much relaxed as ominous. Stewart's Mercury albums made a virtue of melding ostensibly incompatible instrumental elements and musical styles. This track constitutes one of the few occasions on which the mash-up approach threatens to break down: the sunny, fairytale-like lyric never quite gels with the dark fiddle work and the feeling of something terrible lurking over the horizon, while the lengthy non-vocal passages (including a completely instrumental final two minutes) disrupt narrative momentum. Yet the collapse never quite happens. Powell's spiky playing, Waller's drum crescendos, and some typical fat-toned electric guitar work from Wood combine to make for something that is, somehow and simply, an enjoyable listen. Artists don't, of course, always intend the effects their music have, and in this case one wonders whether—had he not been intent on keeping costs low—Stewart might have ordered another take so as to 'fix' the recording's overarching incongruity. If so, his stinginess has worked in the listener's favour.

A brace of Stewart-written autobiographical ballads follows. 'Lady Day' is the Christian Church's name for the Feast of the Annunciation of the Blessed Virgin. It was also the nickname of jazz chanteuse Billie Holiday. It's not known which of those uses of the phrase Stewart co-opted for a composition about Jenny Rylance, a young woman with whom he had an on-off relationship over several years. (By what might seem a bizarre quirk of fate, Rylance next fell in love with—and later married—Steve Marriott, which meant that she was involved with arguably the era's two greatest British blues-soul singers, as well as both front men of the Small Faces/Faces continuum.) The song finds Stewart (in this context, it's pointless to use the neutral term 'the narrator') chronicling a fragmenting relationship. The tone seems contrite and humble, Stewart stating that he refuses to view the time he has spent with his soon-to-be former lover as wasted. The self-effacing mood is bolstered by tender backing, Quittenton and Wood proffering frothy acoustic-guitar swells, Wood picking a keening electric-guitar figure, and an uncredited person maintaining a discreet rhythm on the hi-hat. Powell and O'Flynn provide sympatico violin ornamentation.

Yet examining the songwords more closely unearths a less magnanimous attitude. Stewart repeatedly takes digs, chiding his lover for 'laughing down' at him, not listening to his grievances, and viewing his lower-caste origins as not good enough for her newly elevated status. Moreover, the lyric is mythologically self-pitying, Stewart talking of himself as a latterly visibly aged and stooped figure who makes an unfitting picture for Lady Day's whitewashed walls. It all rather puts one in mind of the unreliable narrator of the Police's 1983 hit 'Every Breath You Take', where a sinister reality is discernible behind the professed devotion—with the difference that, in the Police's case, that nuance was fully intended by composer Sting.

Although his accent bears the hallmarks of his London upbringing, Stewart has always been ostentatiously proud of his Scottish heritage. His adoration of his Leith-raised father compelled him to publicly drape himself from his mid-twenties onwards in tartan scarves and, from a much earlier age, to support not the English national soccer side but Scotland's. 'Jo's Lament' marks the first appearance in his music of his fetishisation of the Caledonian, even if it's here nothing more overt than a thistle-ish tone and mood.

Certainly the likes of bagpipes are out of the question for what is a three-man job. Having said that, Quittenton, Stewart and Wood provide another veritable guitar orchestra. Acoustic, steel and electric guitars—live and overdubbed—are sweetly strummed and imaginatively picked. It provides a bed for a lyric in which the narrator communicates to an old flame that she would laugh if she could see his reduced circumstances and that he is afflicted with a mortal fear of sleeping alone for the rest of his days. In 1970, Stewart was an individual who was, if not yet rich, a recording artist and presumably (and consequently) not lacking in willing bed partners, certainly an enviable position as far as most would see it. He is either harking back to a less successful and confident part of his life, or—more likely—indulging in his habit of reaching for mythmaking and hardship vistas. Perhaps we wouldn't even wonder about the incongruity were it not for the fact that at least part of the song is deeply rooted in personal experience. Not the commonplace and subjective scenes of 'Lady Day'—everybody has exes, and there's always two sides to breakup stories—but the concrete and non-mundane fact of him having fathered a child by the song's subject.

Stewart's first serious girlfriend was one Susannah Boffey. When the pair were eighteen, Boffey fell pregnant. In 1963, this sort of thing was a world-shattering event. Unwedded mothers were considered to be of loose morals, unwedded fathers irresponsible cads and abortion was illegal. Stewart has recalled that the strains the situation put on the relationship caused it to founder. (The fact that he admits that Boffey got so frustrated with him that she broke his treasured steel guitar indicates that—as with 'Lady Day'—there might be dimensions to that split that his brain failed to register.) Stewart states that he doesn't expect Jo/Susannah to forgive him after 'you bore my child then I left you aside'. His observation that hitherto he'd been sure that he had it made hints that he felt that a child and family would be an obstacle to his musical ambitions, but we're left less concerned with the self-interest than the acknowledgement of it and genuine remorse.

The baby was a daughter named Sarah, who—as was the common practice at the time—was given up for adoption. For a long time, Stewart seems to have erased Sarah's existence from his memory. Dee Harrington, despite sharing Stewart's life and home across most of the first half of the 1970s, says of his existent fatherhood status, 'Never spoke to me about that. I wasn't aware of it'. However, in the 1980s, Sarah made contact with Stewart and they were able to build a long-term relationship.

The album almost has a second Faces track in the shape of closer 'You're My Girl (I Don't Want to Discuss It)'. However, Jones, Lane, Stewart and Wood couldn't be joined by McLagan (according to the sleeve notes) 'due to bus strike' (which may be a joke, but—in an era when Britain was subject to much 'industrial action'—could also be true). Written by Dick Cooper, Beth Beatty and Ernie Shelby, 'I Don't Want to Discuss It' was first recorded in 1967 by Little Richard in a percolating soul arrangement augmented by horns and female backing vocalists that failed to make the singles charts. The song was the subject of subsequent covers by Amen Corner, the Robbs, Rhinoceros, the Instigations and Delaney & Bonnie and Friends. Stewart's interpretation perhaps owes a little something to Rhinoceros' blunderbuss approach but otherwise sounds unlike any previous one. The almost-Faces opt for a staccato arrangement while Stewart pretty much invents a new melody line with his vocal track. Lane's thrumming bass is excellent, and the dramatic guitar riff bestowed on the song has its merits, but the overall effect is disjointed and makes for a puzzlingly tentative end to an otherwise often splendid LP.

As with the first album, there were very different cover designs either side of the Atlantic. UK's Vertigo did Stewart proud with an evocative gatefold sleeve. Its monochrome wraparound cover photograph consisted of a grimy longshot of a homeless man, prone beneath an antediluvian-looking lantern, imagery that alluded to both the title track and 'Only a Hobo'. One could argue that the colour spread inside wherein Stewart is lounging in smart clothes is an unfortunate juxtaposition (especially as it's an outside pic that at first glance can be mistaken for being situated in the same street as the one the tramp is lying in). Then again, it could also be said to perfectly epitomise what many found admirable about the artist at the time: the fact that this was a man in a privileged position whose rising fortunes had not caused him to forget the have-nots. Mercury in America went for a slightly cartoonish front cover illustration of a drain on a cobbled street. However, what Mercury's iteration lacked in power, it made up for in musician credits, which were both sparse and inaccurate on the UK version: the back cover provided a track-by-track listing of contributors (and even spelt McLagan's surname right), even if it did forget to mention Waller. Photographs and line drawings of the musicians adorned the inner sleeve. Both editions carried brief, jocular sleeve notes from Stewart and Wood.

The reviews demonstrated the artistic and commercial momentum Stewart was picking up. Bud Scoppa of American magazine *Circus* wrote a review that reflected both widespread admiration for Stewart's common touch and general surprise at the musical direction he had taken. 'It's becoming increasingly obvious that Rod Stewart is an unusually gifted singer and writer . . . *Gasoline Alley* . . . [makes] it clear that Stewart is an artist of originality and sensitivity as well as power', he wrote. 'These songs have an old-timey quality. . . . Several tracks sound as if they were done live in the studio (or a garage for that matter). . . . Considering the fact that Rod was not long ago the lead singer of . . . the Jeff Beck Group, it seems odd that he has now become what could best he described as a folk singer. . . . Although he's English, Rod's free-living attitude most closely parallels the lifestyles of American journeyman folksingers. He has more bread than they did, of course, but he reflects their values in his stubborn refusal to follow trends or lick record company boots'.

It was the gushing but eloquent review of Langdon Winner in *Rolling Stone* that best summed up just what a working-class hero Stewart was becoming. 'The music of Rod Stewart helps us to remember many of the small but extremely important experiences of life. . . . Compassion. Care for small things. The textures of sorrow. Remembrance of times past. Reverence for age. . . . The amazing character of Stewart's work is largely due to the fact that he can recall these fragile moments of insight to our minds without destroying their essence. . . . The tone of his voice and the authenticity of his phrasing let you know that he's doing much more than just singing the required lyrics'. Throwing in a literary reference, he noted, 'At his best Stewart comes very close to Thoreau's meaning in the early pages of *Walden*: "The mass of men lead lives of quiet desperation"'. He then invoked a popular-music comparison point, asserting that Stewart's two albums together constituted 'the most important listening experience I've had since the Band's first album'.

Stewart seemed to be falling on his feet every which way: his stinginess with studio time miraculously translated into admiration for his rootsy, unpretentious sound, and Jenny Rylance's impatience with his self-absorption was translated into Winner perceiving him as the victim.

There were some dissenters. Robert Christgau wrote in the *Village Voice*, 'Stewart's first Mercury album was a landmark that improves in retrospect. Perhaps that's the only reason I find this somewhat flat'. Christgau clearly came to feel that *Gasoline Alley* also improved in retrospect. In a 1981 book that collected his 1970s reviews, he revised his B+ grading of the album to A–, saying, 'Much all-around excellence here—Stewart writes songs with almost as much imagination as he picks them, and his band is as . . . sensitive as his voice'.

Absurdly, the record company chose to promote the album with a single of 'It's All Over Now' (with 'Jo's Lament' on the B-side). They should ideally have been emphasising their artist's considerable song-writing capabilities on the A-side but, if they insisted on a cover version, 'Only a Hobo' or 'Country Comforts' would have been far more likely to make an impact than a well-known song like Womack's. Even more inexplicably, the version of 'It's All Over Now' released gave the lie to the declaration that it was lifted from the album (the single's label even help-fully provided the LP's catalogue number). This was a completely differ-ent recording. That its three-and-a-half-minute length was much shorter than the overlong album version might have been a good thing were it not for the fact that it's a characterless, cluttered version completely lack-ing in the long-player cut's enjoyable spaciousness.

Still, with reviews that seemed to come close to blurring the line between perceiving Stewart as the great white hope of rock and hail-ing him as the Second Coming, *Gasoline Alley* was destined to do well commercially. Its showing at number 62 for one week was the sum total of its UK album-chart activity, but that was an improvement on its predecessor's non-performance in his home country. In the States, the album climbed to the dizzy heights on the *Billboard* Top LPs chart of number 27.

PROMOTING *GASOLINE ALLEY*, Stewart found himself discuss-ing the almost unique position in popular-music history he inhabited: a man with two careers which, though in many ways complementary, also threatened to work against each other.

Holding forth to Penny Valentine of *Sounds* about his complicated relationship with the Faces, he said, 'The trouble is that the Faces' sec-ond album, as far as I'm concerned, has got to be better than *Gasoline*. I'm tending to play down . . . my own albums for that very reason . . . I must admit that I tend to enjoy my own recording sessions best. It's just that I'm producing them and things are arranged round my voice. If there's a mistake, then it's my mistake'. He said he enjoyed Faces record-ing sessions because they were 'a good laugh', but also observed, 'The looning can get out of hand, and now they've built a bar in the studios it's suicide'. He also noted, 'There is the point at Faces sessions of having five musicians and five producers and that can cause a few problems'. He also revealed a gap between him and the rest of the band with regards to priorities. 'The Faces . . . have a much bigger desire to make it in Britain—I think they feel they've got to prove something. Not just to themselves but to the British public. That's why we have a few clashes in the studio'. He said that he would consider a solo tour 'maybe in two or three years', yet also added, 'But I don't know. I don't like the responsibility of being my own master'. He vouchsafed that Mercury were continually urging him to take this path, but he felt he couldn't be in a better set-up than the one he was in, not least because of a support network. 'With Beck even the roadies were telling us what to do. Now there's the record company, the management, the publicity people all pushing for the Faces. That's why I'm sure it's going to work'.

One of the tensions cum ironies of the dual Stewart/Faces career paths was the fact that although, as a consequence of his well-received solo LPs, many more people now wanted to see Rod Stewart in concert, they could only do so by buying tickets for a Faces gig. The band naturally benefitted from this fact. By early 1971, the Faces were selling out three-thousand seaters in America. Without a hit to their name—album or single—and certainly no rave reviews of their records, the Faces became an in-concert phenomenon. This, though, was by no means solely down to Stewart, even though he contributed significantly by draping himself in tartan, kicking soccer balls into the crowds and making a trademark of mesmerisingly twirling his ultra-light aluminum microphone stand. Their collective larger-than-life but simultaneously down-to-earth in-concert personality (they sometimes passed out bottles of Mateus Rosé) quickly generated a live prowess on a par with that of the Rolling Stones and the Who. The Faces' tendency to inebriation inevitably meant lots of bum notes, but that mattered less to their audiences than the fact that they seemed the very antithesis of the fast-developing corporatisation of the rock industry. Their proudly glittery stage clothes, meanwhile, defied the growing division between glamorous pop and dowdy rock that was lately developing. 'They were a good live band—a good *fun* live band', says Altham. 'They created a good atmosphere on stage'. 'The Faces were a shit-hot band', says Ray Jackson. Critic Lester Bangs said (in his inimitable more-emotional-than-grammatical style), 'I am possibly the world's worst audience: I'll sit blankly staring at Levithan field goaling the parted Red Sea waters, and The Faces actually managed to get *me* on my feet dancing up and down on my shuddering chair as I clapped and whooped like a born-again fool'.

Stewart himself was anxious in his 1970 *Rolling Stone* interview to emphasise that the Faces were a group. Asked if he saw himself as its leader, he said, 'No, very far from it. . . . It's probably something I brought upon myself, because *Gasoline Alley* was so big, and I feel like a lot of the people are coming to hear the numbers off that album. It's weird, really, I shouldn't worry about it, but I do. And I want this band to be really successful'. Despite this touching loyalty, the image had begun to take hold of the Faces riding on Stewart's coattails. There was, of course, one surefire way to prove it a misconception: by the Faces putting together a great album of their own.

Moreover, this was a task it would clearly be simplicity to achieve. Stewart's studio band was a loose collective, whereas the Faces were constantly working and thus had the almost telekinetic communication of the well-oiled road band. The Faces boasted four songwriters in Lane, McLagan, Stewart and Wood, whereas the solo Stewart so far was dependent on himself and Wood. Moreover, the Faces contained within their ranks much the same personnel that had conjured such magic on Stewart's albums.

There was a good augury for the Faces' second album. In November 1970 came a UK single that was a lovable scamp of a song. A Lane/Stewart/Wood creation, 'Had Me a Real Good Time' is a good-natured, proletarian vignette involving the narrator being invited by a young lady into 'a high-class world', his means of transportation to her party, his bicycle. Once there, he declares that he was glad to come, he'll be sad to go, but while he's there he'll have him a real good time—a statement sweet in its innocence, unpretentiousness and gratitude. Wood's girthful, distorted guitar and McLagan's barrelhouse piano propel a poundingly anthemic melody. The instrumental B-side 'Rear Wheel Skid' has a rough power.

The Faces' US-only single early the following year had less logic, being a cover of Paul McCartney's 'Maybe I'm Amazed'. Not only was it a well-known song but the Faces had plenty of people in their ranks capable of writing new material. Stewart and Lane share vocals. B-side

'Oh Lord, I'm Browned Off' has no power, rough or otherwise, being an okay-ish instrumental.

That second album, *Long Player*, duly appeared in February 1971. After the promise of the UK precursor single, the opening track was a depressing affair. 'Bad 'n' Ruin'—a McLagan/Stewart co-write—possesses a scraggly and pedestrian guitar introduction which Stewart soon follows with an apropos-nothing elongated whoop. The track meanders through similar nondescript instrumentation and mechanical expressions of excitement for fully five and a half minutes. Its lyrical motif— 'Mother, you won't recognise me now'—is an attempt at bad-boy, beautiful-loser mythology that comes off as meaningless and rote. Things rarely get much better from there.

'Tell Everyone' is a Ronnie Lane composition, but its vocals are handled by Stewart. Like much of Lane's compositional work, it's affectingly tender ('To wake up with you makes my morning so bright'), but the accompaniment here is sluggish and boring. Rod doesn't help with another of his yelps of unearned euphoria.

'Sweet Lady Mary' is credited to Lane, Stewart and Wood, but one suspects its mainly Lane's creation: 'With every footstep one more tale is told' is the type of eloquent expression of compassion to which the bassist was prone; Stewart's sensitivity is more colloquial. Along with the sweet poetry are simpatico Stewart vocals and some lovely pieces of instrumentation, including sky-straining slide guitar, but the track carries on for nearly six minutes and is constantly struggling against a murky mix. The sweet la-la-la vocals from Lane that draw it to a close are pretty much the best element. Lane handles the vocals on his solo composition 'Richmond', an acoustic pine for his leafy English domicile. A bare, percussion-less recording with a prominent acoustic slide guitar part, it's slight and nondescript.

The version of 'Maybe I'm Amazed' that closed side one was one of a pair of tracks on the album recorded at the Fillmore East. Perhaps omitting the band's studio single version of this song for an alternative live rendition displayed an admirable value-for-money ethos. Perhaps also involved was a wish to capture on a record release the live prowess for which the Faces were becoming celebrated. However, a ballad that involves no audience participation hardly seems the right recipe for the latter objective. Moreover, when Stewart's opening dialogue sees him virtually chiding the crowd ('If you don't know it, I really don't know where you've been, so you should know the tune') puts one in mind of the rock critic who opined that behind the Faces' bonhomie lay a thinly disguised contempt for their audiences.

Side two opens with a remix of 'Had Me a Real Good Time'. The slide and pedal streel guitars underpinning 'On the Beach' (sung by composers Lane and Wood) instantly disappoint on the grounds that the album has already had more than its quota of such undynamic, droning roots music for what is supposed to be the product of a rock 'n' roll band. It's also the second track in a row that restarts after a false ending halfway through, with the difference that the listener wasn't disappointed by the resumption of 'Had Me a Real Good Time'.

Big Bill Broonzy's 'I Feel So Good' is the other Fillmore East recording. It's pointless in the way that all concert recordings are: you had to be there, what's heard on record is a soundboard product not experienced by many (or even necessarily any) in the venue and the historical inaccuracy will have been compounded by flub-correcting studio overdubs. However, at least some justification for its inclusion is provided by the semblance of atmosphere engendered by the call-and-response Stewart initiates with the audience. Nonetheless, nine minutes is a hell of a long running time for what started life as a sub-three-minute ditty by the Chicago bluesman.

'Jerusalem' is a pointless two-minute closer but at the same time not out of kilter with the acoustic, cawing roots music and general aimlessness that has preceded it.

Across the forty-five-minute album, the potential suggested by so much intrinsic talent and by such an exciting live reputation culminates in precisely one above-average song and a remainder that the listener is indifferent about ever hearing again. As well as undistinguished, everything seems vaguely lo-fi. Far more care seems to have been lavished on the packaging than the contents. In the UK, the album—in keeping with its generic title—appeared in a sleeve designed to resemble old-time phonograph records: an artificially aged rough card adorned by nothing except art deco lettering and patterns, with a central hole in the material through which could be seen the disc's label. (The American sleeve did something similar but less effectively, employing a dull brown colour scheme and an approach that didn't communicate the pastiche being tilted for.)

Richard Williams of *The Times* liked what he heard. 'Its uncomplicated maturity will surprise those who remember the Small Faces as purveyors of hot, strong rock in the mod tradition. . . . In a way they are a British version of the Band, performing in a very reticent manner material which at first hearing sounds slight, but which grows apace in the listener's mind'. John Mendelsohn of *Rolling Stone* took a contrary point of view. While he said that the band's live activity made them candidates for being 'very enormous indeed', he decided that 'we all have reason to be a trifle disappointed with Faces' new *Long Player*', even if it was 'consistently good casual fun and occasionally splendid'. He stated that the band lacked 'a clearly-defined sense of direction'.

The *Village Voice*'s Robert Christgau was initially enthusiastic. Adjudging *Long Player* 'a minor triumph', he said, 'I think this is the best of Stewart's records, not on the basis of song selection—both Mercury albums reach higher peaks—but because the instrumental groove is so vital and, yes, funky'. However, he later considerably downgraded his original A– rank to a B. In his 1981 book, *Rock Albums of the '70s*, he wrote, 'Stewart is a pop craftsman solo; with the Faces he's a boogie man. Boogie's not a bad idea . . . but as exciting as it is theoretically . . . it doesn't have much staying power. That's partly because they play it too loose and not quite fast enough. And partly because Stewart reserves his popcraft for solo LPs'. Christgau was cheating a little: in this pseudo-contemporaneous review, he was retroactively projecting a perception about Stewart that would begin to dawn on critics and the public from May 1971 onwards, when Stewart's third solo album appeared and transpired to be not just a significantly superior release to *Long Player* but a titanic classic.

3

EVERY PICTURE TELLS A STORY, DON'T IT?

THAT THIRD ROD STEWART ALBUM was *Every Picture Tells a Story*. As it is by common consensus one of the greatest albums ever made, it merits prolonged examination.

Once again, sessions took place at Morgan Studios, Willesden, northwest London. Although Lou Reizner had nominally had a production role on his two previous long-playing efforts, it was Stewart who took the helm for *Every Picture Tells a Story*, something he may have been inspired to do through his production work on one side of *It Ain't Easy*, an album by his old colleague Long John Baldry also released in 1971. 'The other side was produced by Elton John', says mandolinist Ray Jackson, who played on both albums. 'The sort of smulchy side was Elton John's side and the raucous bluesy sort of music was produced by Rod Stewart'. The album contained a version of the Faces' 'Flying', although it appeared on the John-produced face, not the obvious side. Although Jackson notes of Stewart and Baldry, 'They were within the same management', it should also be pointed out that Stewart perhaps felt he owed Baldry a favour, and not just for the employment he'd previously given him. It was under Baldry's aegis that Stewart's voice was first heard on record, him appearing on the B-side of a 1964 Hoochie Coochie Men single and on a track on the *Long John's Blues* album of the same year.

As to *Every Picture Tells a Story*, Pete Sears says Stewart's production role was not an in-name-only proposition. 'He produced it, alright', he insists. 'Mike Bobak certainly added a lot, but Rod decided which tracks were the best and how to go about recording them'. 'I don't think he was, really', is Bobak's comment on the notion of Stewart being the producer. 'He just used to go down and sort all the songs out. When I mixed them, he was in the bar. He only just came up after I'd mixed them and said, "Okay I like that", or "I don't like it—do it again". In those days engineers had a different role. These days, they might be called producers. He was always in the studio, he was never up in the control room'. However, Bobak does say that Stewart did evince a thoughtfulness and a proactiveness about the soundscapes being created. 'I used to give him a rough mix of the evening's work and he used to take it away and ponder over it and come in with a mandolin player or whatever he felt was necessary to finish it off'. Reizner, in fact, told Tremlett something similar: 'All the sessions that I did with Rod were very exhausting sessions because once he was actually in the studio he was quite meticulous, and he always had his own way of wanting to do things; he liked to get a very dry sound'.

By this point, Bobak was beginning to reassess his estimation of Stewart as 'one of the lads'. While Stewart wasn't yet a household name—the success of this album would bring about that—a dark side was already beginning to emerge. Bobak says, 'The more famous he got, he got more and more unpleasant. As they do'. He recalls of Stewart's attitude, 'If it sounded good yeah, and if it didn't, he used to shout at me. He lost his temper quite a few times. When he didn't like the way things were sounding, he'd blame me. I wasn't playing it. I don't know how he thought he could blame me. But he did'. He also recollects Stewart during these sessions for some reason pouring a glass of water over a young engineer named Phil, who was distraught.

Pete Sears recalls Stewart's recording modus operandi as being as highly casual as ever. McLagan recalls that the new songs would be presented to the musicians by Quittenton accompanying Stewart on acoustic guitar while Stewart sang. The work done by the band on arrangements was, the keyboardist says, 'absolutely none'. He adds, 'He was quite happy with mistakes on tracks. He didn't mind. He wanted to get to the boozer'.

Indeed. Morgan was in Stewart's North London stamping ground, but the fact that it was his—and the Faces'—studio of choice may be more down to the matter of it boasting an almost unique feature. The bar Bobak refers to was fully licensed and located in the studio building itself. 'It was like a pub with a draught beer and sausage rolls and the whole thing', says Sears. 'We'd have a few before and have a few afterwards, so that was an interesting way of doing recording. We were never completely drunk or anything, but whether alcohol had any contribution towards the overall sound of the album I don't know. Probably did on some level'. The presence of the bar also facilitated musicians being on hand even if not immediately required. 'I was just there a lot of the time for that particular album', Sears recalls. 'I think he liked to have the core group of musicians available . . . in case he decided to use that instrument or something'.

Morgan Studios was a new recording venue, founded in 1967. It took its name from one of the four owners, Barry Morgan, most famous for being the drummer with chart act Blue Mink. Of the recording space itself, Mike Bobak says, 'That was the upstairs studio, which was maybe forty foot by forty foot. High ceiling'. The room was carpeted: 'It was quite 'live' in there'. Sears says, 'As you walked in, the piano was off to the right and then you went up these little stairs on the left to get to the control booth, which was overlooking the studio. It wasn't like many studios where the control booth is on the same floor. I liked it being upstairs, in a way. It was separate. You didn't get that sense you were being peered at like you were on television or something'.

This time around, the usual musicians—Stewart, Wood, Quittenton, Sears, McLagan, Waller and Powell, and, collectively on one cut, the Faces—are augmented by bassist Andy Pyle, slide guitarist Sam Mitchell, bassist Danny Thompson, mandolinist Ray Jackson and vocalists Madeline Bell, Maggie Bell and John Baldry. (We can safely assume that the sleeve credits for Messrs. Martell Brandy and Mateus Rosé are jocular.) With the exception of Thompson, all the newcomers had worked on *It Ain't Easy* (as had Waller and Wood).

Stewart kicks off the LP with the title track, a picaresque story that's a writing collaboration between him and Wood. The music is a typical early-Stewart combination of explosive rhythm but largely acoustic instrumentation. In fact, it's remarkable what a dramatic and epic

49

soundscape Stewart and colleagues conjure from such minimalism. This is primarily down to a portentous melody, Stewart's grave but stirring vocal, and Waller's panoramic drum rolls.

There are other Mercury-Stewart hallmarks, none of them obviously assets. The six-minute song has little structure, possesses no chorus and has a casual, sometimes contrived, rhyming scheme. In the vein of such sloppiness is the issue of it being unclear what Stewart means in his use of that title phrase, which itself is utilised only as a fade out. Yet, as so often with early Stewart, these faults are things one doesn't notice in the moment because the overall effect of what one is listening to is so enjoyable.

Lyric-wise, the song is partly based on Stewart's teenage years spent travelling light (especially of pocket) in Europe. The narrator's memories of combing his hair a thousand ways in a vain attempt to kid himself that he's matinee-idol material has the verisimilitude of direct experience, as do his anecdotes about Paris and Rome (where his body stunk but he got his funk, apparently). However, it seems safe to assume that the denouement is not drawn from true life. For some reason, he finds himself making his way back to England via what seems the circuitous route of China. On the Peking ferry, the protagonist discards his I-walk-alone philosophy after finding true love in the arms of one Shanghai Lil (who never used the Pill, apparently). Unlikely though this exotic flourish to a so-far commonplace story might be, it's also moving. Stewart calls off the backing musicians to create an aural space for him and the 'vocal abrasives', as the sleeve puts it, of Maggie Bell, a raspy-voiced chanteuse who could be posited as the distaff equivalent of Stewart. Together, the two of them declare that the narrator had hitherto firmly believed that he didn't need anyone but himself. When he then observes, 'Look how wrong you can be', it creates one of those lip-trembling moments at which Stewart is so good: it's calculated and verging on overblown, but ice would have to be running through one's veins for one not to respond in the emotional way Stewart intends. Rock critic Greil Marcus was certainly one person swept up in the narrator's Damascene conversion. The *Rolling Stone* stalwart later wrote, 'There's a moment . . . when you can hear a soft, spontaneous "Hey . . ." out of one speaker; it's as if one of the musicians was so caught up in the story Rod was telling that he couldn't help but wish the singer and his lover well. I know no friendlier moment, not on record, not in real life, and it may sum up everything Rod Stewart and his band had to say'.

'Seems Like a Long Time' was written by Ted Anderson, a songwriter whose compositions had been recorded by the New Society, the New Christy Minstrels, Maffitt/Davies, the Hager Twins and Michael Johnson. 'I remember the opening line—"Nighttime is only the other side of daytime"—coming to me driving home to Kansas City from a coffeehouse gig in Chicago in early 1970', Anderson says. 'It seemed like a portal to me, and I followed it into the chorus. That's when I knew I had a song. Then, of course, you're stuck trying to resolve and get out of it. I do think that the chorus has a haunting, empathising, maybe comforting, sort of communal feeling which I attribute to the times, the era if you will. And honestly, I consider myself as a conduit, more of an observer, actually. Yes, I wrote the song, but I've always felt uncomfortable taking credit for it'.

'Seems Like a Long Time' was first recorded in 1970 by folk duo Brewer & Shipley. Michael Brewer describes Anderson as 'an old friend of ours'. Although he says Anderson 'played in coffeehouses and was a songwriter', he adds, 'I don't believe he ever recorded'. 'Seems Like a Long Time' was one of the things Anderson would perform, but Brewer says, 'He would never perform it the same way twice and it wasn't really a song yet. It was more of a song idea'. However, Brewer and his colleague Tom Shipley liked what they heard. 'So we just gave it an arrangement and a structure and whatever to suit ourselves and then we recorded it onto an album called *Tarkio*. We just thought it had a lot of potential so, the version we recorded, we basically finished writing the song'. However, he points out that the message is Anderson's alone. 'It was definitely Ted's lyrics'.

Brewer & Shipley would hit big in the States in 1971 with their pro-pot number, 'One Toke Over the Line' (also a track on *Tarkio*), something that caused US vice-president Spiro Agnew to brand them a national menace. 'Seems Like a Long Time' further bolstered their hippie credentials, because the way that Anderson chose to 'resolve' his inspired opening was by inserting a reference to an issue that was causing America—especially its draftable male youth—anger, fear and aching melancholy. Anderson's lyric observed that while wartime might only be the other side of peacetime, those who had seen how wars were won understood just what a long time that gap seemed. Such references may sound nebulous and not particularly political today but, in the context of the era, had an unmistakable and powerful topicality. 'The time had a whole lot to do with why we thought the song was really good', says Brewer. 'Definitely it was influenced by the Vietnam era'.

Brewer & Shipley's version was a slick and full-bodied recording with cascading acoustic guitar and a prominent piano part. It wasn't released as a single, but Shipley notes that it had quite a lot of exposure anyway, and that this was presumably the means by which the song became even more well known: '[*Tarkio*] was the one that had our biggest hit on it, and I guess Rod Stewart's people, or Mr. Stewart, heard it'.

Mr. Stewart turned the song into something of an epic, if a delicate one. The track starts quietly with Sears' sonorous piano and a slow but dramatic drum roll. Waller excels himself again, maintaining a busy presence without intruding on the tender mood. Sensitively thrumming bass provides another pleasingly simpatico ingredient. In a central minute-and-a-half section, the chorus is repeated over and over, relieved only by a raspy guitar solo from Wood. Yet the repetition doesn't become tedious because the chorus is ever more ornate, incrementally spiraling to the heavens courtesy of harmonies from Madeline Bell, then in the band Blue Mink. The smoother-larynxed Baldry adds a 'Yes, it does' refrain in a soothing Greek-chorus addendum. Adroit touches of echo contribute to the transcendent quality. The recording settles down for the last, Vietnam-alluding verse, following which Sears provides a delicate finale with a wispy piano phrase.

As Stewart and Faces fans, Brewer & Shipley were thrilled to find themselves a recipient of a cover version by him (leaving aside the fact that they weren't the composers). They were even more thrilled by how good it was. 'We had other songs recorded by artists', Brewer notes. 'People are going to give it their own interpretation. It's not always our cup of tea. We wrote and recorded a song called "Keeper of the Keys" on our first album and a group called H. P. Lovecraft recorded it and they invited us into the studio to hear it and we didn't really care for it very much'. They 'loved' Stewart's version of 'Seems Like a Long Time' because it had 'a lot more energy to it'. While Anderson says of Brewer & Shipley's original, 'It's more folky and resembles the way I originally conceived "Seems Like a Long Time"', he says Stewart's version is 'very compelling, very moving, a fully realised rendition. . . . I to this day always feel like I'm hearing it for the first time'.

Stewart's interpretation was rewarding for Anderson for more than those reasons. 'We were all living in Kansas City at the time', says Brewer. 'I remember him going out and buying a new Volvo'. Brewer adds of himself and Shipley, 'We owned the publishing on the song for probably a couple of years and let him have it back, but I know for a fact that he made a few dollars. So did we. Then we sold our catalogue to BMG a number of years ago and Ted did the same thing with that song'.

Brewer & Shipley never met Stewart, but Anderson was introduced to him after a Faces concert in St. Louis in 1972. He thanked him for recording his song. Stewart's reaction? 'There you go'.

Sadly, a similar financial fairytale didn't revolve around the inclusion on *Every Picture Tells a Story* of 'That's All Right'. Following the previous two albums' jams on rock 'n' roll evergreens, Stewart and co. provide a five-minute vamp on a song made famous by Elvis Presley in 1954 but written by Arthur 'Big Boy' Crudup and first released in 1947. Noting the LP's spectacular success, John Carter—head of the American Guild of Authors and Composers, which represented Crudup professionally—took an active interest in why previous administrators had failed to provide Crudup what he was owed from covers. With Crudup now semi-retired, he tried to reach a settlement with publishers Hill & Range to at least ensure he could have a comfortable old age. Unfortunately, a deal was only struck several years later when Hill & Range began negotiations to sell their catalogue to Chappell Music. Upon being apprised of the legal dispute between Crudup's people and Hill & Range, Chappell put the deal on hold pending its resolution, prompting Hill & Range to immediately offer a first payment of $248,000. Sadly, it was only Crudup's heirs that would benefit: he had been dead since 1974.

For Stewart's generation of musicians, Crudup's song was a touchstone. The 1954 cover credited to 'Elvis Presley, Scotty and Bill' was not the first Elvis song most people heard—that accolade goes to 'Heartbreak Hotel', his 1956 debut for the major RCA label after they had bought his contract from minnow Sun Records—but every music fan was aware that it had been Presley's debut record and every musician grasped that its melding of black blues and white country was the very essence of rock 'n' roll, a form of music that by the 1960s was central to most young people's lives as both a means of pleasure and through the libertarian social revolution that was considered to be intertwined with it.

By 1971, there had already been around two dozen recorded versions of the song, variously billed as 'That's All Right' or 'That's All Right Mama' by, among others, Marty Robbins, Carl Perkins, Snooks Eaglin, Billy Fury, George Hamilton IV, the International Submarine Band, Shocking Blue, Albert King, Al Kooper & Mike Bloomfield and Canned Heat. It's doubtful if Fury or any of the English musicians who covered it properly understood that, in American popular song up until around the 1960s, 'mama' was a term of endearment addressed to a romantic partner in much the same way as the more common and enduring 'baby'. During the early 1960s, Bob Dylan was one of the few to shrug off the self-consciousness Sigmund Freud's work had injected into such lover/ mother terminology overlaps and continue to employ it. Crudup's song, in fact, provides an unusual address-form intersection for the two female figures most central to the majority of male lives: in a verse that frames ones in which Crudup is squabbling with a female partner, he receives advice from his parents, but mainly his mother, about the perils of his love life. (Such a peculiar, quasi-disturbing mash-up might be said to be apposite for Presley, who had such a famously intense relationship with his own mom.)

With so many having tackled 'That's All Right', it was by now less holy ground than hoary old chestnut. Some may even have groaned when they saw it on the *Every Picture* tracklisting. That being the case, perhaps a loose arrangement in which the song merely formed the backbone to displays of virtuosity was the only logical place for 'That's All Right' to go. The trouble is, previous Stewart-album jams had been either only partially successful ('It's All Over Now'), possibly accidentally successful ('Cut Across Shorty') or unsuccessful to the point of laughability ('Street Fighting Man'). Symptomatic of the confluence of artistic ambition and achievement with which this album is blessed, for the first time a Rod Stewart jam is not just a success but an unequivocal one.

'He wouldn't play us the original track if it was a cover', Sears says. 'He'd just play it on the acoustic guitar in the afternoon. We subliminally knew vaguely how the song went, of course. Nobody really tried to give it any feel. Because of the combination of musicians that he'd assembled, it came out the way it did'.

A flashy acoustic guitar intro gives way to a casual, knockabout rhythm perfectly maintained by Waller (absolutely on the top of his game on this LP). Stewart's delivery is similarly relaxed, albeit passionate, with him throwing in a little personal touch by addressing 'mah mama'. An acoustic guitar break segues into a high-spirited piano run. The last minute and a half of the track is given over to multiple repeats of the title phrase at the end of which individual instruments are given a turn in the spotlight, including — and deservedly — Waller. Just when this threatens to get repetitious, proceedings are called to a halt at the four-minute mark with a delightfully quivering guitar line.

'That's All Right' segues into a version of the hymn 'Amazing Grace' on which Stewart is accompanied only by the National Steel guitar of either Wood or Sam Mitchell (accounts vary). In an era when musicians were less savvy about mechanical royalties and the need for formal attribution, the song wasn't included in the tracklisting of the American edition. In the UK, the disc labels of some editions did list it, stating it to be track '3b' and crediting the arrangement to Stewart but erroneously stating it to be traditional, although this didn't really matter considering it was by now out of copyright, both lyric- and melody-wise. The lyric has been set to many different melodies since John Newton wrote it in 1772 as a paean to the God he considered to have saved his soul. 'I was going to record 'Amazing Grace' and call the album that, and then she went and recorded it', Stewart revealed to Pete Frame of *Zigzag*. The 'she' was Judy Collins, who had included it on her 1970 album, *Whales and Nightingales*, and released it as a single. (Other plans Stewart had for the album that were abandoned — according to Steve Turner, who interviewed him for *Beat Instrumental* while the LP was being recorded — were the inclusion of versions of the Etta James hit 'I'd Rather Go Blind', Jagger/Richards' 'Out of Time' [taken to no. 1 in the UK by Chris Farlowe in 1966], and the Who's meaning-of-life quest 'The Seeker'.)

Although religiosity — with its authoritarian and censorious associations so inimical to the freedom-loving spirit of rock — was somewhat taboo in 1970s musical circles, the track has a certain logic in being suffused with the humility and devotion which then characterised Stewart's songwriting and singing style, albeit usually directed at lovers rather than the Almighty. In fact, drowned might be a more accurate word than suffused, for Stewart's wrenching performance comes perilously close to he-protesteth-too-much territory. 'Amazing Grace' is not an objectionable listen, but it's lucky that it lasts just two minutes, lest the listener be tempted to cry, 'Yeah, Rod, you're sensitive—we *get* it'.

Since he'd demoed it in 1962, Bob Dylan's 'Tomorrow Is a Long Time' had been the subject of several covers. Most were obscure, but Elvis Presley had somewhat unexpectedly included a version on the 1966 album *Spinout*. Dylan—who, like so many musicians of his generation, had been largely inspired to become a professional musician because of his adoration of 'the King'—cited it in a 1969 *Rolling Stone* interview as his favourite of the countless cover versions of his songs. This is almost certainly why Dylan chose to finally release a version himself, a live rendition on his 1971 compilation *Bob Dylan's Greatest Hits Vol. II*. For his part, Stewart himself had come across the song on the same Hamilton Camp album on which he had discovered 'Only a Hobo', with Paul Nelson possibly playing a part in him hearing that record in the first place.

Stewart's version—originally rendered as 'Tomorrow Is Such a Long Time' on the sleeve's tracklistings—is heart-melting from the first second, when a strummed acoustic guitar blends with the pedal steel of Wood and the fiddle of Dick Powell. Stewart's contribution is not just sensitive but unusually unshowy, him for once dispensing with his trademark 'whoohs' and 'wait a minutes' and focusing solely on message and emotion. Bobak makes his own subtle but considerable contribution to this exquisite tapestry. The interlock of Stewart's double-tracked voice—one in a higher key than the other—is quite remarkable, yet typical of his talent for meshing. 'The use of reverb and echo, or lack of', marvels Sears of Bobak. 'I don't know how he did it, but the separation in the instruments was astonishing'.

The first track of the original vinyl's side two was an acoustic guitar instrumental fragment called 'Henry' in which Quittenton gets to show off his classical training. (UK labels listed it as track '0', a drollery that ensured Quittenton got his compositional and publishing dues.) This led into the track that is now considered the album's keynote but which nobody seemed to recognise as such at the time.

'Maggie May' was written by Stewart and Quittenton, the first time the artist had shared a writing credit with anyone but Wood on his solo work. 'Martin had never been in the music business, but he just got lucky writing two great songs with Rod', says Gaff. 'When I say he got lucky, obviously Rod thought he contributed terribly well to them, so . . .' 'He was a quiet, sort of unassuming chap', says Bobak. 'I would say he [was] slightly lacking self-confidence. Not his technique, just his personality'. 'He and I had a band on the side, playing instrumental music during 1973', says Sears. 'He was very much a recluse in his character, but a brilliant musician and writer. . . . He was very much an introspective, intellectual person, and extremely serious about his playing and considered himself, I think, more of a folk-jazz musician'. Quittenton would, in other words, seem to have been the polar opposite of Stewart. 'I don't think they really hung out together or anything like that', says Sears, but adds, 'They certainly got on well in the studio . . . Rod had great respect for him'. Waller didn't find it surprising that two such apparently disparate souls should coalesce. 'Rod can be quite quiet, you know', he says. 'You shouldn't believe what you read in the newspapers, a lot of old rubbish'. 'He quite liked people like Martin Quittenton', says Dee Harrington. 'Mike Bobak was the same kind of character. He'd have those studious-type, thinking people who were very unlikely to be in that position around him'.

The creation began in Stewart's sitting room. 'He just asked me if I had any ideas for songs', Quittenton told Ewbank and Hildred. 'We just started messing around with a few chords and up came "Maggie May". I thought up the twelve-string guitar introduction to the song while I was on the tube [subway] on the way to the studio'.

Structurally, 'Maggie May' is very similar to the title track—that is, a semi-autobiographical nearly six-minute romp that is indisputably a rocker despite using mostly acoustic guitar and highly memorable despite having no actual chorus. '"Maggie May" is based on the truth', Stewart told *Q* magazine. 'It was my first shag . . . and it lasted precisely 28 seconds. It was the [Beaulieu] Jazz Festival and I lost my virginity to this rather large girl and I don't think her name was Maggie'. One doesn't quite know how to reconcile this sweet anecdote with an equally moving one Stewart offered Philip Norman of the *Sunday Times* in 1974: 'We had a piano at home that nobody played . . . I had my first bunk-up underneath that piano. This girl and me were going on the march to Aldermaston, banning The Bomb, and I whopped one up her underneath the piano'. However, Stewart repeated the Beaulieu Festival anecdote in his 2012 autobiography.

As with so many instrumental passages on this record, the opening chords—a moaning acoustic guitar and purring bass—seem to possess an emotionality in and of themselves, conveying a curious melancholy. This is an impressive and arresting enough introduction, but then comes a piece of conceptual genius when a rat-a-tat of drums reminiscent of an attention-demanding knock is followed by the narrator's demand that the titular Maggie wake up in order to hear his grievances about her.

The song is neither loving nor lovelorn but instead condemnatory, albeit a condemnation tinged with sadness and a slightly supplicant tone consistent with it being an address by a younger person to someone his senior. As ever with Stewart's compositions of this era, there's a considerable amount of clumsiness and laziness. He turns cartwheels with preposition simply in order to rhyme 'jokes' with 'coax', an effort doubly preposterous because 'coax' forms part of a formal phrase out of character with the prevailing Holden Caulfield-esque colloquialism. Other times he can't even be bothered with conventional structure, each and every verse trailing away on a non-rhyming line.

Also as ever, however, the deficiencies are more than offset by touches that are truly inspired. The exposition is dexterous, the narrator establishing his age by pointing out that, as it's late September, he should be back at school, and conveying the age gap between he and his lover by reflecting how the morning sun mercilessly betrays her age.

Maggie has made the schoolboy narrator in turn both a man and an old man, grateful for being initiated by her into the adult world of sexual relations, but subsequently dismayed at her exploitative treatment, belatedly realising that her luring him away from the family home was an expedience to stave off loneliness. This melancholic tale is delivered in an incongruously uptempo manner, yet the swelling melody underscores the sadness and regret.

Stewart's fatuous and sublime tendencies come triumphantly together in the final verse. Its first and fourth lines are beautifully sorrowful. With his assumptions about and faith in humanity in tatters, and the new life he had embarked on and sacrificed so much for revealed as a dead end, the narrator is fearfully contemplating his options. He morosely concludes that one of them is collecting his books and returning to the now childish-seeming environs of school. After pondering another couple of options, he exasperatedly dismisses all such thoughts to exclaim to Maggie that he wishes he'd never seen her face. Sandwiched by those two naturalistic and moving passages are ones of utter inanity. In them, the brace of other routes the boy contemplates are those of becoming a pool player and working for a rock band. The pool player option is clearly thrown in simply because 'pool' rhymes with 'school'. While providing a helping hand for a rock 'n' roll band (we infer as a singer rather than a mere roadie) is, from our knowledge of Stewart's life and career, realistic, the way that it's presented as an afterthought is not. Yet it all works. The image of stealing his daddy's cue to embark on a new career is a delightful turn, a peek into a demimonde of ducking and diving in a quest for riches. The contrived rhyme delights us in its effrontery, and the tender familial reference provides a moving and vulnerable touch amongst the song's overarching mood of reproach. The rock singer option has more of the same rake's-progress air.

The icing on the cake of the verse is the subtle flourish of celeste washes, which provide another of the special moments that listeners love to sit waiting for, adding to ones the song has already racked up (the call for Maggie to wake up, the exquisitely bizarre line about the cue, and the climactic declaration that the narrator wishes he had never seen Maggie's face). 'I thought that was an interesting choice with celeste because I hadn't really heard that since Buddy Holly', recalls Bobak in reference to the bespectacled 1950s rocker's 'Everyday'. Bizarrely, both Sears and McLagan are under the impression that they performed this part. 'In every studio back then, there was always a beautiful Hammond B3 and Leslie, a grand piano, a celeste, harpsichord', says McLagan. 'In the decent studios, they were always equipped with keyboard instruments. It was just sitting there. It seemed like a good idea'. Sears, though, has just as distinct memories of providing the part. 'Every now and again you hear this little tinkly thing at the end on the downbeats of the sound', he reflects. 'It's quite loud in the mix actually. It almost sounds like a toy piano. That's what I played on "Maggie May"'. Not entirely seriously, he adds, 'It's the reason it was a big hit, I'm sure'. Giving credence to Sears' story is the fact that he receives recompense for his contribution. 'He paid me well, I was happy with it, but I got paid as a session musician', he says. 'But several years ago in the UK, they passed some new law that said that even if you're hired as a side musician you could get royalties. So I do get royalties on that song now'. One thing that we can be sure McLagan contributes is the swoops of organ throughout the track. 'I was channeling Al Kooper', he says. 'I'd always loved Al Kooper's playing with Dylan'.

Despite that celeste decoration, Stewart still wasn't satisfied with the recording. It was only when Ray Jackson, mandolin player with folk-rockers Lindisfarne, came into the studio to do overdub work on another track, 'Mandolin Wind', that the artist felt that it truly began to take shape. By this time, the rest of the album was finished and the only people in the studio were Jackson, Stewart, Bobak and Stewart's girlfriend Dee Harrington. 'Nobody thought it had any merit because it wasn't finished', says Jackson of 'Maggie May'. 'It was going to be left off. It was only after the mandolin was put on that the song was completely transformed, because it didn't have a middle eight, it didn't have a chorus, it was just a sort of a vocal track all the way through really, with a couple of bridges in-between and a long end piece which had nothing on it at all. He asked me to think of something to go on there with the mandolin while I was in the studio and I ended up multi-tracking the mandolin about twelve times and coming up with a basic tune to put on the end of it. . . . They liked the sound of it so much that they thought, "Yeah, we would like that thickened up a bit". Made it almost into an orchestra'.

'Mandolin Wind' itself—which follows 'Maggie May' on the album— is perhaps Stewart's most extraordinary composition. Having raided the Elton John tranche of songs that became *Tumbleweed Connection*, Stewart seems to have been inspired by their spirit for this solo composition, in which he assumes absolutely convincingly the persona of a Wild West homesteader. 'Rod's much better at writing about imaginative and fictitious things than I am', Ronnie Lane noted to Jonh Ingham of *Phonograph Record* in an article published in January 1972. 'I can't do that sort of thing at all'.

The sleeve credits Stewart only with the track's vocals and acoustic guitar, but the scrubs of banjo that gently propel it are also presumably his. The redemptive quality of love is the theme of a creation that sees the narrator giving thanks in the second person to a companion who stuck with him through a winter so brutal that buffalo died in frozen fields, leading a man averse to displays of emotion being reduced to tearful supplication before God. Now that the worst is over, the narrator can even inject levity by telling his lover that all he has is hers with the exception of his steel guitar. It all has a sepia-toned authenticity. Perhaps the only lyrical misstep is the title phrase, Stewart using an instrument that produces such soft tones as a simile for the pitiless conditions his character endured.

Once again, the singing and musicianship is utterly simpatico. Wood's sweetly mournful pedal steel gives way to a Jackson mandolin solo that is ebullient. 'Rod had a specific melody which he wanted, and he sang it to me over the headphones in the studio', says Jackson. Thirty seconds before the end of this five-and-a-half-minute track, a so-far drumless affair is taken into the fade by a quick-stepping Waller.

Stewart was justifiably proud of the track, later commenting, 'I always thought the best song I've ever written is "Mandolin Wind". If someone recorded that in forty- or fifty-years time, I'd be very happy'. Someone rather illustrious recorded it somewhat quicker than that: the Everly Brothers issued a version on their 1972 album *Stories We Could Tell*.

Proving that it takes all sorts to make up the world, Bobak dissents from the widespread admiration for Stewart's ability to inhabit somebody else's clothes. 'When we were mixing it, he said, "What do you think of that?" I said, "It's very good, I like it. I think the words are a bit silly, though". . . . Buffalo dying in the frozen fields and all that stuff and we were sitting in Willesden High Road. . . . He didn't like that at all'.

The album's Faces track—yet another established tradition in a solo career only three albums old—is a cover of '(I Know) I'm Losing You'. The Temptations' 1966 hit was the original release of this song by Norman Whitfield, Eddie Holland and Cornelius Grant. However, it may not have been that which provided the template, as Stewart's version seems to owe more to the larger-than-life 1970 rendition by another Motown act, Rare Earth, which was actually the bigger hit Stateside. The Faces' version trumps both of them, and this dark, haunted recording constitutes one of the few occasions on which they translated their stage prowess to recording tape—a fact that, for some, makes it an outrage that it appears on a Rod Stewart solo album.

There was probably nothing sinister in the Faces being credited in the sleeve notes only with 'musical development', this presumably being down to the contractual issues referred to by McLagan and Jackson earlier. Gaff also offers another reason. 'The reason it probably wasn't credited is Mercury wouldn't do it', he says. 'They didn't want to give Warners publicity. Mercury were almost a small-time record company with small ideas, compared to Warner Brothers'. The fact of the track appearing on *Every Picture* in the first place is a different issue. 'We used to do it on stage', says Jones of the song. That a feature of the Faces' set didn't end up on a Faces LP came to seem a disturbing part of the syndrome of Stewart's solo works always being superior to Faces outings. 'I assumed it was for the Faces, really', says Bobak. 'And then it suddenly appeared on that album'. 'He wanted to cut that song and I don't know why he used the band', says Ian McLagan. 'It was nice that he used the band. It's a difficult situation. In retrospect, I really feel that should have been on a Faces album, but it was cut on his time'.

Opinions, though, differ. 'It was definitely a Rod Stewart track', says Gaff. The manager goes further in disputing conspiracy theories: 'He would put a track in which they were all involved on his solo albums. . . . I think he would have preferred not to use them at all. Because he had one idea, they had another idea. Rod was very kind. A lot of people don't realise it, but he was terribly fair and he would do that for them, and they never did anything for him'. The way Kenney Jones tells it, there was nothing dubious or surreptitious about the process. 'Rod called up and said, "Are you doing anything tonight?"' he recalls. 'I said, "Well, I'm just at home watching the TV, why's that?" He said, "Well, I think we might try and do 'Losing You'"'. Adding a nuance to the whole saga, it has to be said that 'Losing You' is a very un-Faces-like recording. The slickness, large scale and echo-laden atmosphere that attend the entire proceedings are alien to the casual and raggedy aura that almost always hung over product released under the Faces' own name.

'My house was West Hampstead-way', says Jones. 'It took about a minute to get there, five minutes. I was watching a film and I bombed on over there, played "Losing You" and I said, "See you later guys, bye", and I went back to watch the end of the film'. In that brief visit, Jones had laid down something remarkable: given a shot at replicating the extended drum section that formed part of the Faces' live version, he rose to the occasion spectacularly. 'That was a particularly good drum sound that day', says Bobak, who placed Jones literally beneath his feet. 'I got him to set up his drums underneath the control room and got a bounce off the low ceiling, which made it a bit live-er sounding'.

'If you like drum solos', sniffs McLagan. 'It was always the worst part of the show for me. I'd go and have another drink at the back of the stage while he played an endless solo'. 'It was never meant to be a drum solo', says Jones. 'Never in a million years. The drum solo happened after that record became very popular in America. It was always meant to be a drum break while Rod sort of chanted a few vocals over it, which is more like what's on the album, and then it turned into a drum solo slowly after that. If I was going to do a drum solo, I'd do a damn sight better one than that'. He adds, 'It became a Faces stage song and it's known more for the Faces than Rod, funnily enough'. Although, like the other Faces, Jones could be said to have been acting as Stewart's session drummer that night, he says, 'The thought never crossed my mind to charge him like I would somebody else'. Nor did Jones get round to registering for performing rights royalties. 'I must actually put that in. I mean, I could sit down forever and I should do really, but time's too short. I'm proud that I played on it and that was that'.

Wood's opening staccato guitar phrase is sheened and larger-than-life. Doom-laden fragments of instrumentation—a menacing bass, a broiling piano—further set the scene for Stewart's vocal, which is at an anguished pitch from its first appearance. The narrator is in a state of sweaty paranoia, convinced that his lover has transferred her affections elsewhere ('Can feel the presence of another man!'). His anguish is only worsened by the frustration of the fact of having nothing with which to prove his suspicions. A respite in the torment comes on the two-minute mark. The silence and soothing male harmonies in this brief lull are followed by an exquisite piano ripple that provides the cue for a re-entry of instruments, including Jones' bulldozing drumming. At 3:40, all decks are cleared for Jones, who for a full half-minute fills the soundscape with a frenetic exploration of his kit. His colleagues rejoin the fray for an almost unbearably exciting final minute as Jones powers the song forwards at a gallop.

Stewart's vocal is perfectly judged throughout, expertly deploying stylised lead-vocalist archetypes for punctuation, supplementation and counterpoint: the yelp with which he accentuates the drama of the introduction of McLagan's piano, his giddyap-like exhortations to Jones and—following Jones' exhausted drum-clatter finale—his muffled 'Whoo!' sign-off.

Tim Hardin was a big favourite among many 1960s bands. His jazz-inflected folk albums *Tim Hardin* (1966) and *Tim Hardin II* (1967) contained a treasure trove of sensitive ballads like 'If I Were a Carpenter', 'Misty Roses', 'Red Balloon' and 'How Can We Hang On to a Dream' and was raided for cover versions by Bobby Darin, the Four Tops, the Small Faces and others. Artists tended to use Hardin's spare originals almost like demos for chart-friendlier extrapolations. 'Reason to Believe' was one of the highlights of Hardin's debut, a miniature beauty that in its brief two-minute span undemonstratively communicated the heartbreak and self-deception of a man who has been lied to 'straight faced' by his lover but wants to find a way to put the betrayal behind him and salvage the relationship. Quickly attracting a dizzying number and variety of covers, it was recorded by, among others, Marianne Faithfull, Rick Nelson, Ian & Sylvia, Gary Lewis & the Playboys, the Youngbloods, Scott McKenzie, the Nitty Gritty Dirt Band, Peter, Paul & Mary, Glen Campbell, Peggy Lee, Cher, Andy Williams, the Carpenters and Ramblin' Jack Elliott. Amongst the best versions was a sweet, understated rendition issued by Bobby Darin on a 1966 B-side.

Late to the party Stewart might have been, but he more than made up for it. His version of 'Reason to Believe' is used to close the *Every Picture* album, yet, despite the aesthetic sumptuousness of what precedes it, is possibly the best thing present. Folk supergroup Pentangle's Danny Thompson is drafted in to provide upright bass on an utterly exquisite reading.

Despite an overarching delicacy, the soundscape is rich and full, utilising piano, organ and drums. Downstrokes on an acoustic guitar provide a soft thrust. The instruments are introduced one by one, incrementally intensifying the drama. Stewart's gravelly tones maintain the original's understated air but inject an additional degree of emotionality. What truly ramps up the pathos, however, is Powell's beautiful violin solo at the midway point. If the false ending that occurs just past the two-and-a-half-minute mark had been real it would already make the recording longer than the original, but such is the aural gorgeousness that the listener doesn't mind in the least that the track resumes to continue for another minute and a half.

With the album's recording completed, the mix was attended to. It involved no more agonising than had laying down the tracks in the first place. 'All the mixing was done in two days, the whole album', says Bobak, who adds that Stewart would emerge from the bar to say 'Yes' or 'No' or 'Didn't like that bit of guitar, lose that'.

As ever, the contents of the album were a complete surprise for Stewart's manager. 'I must be the only manager in the world that never heard an album until it was dropped on my doorstep', says Gaff. 'Usually I'd be sitting waiting three or four or five or six in the morning, whether it was Los Angeles or London or whatever, for the final album. I never went to a studio. I hated studios and Rod hated me going. He had a great attitude towards it. He figured the best time to hear the album was when it was finished, which was correct. He wouldn't let anybody near it except those directly involved . . . I was delivered the album and I had to go out and sell it'.

The album was housed in a deluxe fold-out sleeve designed by John Craig. Around four years older than Stewart, Craig had met the singer at the time of the release of his debut album. It was the briefest of chats and Craig never got to actually talk to him after that, primarily because he left Mercury to go freelance, but their professional paths did cross again courtesy of Jim Ladwig, who left his post as a Mercury art director to become co-founder with Don Hosterka of Album Graphics Inc. This Chicago-based company's mission was to exploit the increasing interest of record companies in turning albums into elaborate, covetable artefacts. Stewart was one of their clients. 'They started to do these deluxe fold-up packaging things', says Craig. 'They were doing some die-cut packaging too. They actually did the packaging for the Stones zipper cover'. The real-flies sleeve of *Sticky Fingers* Craig mentions appeared just five weeks before *Every Picture Tells a Story*.

'Jim used to go over to Europe to see Rod and present him with different ideas', says Craig. 'I knew the *Gasoline Alley* album pretty well, I knew the yellow album [*The Rod Stewart Album*] pretty well, so by the time *Every Picture* was coming up, I was knocking on the door saying, "Hey, I want to do this one". I would present them with some ideas and then he would present them to Rod, and then we would go back and forth from there'.

The front cover of *Every Picture* would feature a quintessential image of Stewart in performance: emoting with closed eyes, hand clutching his microphone's stand, his rooster hairstyle backlit. At first glance, and even under protracted scrutiny, the image looks like a painting. 'It's actually a photograph', says Craig. 'It's a photo that was backlit so that it was very soft around the edges. I would convert the black and white photos to a sepia tone photo, and then colour it with oils and coloured pencils'.

Many have wondered about the meaning of the stylised 'Classic Edition' heading at the top of the front cover. It was co-opted by Craig from a type of artefact common in the days of 'parlor music', when many homes had a piano. 'Sheet music', which contained the notation for playing tunes, was a huge business in and of itself: the very first music charts did not register sales of recorded music but that of sheet music. The prosaic notation within these pamphlets was complemented — and in some ways 'sold' — by title pages with fancy typography and colourful illustrations. 'It actually was part of the sheet music and it just sounded right and looked good and why not leave it there', says Craig of the classic edition legend. Also cannibalised from similar sources was the border and the lines fanning out from the central image. They and the lettering were all rendered in Art Deco style, a geometric and futuristic design type that had come to prominence in the 1920s. Craig: 'At that time, it was just getting its first revival and there was a large show of deco objects touring the country. It was a very sophisticated design, but it also trickled down to mass culture. . . . Some of it was based on Aztec design, so you have a lot of zigzags, a lot of sharp angles, a lot of very flat surfaces too'. Craig says of the Art Deco revival, 'Basically it was sort of a reaction to the fluid Art Nouveau style where everything was curvy and organic'. The Art Nouveau style had been extensively used on the famously ornate and florid posters advertising the gigs of the bands that might be termed the San Francisco Class of '67.

Instead of a conventional tracklisting, the album's back cover presented the song titles and compositional credits on sheet music mock-ups. Notes Craig, 'I stayed with the whole sheet music idea to illustrate the songs on the back, just converting the titles to images that fit. . . . That [album] title applied better for me there. It was mostly just to feature Rod on the front and they had this photo they wanted to use, so that wasn't the picture that told the story so much. I tried to make the other ones tell the story'. Craig was using designs from sheet-music covers that had become public domain since their first appearance in the teens of the twentieth century. As such, they all by now possessed a period charm, especially when set against the earthy and informal phraseology and culture of rock music. Some of the images he co-opted were apposite: '(I Know) I'm Losing You' featured a design of a man sitting in an armchair, the image of his absent lady love hovering above him in a thought balloon. Some seemed arbitrary: 'Mandolin Wind' was illustrated with fluttering bluebirds. Some could be taken either way: the smiling belle chosen for 'Maggie May' could be viewed as inappropriately cheerful or suitably callous. It should be noted that Craig can't remember if he received a pre-release copy of the album to work from, so his choices wouldn't necessarily reflect knowledge of song content.

The album jacket's unusual deluxe format gave scope for two fold-outs. One of them featured a colour photo of Stewart singing onstage, the other proffered photographs of some of the players (Stewart, Wood, Waller, Quittenton and Sears, although strangely not McLagan) atop sleeve notes by Stewart and a more formal tracklisting.

There's another odd omission. Stewart's sleeve notes state, 'The mandolin was played by the mandolin player in Lindisfarne. The name slips my mind'. 'He was a bit like that', says Bobak of Stewart. 'I don't think he cared'. 'I was a bit disappointed when I saw the sleeve notes', admits Jackson of his name's absence. 'He could have easily looked at the John Baldry album and found it. I wasn't too bothered because Lindisfarne were just sort of approaching the breakthrough stage and I thought maybe Lindisfarne's name would benefit better than my own name at the time. So I didn't kick up a stink about it that much'. In fact, it was more his work on the album, especially 'Maggie May', that gave Jackson cause for disgruntlement. When 'Maggie May' started receiving radio play, he found that his handiwork wasn't always audible. 'There's times when the end bit was cut', he says. 'They would fade it because it was too long for the program formatting'. To add insult to injury, he found his part being mimed on the influential BBC television chart show *Top of the Pops* by a DJ with no ability on the instrument. 'I did the first one. The second one I think I was out of the country, so I wasn't invited and John Peel was seen on it. 'Bit pissed off, but what can you do?' Meanwhile, Jackson's remuneration was something he retrospectively came to view as unsatisfactory. 'I was quite wet behind the ears at the time. I knew what the Musicians' Union rate was, but I didn't know porterage or overdubbing was actually extra on sessions, so I never charged for those'.

Although the sheet music conceit is impressively executed, the front cover of the album seems a little low rent, like something a teenager has done with colouring pencils. It seems even more unbefitting now that *Every Picture* has come to be seen as a classic album. To Gaff—who admits he had absolutely nothing to do with Stewart's cover designs—it's largely immaterial. 'I've seen great, great covers with shit albums that nobody's ever seen again', he reasons. 'At the end of the day, you can't see the cover over the radio and, when people buy it, it suddenly becomes a great cover. It's the power of suggestion'. One problem that eventually arose from the cover that is not Craig's or anyone else's fault (except perhaps younger generations of music company employees unfamiliar with the LP) is an explanatory sleeve note stating, 'Front cover photo: Lisa Margolis. From a performance at the Fillmore East, New York'. On some subsequent reissues, the second sentence has become detached from the first, leading consumers to be given the impression that *Every Picture Tells a Story* is a live album.

Although Craig was only into his 'third or fourth year of working professionally', his design would soon be resident in millions of homes worldwide. 'It was pretty certainly the biggest thing I've done, most recognisable thing, at that time. Change my life? Um, no. Mostly with friends that would be surprised when they knew that I had done it. They sort of look at you a little differently. I had a friend I had known a long time and he said, "I didn't know you did that. I love that album"'.

So did a lot of people. *Every Picture Tells a Story* was released on 28 May 1971. For the first time, a Rod Stewart album appeared on the same label in the UK and the States, with Stewart switching in his home country from Vertigo—more associated with less commercial types of rock— to its corporate stablemate. This didn't, though, engender a transatlantic consistency on every level: much of John Craig's efforts on the cover were for naught in less prosperous Britain, where the deluxe packaging was dispensed with. The UK iteration came housed in a regular sleeve, with a cropped version of the colour photograph of Stewart from the interior of the US edition slapped on the back with the artist's sleeve notes and a perfunctory tracklisting. The sleeve notes on either edition, incidentally, gave no hint of maltreatment of Mike Bobak and Phil, thanking both for their 'engineering abilities' and stating, 'Bless their cotton socks'.

In terms of reviews, John Mendelsohn of *Rolling Stone* called the album's quality remarkably wrong. He complained that *Every Picture* was 'equal parts magnificent splendor and pleasant inconsequence'. He had extremely high praise for the backing band ('Together these gentlemen interact ingeniously, producing accompaniments as rich in texture as those of the *Highway 61* and *Blonde on Blonde* bands'). However, he cavilled about the lack of Stewart originals. 'If Rod Stewart ever allows himself the time to write himself a whole album, it will be among the best albums any of us has ever heard'. His words were somewhat undermined by his utter wrong-headedness about the cover versions, him dismissing the sublime 'Seems Like a Long Time' and 'Tomorrow Is a Long Time' as 'massively inconsequential, nay, downright trivial, fare'. His review goes down in history as one of those look-how-wrong-you-can-be (to use a Rod Stewart phrase) slatings (to use a Britishism for 'severe critique') of classic albums.

Robert Christgau was one of the vast majority who called it right. 'Finally, the album that does him justice', he said in a *Village Voice* review that had only one criticism: 'Sometimes his band plays out of tune', although he added the playful caveat, 'almost as bad as the old Rolling Stones'. He awarded it an A grade. As with previous Stewart albums, he subsequently revised his grade. This time, it was upwards to the maximum A+—in other words, a rare example of a perfect album.

British weeklies were just as ecstatic, *Sounds* saying the LP was 'practically impossible to fault' and *Melody Maker* predicting, 'You won't hear a better rock and roll album in 1971', the latter quite a statement considering that the previous month had seen the release of *Sticky Fingers*.

From there, reverence for the album only increased. In a poll among music critics and disc jockeys for *Critic's Choice*, a 1978 book compiled by Radio One DJ Paul Gambaccini to find the best two hundred albums ever made, *Every Picture Tells a Story* came in at number 46. Forty-two years later, when *Rolling Stone* magazine presented its '500 Greatest Albums of All Time' poll, the record—despite massive expansion of the pop canon and a considerable fading from the popular consciousness of the fact of how 'credible' Stewart had once been — still made number 177.

'There was something about it', says Sears of the album. 'There was definitely a magic in the spontaneity and combining of styles. It came together in a very spontaneous way and it was fortunate, one of those synchronistic things where you just get a certain group of people together and they create something that's unique. That's what it felt like to me at the time and I think that album still stands up today . . . I'm happy to have played and been a part of it'. 'I didn't appreciate it at the time, but I can see why it is', says Bobak of *Every Picture*'s classic status. 'I think the key to it is because it sounds so spontaneous. It doesn't sound hours of work [have] gone into it, but it sounds great at the same time. A certain roughness about it'. Jackson agrees that it deserves its classic status. 'Not only because of its sales but the fact that it had a certain cachet which was different from other things that were flying around at the time. Rod Stewart was out on a limb'.

Stewart himself has often given the impression in subsequent years of not understanding what made him so good in his Mercury period. However, even he has said, 'I never get tired of listening to *Every Picture Tells a Story*'.

With such good reviews, the album understandably began to shift units. Within a month, its half a million sales had put it in *Billboard*'s top 20. In the UK, it made the top 10 by the end of July. Nobody, though, had thought to try to boost sales by releasing a single from it. It seemed clear at this point that Stewart was an albums artist. Moreover, such a status was increasingly desired, with more and more recording acts and their managers feeling that singles were for teenybopper bands. Moreover, more than ever before, albums were within the public's financial reach. The Stones sold more copies of *Sticky Fingers* than they did its accompanying single — an inversion of sales traditions that was particularly noteworthy considering that said single, 'Brown Sugar', was a UK number 2 and a US chart topper.

Perhaps it was the potential for publicity engendered by the Faces embarking on 9 July on their fourth major US tour (sharing the bill with heavy metallers Deep Purple) that motivated Mercury to ignore the mildly seven-inch-hostile temperature and pull a single from the album. They chose 'Reason to Believe'.

'I must admit I'm not a fan of that recording because I really did love Tim Hardin's first two albums', says McLagan. 'I was a huge fan of his and I just thought it was a bit overdone'. As for the criticism that the original sounds more like a demo tape than a finished product, McLagan says, 'That's what I love about it, though'. He adds, 'I actually met Tim several times and at one point he came to one of my sessions in LA and I said, "I've got to ask you—who played piano on all your tracks? It's beautiful", and he said, "That's me". I said, "I love you". He said, "Well, I'm just playing what I know, really". I said, "Well that's why it's so special: it's not overplayed, its extremely subtle and very essential"'.

To pretty much everybody else, Stewart's interpretation of 'Reason to Believe' was stunning and, as such, must have seemed a pretty logical choice for release in the 45-rpm format. The record, of course, needed a B-side. The one chosen was 'Maggie May'. 'I don't know why the record company didn't put it on the A-side, because it was clearly the better song', says Bobak, who says of 'Reason to Believe', 'I was thinking to myself, "Well, it's someone else's song—he's just covering it"'. 'We shoved it on the B-side because we didn't like it, particularly', recalls Gaff. Gaff could have added that placing a Stewart song on the flip was an adroit move, for if 'Reason to Believe' did become a hit, Stewart would reap a piggy-back royalties bonanza. The very fact that it was shoved on a flipside, incidentally, would have made many Britons, without hearing it, assume that 'Maggie May' was a well-known saucy folk song about a prostitute who robs a sailor, a snippet of which had been heard on the Beatles' *Let It Be* album the previous year. Although it would seem logical that that is where the Stewart/Quittenton song got its title, there's no mention of the woman's surname in it and no thematic, lyrical or melodic connection between the two.

While Gaff may be exaggerating in suggesting that Stewart and his camp 'didn't like' 'Maggie May', it was understandable that it was felt that a structureless, chorus-less, five-minutes-plus song was not hit-single material. The thing is, neither, apparently, was 'Reason to Believe'. It made reasonable but not spectacular sales progress, and any success it did have wasn't necessarily hugely beneficial to the parent album. *Every Picture Tells a Story* was already at number 5 in the UK albums chart on September 11, the very day that the single nudged into the country's top 20 and was on its way to the US top 10 in the month of the single's release. However, a remarkable synergy then began to take place. A DJ in Cleveland (according to most sources, although Gaff feels it may have been Philadelphia) had turned the record over and generated one of those instances of snowballing interest—the pre-digital version of going viral—that ultimately results in record companies bowing to public demand.

'Did I see it? Not in a million years', says Gaff of the success of the new A-side (de facto and then literally) 'Maggie May'. 'Before I knew what was happening, they'd turned it over and I got this call from Mercury in Chicago to say, "Jesus I think we've got a hit on our hands", and of course the rest is history. They had turned it over everywhere'. When Gaff says 'the rest is history', he could just as accurately say that the rest *made* history: when for three weeks that October both 'Maggie May' and *Every Picture Tells a Story* simultaneously sat at the peak of their respective charts in both Britain and America, it was the first time this feat had ever been accomplished. The album was number 1 in the *Billboard* Top LPs chart for four weeks and 'Maggie May' number 1 in the *Billboard* Hot 100 for five weeks. In the UK, *Every Picture* enjoyed six non-consecutive weeks at the summit and 'Maggie May' five straight weeks at the top.

Mercury followed up 'Maggie May' in several territories (but not the UK) with a single of '(I Know I'm) Losing You' in the winter of 1971. The record—which usually had 'Mandolin Wind' on the flip—was stated to be by 'Rod Stewart with Faces', a shared-billing first that possibly resulted from a sub-clause of the gentlemen's agreement between Mercury and Warner Bros. Stewart's colleagues may have been irritated by the second-banana status this implied but must have been at least a little gratified that it formally alerted the world to the fact that they'd played on this rip-roaring recording. It made it to number 24 on *Billboard* and might have gone as high as it deserved if it weren't for the fact that so many members of the public already owned the album.

The people around Stewart had different reactions to these extraordinary events. 'I recognised Rod's talent straight away, otherwise I wouldn't have asked him in the band', reflects Jones. 'I'm not surprised that he had success when he did'. 'In the music business nothing should ever surprise you', says Gaff. 'We were all delighted . . . I can't even remember how I felt. All I know, the work got more strenuous, much tougher.

You're in the middle of it all and you don't know how you got there, how it all happened, and you've got work to do. You have to get on with it. It all sounds a little simple, but that is really what happens. It all builds up so quickly and you're able to have a bigger car to get to the airport and you can fly first class, but the fucking travelling gets harder and the work gets harder and the decisions get harder and everybody wants a piece of you. Not just a piece of the artist, but a piece of the manager as well'. 'I could be very clever and say, "I knew 'Maggie May' would be a number one"', says McLagan. 'It was a pleasant enough tune. The thing is, at that point you're just latching onto what's going on. You're not thinking any further ahead than that, just making sure you know where the chords are going and what you should be playing. I could see it was good . . . I'd like to think I'd have picked "Maggie May", but I don't know why "Every Picture" didn't come out [as a single]'. Sears offers, 'I knew it was a good song. It really felt right, felt really good, when I was listening to it back, but it just felt like another song on the album at the time. The whole album felt good and flowed well together and there's a lot of strong tracks on that album, and I wasn't really thinking in terms of what would be a hit single'. 'When "Maggie May" became a big hit I couldn't, at the time, see what the fuss was about', Quittenton reflected to Ewbank and Hildred. 'It took me a long while to realise it was actually a very good popular song'. It certainly rescued the co-author from straitened circumstances: he currently had a part-time day job in a Sussex music shop.

'It was the Faces that actually broke Rod, as far as I'm concerned', says Jones. 'By that time we'd established ourselves with the Faces and we were promoting Rod *and* his solo album'. Whether or not that's true, Rod Stewart was suddenly a colossal figure in music and popular culture. A new word going around at the time was 'superstar'. At the advanced age of twenty-six, Rod Stewart was now most definitely one.

4

HAD ME A REAL GOOD TIME

STEWART'S STRATOSPHERIC ASCENT was no doubt sweet in itself, but he had the pleasure of embarking on it in company. Come the summer of 1971, he had a new romantic partner in his life.

Stewart met Englishwoman Dee Harrington in late July as a consequence of her being currently domiciled in the United States, where she cooked an English dinner for the homesick Kenney Jones. The drummer repaid the favour by inviting Harrington to a party hosted by the Faces at a club. Harrington went along, although she knew little about the band. Being a leggy blonde, she caught the eye of Stewart, who of course has always had a preference for that 'type'. 'Rod asked me to dance', Harrington recalls. 'We had a dance, and he took me out of the club. He just said, "Let's leave"'. Harrington found Stewart 'an interesting person to talk to, a lot of fun. A type of person to make you laugh and tell a joke. Just lovely'.

The following night, Stewart took Harrington to a Faces gig at Long Beach Arena. 'That's the first time that I saw him and the Faces play', she says. 'I actually had worked as a PA for a small record label, so I was used to being with people in the music business. But the performance—I always remember thinking, "My God, the gig's fantastic". He was very in control'.

Harrington hailed from the upscale town of Harrow (part of London since the mid-1960s) and was the daughter of a Royal Air Force squadron leader. Her bourgeois background might suggest that she and Stewart had little in common, but the two found themselves very compatible. The bedrock of their relationship was music. 'I loved the same music he loved', says Harrington. 'That was the black American soul music which he got all his inspiration from. The music is what carries you through in life a lot'. Things snowballed quickly. In November 1971, Stewart asked Harrington to marry him. 'I was so shocked. You don't actually marry people in the '70s—you lived with them. And I'm twenty-one. I don't even know who I am. But I loved him. We wanted to be together'. She feels that the fact that the proposal was made in New York had its own significance: 'That was his way of showing me, "Whatever I might be doing when I'm out here, I want you to be with me". That seemed to work for us both. . . . He made a commitment to me that he'd never done before with a woman, and I had to listen to that, really'. So started a long engagement. 'I didn't feel this overpowering need to go up the aisle, because I didn't know who I was', Harrington says. 'So I grew up with a rock star'.

As they began living under the same roof, Harrington increasingly began to perceive an intelligent and sober side to a man whose public image was a hedonist concerned mainly with alcohol, football, fast cars, music and blondes. Stewart may have failed the eleven-plus examination that dictated the quality of secondary (high) school education for his generation of British children, but Harrington says, 'I would say he's probably the most sensible man I've ever met. He's very business oriented. Always clever about investments and having good relationships with his lawyers and his accountant and being in control. He wasn't somebody that got some money and then just blew it away. . . . He's the one person that I've known in my life that you could ask, "Do you think this is a good idea?" and he'd have a good answer'. Stewart's first managers, John Rowlands and Geoff Wright, found this out when they offered him a contract in 1964. Wright told George Tremlett, 'He had the document for about two weeks before he signed it, and during that time he discussed it with his brother who was an accountant—and I think that's why Rod was always so shrewd with his money. He always had his brother to turn to for advice'. No doubt it was his brother's counsel that led Stewart to assert that Rowlands and Wright should not receive a percentage of the money he earned with Baldry on the grounds that that income stream existed before he retained them. Guitarist Jim Cregan would work with

Stewart from the late-1970s onwards. He notes, 'He bought all those Tiffany lamps back in the day when Tiffany lamps were not anything special, and he sold at the top of the market. He collects pre-Raphaelite paintings. He's very knowledgeable about quite a lot of things that people wouldn't imagine'.

Not that Harrington didn't find that Stewart had his oddities. 'Rod never liked using the telephone', she recalls. 'He'd never pick the phone up in the house. [This was] before the days of answer phones, before mobile phones. If you got a call from him, it was such a shock'.

There were other sides of Stewart's character hidden from public view. One was a generosity at odds with an image he actively cultivated of a man who never 'stood his round' (paid for the drinks). She recalls Stewart reading a story in tabloid newspaper *The Sun* about a young boy with calipers on his legs who was a fan of Arsenal Football Club, the soccer team located in Stewart's North London home turf whose matches he regularly visited with his father. He told her, 'I'm going to get the office to get in touch with him and we'll get him to come and stay with us and then I'll organise things to go and meet all the Arsenal people'. Stewart was as good as his word. On another occasion, he responded to the grave matter of Faces fans being injured by a bomb planted by the IRA near a ticket office where they were queuing. Harrington: 'He said, "We're going up to the hospital. I've organised with the office to [tell] the hospital not to let anyone know that I'm going to go up there". These things were always really important'.

Harrington notes of Stewart's tightwad image, 'He was never mean with me. I can't say anything bad against him over finances'. In fact, Harrington herself was sometimes the one who was careful with the pennies. 'I sent back bills that would get sent to us from [nightclub] Tramp where Paul McCartney would have [a] table. I said, "Well, we're not paying for all that. You can get half of that from Paul McCartney". What happens is some people just go, "Well, we'll get him to pay that because he's got the money"'.

Another hidden aspect of Stewart was an unlikely hobby. 'He spent a long time on his model trains', says Harrington. 'That was his quiet thinking-about-everything time'. When the pair moved to bigger premises, Stewart devoted an entire room to his hobby, and spent large chunks of time there. Horsewoman Harrington would go out riding. 'I came back a couple of hours later, he'd still be there'. Cregan would find Stewart was still obsessed with this pastime long after Stewart and Harrington had gone their separate ways. 'He's got such an eye for detail', he notes. 'The days before they had CGI, you'd have model builders go in and build a model of a city or a model of a town or a house. . . . He could have been one of those guys. . . . He's that good. The back garden of the houses that back onto the railway have got used tires or bits of bicycles. Every old building that's got an air conditioning unit in the window has a little streak of rust coming down the wall beneath the pipes. You can go in as tight as you like, the detail is staggering. It's all about the buildings for him. It's just that the trains are an excuse to build all these buildings'.

Stewart's main preoccupation, though, was his job. 'He was so musical', says Harrington. She recalls him practicing a lot. 'Harmonica and banjo and guitar'. For someone who was never a prolific songwriter, Stewart was attentive to composition, and continually so. Harrington: 'He wasn't, "Oh, I've got to sit down for the next ten weeks". . . . He was always writing. . . . He basically would write all the time in his mind and then he would place stuff together because he would hear somebody say something and go, "That suits me. I could incorporate that in that other song that I've been writing for a couple of years"'. Some Faces wives insisted that the second syllable of the female in the title of the song 'Cindy Incidentally' betrayed it as a message to Harrington, but she says, 'I never felt that whilst we were together he wrote about me in any particular way'. Her later experience as a music-industry manager made her conclude that this was not unusual. 'I don't think it's always about one person. Because you're writing a song all the time, to make it work you might bring something else in that fits better than the reality'.

Some people—including then-staunch fans of Stewart like Robert Christgau and Greil Marcus—felt that Stewart's lack of original material, casual approach to songcraft conventions and child-like preference for grid-like album formulae meant that he was an accidental genius, someone who didn't really understand why or how he was so good. From what Harrington says, though, there was considerable thought behind what on the surface appeared hand-to-mouth methodology, certainly as far as choice of song goes. 'He's not like a lot of artistic people who just like lots of things and they're never going to be hits and they don't suit them', she says. 'He was clever about his own identity and his own presence in music, not just singing anything'.

Harrington says that Stewart reacted well to his sudden fame and wealth. 'Remarkably so'. Although he was naturally pleased about his success, she remembers his feelings as being less euphoria than relief. 'At last—somebody likes his music. He was so happy about that'. She also says, 'He didn't change much in his life'. Part of the reason for this was simple lack of time. 'Two albums a year, one Faces, one Stewart. Faces touring. The Rod promotion, Faces promotion. It was endless. You don't get to sell those records by not being out there. . . . He didn't really have much time to be that rich guy. He was working'. Another reason for Stewart not transforming into the lord of the manor was a careful and loving maintenance of his roots. 'He's very, very into his home, Rod. Every weekend, he would go and play football with the Highgate Redwings, who he played with when I first knew him. Sometimes I went and then we'd go to the pub afterwards, we'd have a drink with the boys, but then we'd go and see his mum and dad. We were always going to see his mum and dad, his sisters. . . . [His brother] Bobby lived just up the road from the house. . . . There was a deep family feeling there. . . . Even when we lived in the big house, he loved his home. A lot of those guys from that time, they'd all be out partying, Class-A drugging it, but he held on to that side for quite a while'.

The big house to which Harrington refers is Cranbourne Court, a thirty-two-room Windsor mansion set in seventeen acres which Stewart took possession of in the second half of 1971. 'He had a beautiful house, which I didn't really want to leave, a mock Tudor in North London', says Harrington. 'We moved because [he'd] had "Maggie May" and we couldn't get out of the house. That's why we ended up in the countryside in twenty acres of land where nobody could see the house'. She notes, 'He also had a house in Muswell Hill that he let John Baldry live in. And he got a house for his mum and dad in Muswell Hill. I helped to decorate that. Also, he bought an investment townhouse in Highgate'. One impetus for taking possession of so many buildings was that, in high-tax Britain of the 1970s, buying property was one of the few ways to legitimately keep one's income from the Inland Revenue. Cranbourne Court is a perfect case in point. Harrington: 'It's ridiculous when you think about it. His accountant said, "You've got to spend some money on buying a house. It's got to be a hundred thousand pounds". It was bought off Lord Bethell, who obviously had fallen on hard times'. That a long-haired young man with a London accent was more solvent than a Lord-in-waiting to the Queen was certainly a barometer of changing times.

'We had an idyllic life', says Harrington of their new domicile. Cranbourne Court's expansive grounds became the couple's private playground and a means for Stewart to lavishly indulge his common-law wife (to employ a phrase then in vogue). 'He knew that I loved riding horses. He said, "You build stables and do whatever you want with the fields". He knew that I would have nothing to be doing stuck out in this house in the middle of nowhere. He knew that that would consume. He was clever about that'.

Harrington feels part of this strategy on Stewart's part was down to his insisting that she had no role outside the home. 'He would never let me go to work. He'd say, "People will talk about me and they'll say, 'That man in that house with all that money lets his wife go out to work'". He would say I didn't need a job. Well, no, I didn't need a job. But I needed to be somebody. You don't want to be that boring person [when] the other person's always got so much to say'. She also says of what might be termed Stewart's domestic strategy, 'He came and went with all these recordings, his promotions, his football with the guys in Highgate, but it enabled him to operate in some kind of normality. He is freed up from anything else other than having a relaxing existence'.

While some might view Stewart's attitude as chauvinism, Harrington didn't generally feel belittled, and, if anything, felt deified. Stewart invited to dinner the Sunderland soccer team—'giant-killing' victors in the 1973 Football Association Cup final against the mighty Leeds United—and was furious when they arrived late. 'He loved my cooking. "How dare you arrive late? Don't you see Dee has been cooking all night long?" He would place me on the pedestal a bit'.

STEWART HAD THE GRAND SLAM OF SUCCESS and credibility. He was both a superstar and a man of the people, a rock musician and a pop star, a heavyweight artist and a teen idol.

As with many cultural idols, he proliferated. His haystack haircut (or perhaps dragged-backwards-out-of-a-haystack) was an expanded version of the blonde explosion that was the style of his idol and friend foot-baller Denis Law, but it became perceived as uniquely his. Many was the barber that found customers asking for 'a Rod Stewart'. Meanwhile, his penchant for draping himself in tartan scarves was copied by both sexes, long before it became the badge of identity of Bay City Rollers followers.

In respect of visiting the States, Stewart had been a grizzled veteran to ex-Small Faces Jones, Lane and McLagan's novices. However, matters were reversed when it came to another aspect of his and his fellow Faces' snowballing careers. Recalls McLagan of Stewart, 'On a plane once I said, "What are you doing?" He said, "Reading my fan mail". I said, "Ah, Jesus Christ". I took the piss out of him. But then, he hadn't had any. We'd been through all that and sort of got over the novelty and it was like a fresh thing for him and he was excited'. McLagan believes that the fact that Stewart was one of the last of his contemporaries to make it had a significant psychological effect. 'He'd never given up trying, and the tim-ing was right', he says. 'He jumped on it. He thought it was all going to die the next day so he might as well just cash in on it. I'm sure of it. He was very insecure about it'.

There are, though, nuances to this. In 1974, Stewart seemed to admit to the *Sunday Times'* Philip Norman that there might have been self-sabotage involved in his slow progress. 'People tried to help me, to record me, but I wouldn't turn up for the session or something', he revealed of his pre-fame days. 'It's easy living with failure. It's not so easy to live with success'. Which is not to say that the aching longing for success Stewart felt in the first half of his twenties wasn't genuine. In any case, in time it was replaced by almost a gratitude that it took so long. In 1973, he reflected to Penny Valentine of *Sounds*, 'I was lucky that all this started to happen when I was 24. When I knew . . . to say, "Hold on, steady your-self" instead of going out and getting drunk every night'.

There are also nuances to that success and credibility grand slam. For all his talent, it has to be said that in some ways Stewart's success was odd. He was a very unusual rock star for the time in not being able to fill up an album with original songs. It made him almost a throwback to a pre-Beatles era of young recording artists being mere mouthpieces for often middle-aged Tin Pan Alley songwriting hacks. Had it not been for the mitigating factor that he also contributed to Faces songs (i.e. it could be said that, cumulatively, he wrote or co-wrote a whole album a year), and the even bigger mitigating fact that critics loved his music to death, he would have been considered, to a greater or lesser degree, to lack credibility.

There was also something in his career that was less a nuance than an awkwardness, one that would develop into a timebomb. Gaff says of Stewart and the Faces prior to *Every Picture*, 'The two careers were very much in parallel. Nobody'd had a hit. I'd say it was 50/50', although he does add, 'To be honest I think Rod was getting more airplay'. The tail, though, was now wagging the dog.

The ratios suddenly changing was not, of course, all to the Faces' disadvantage. The Faces were pulled along in Stewart's glittering slipstream. Teenage girls who wanted to see their chart idol had no option but to go and see the Faces and to rub shoulders with the some-what different, more testosterone-charged demographic that the Faces attracted; the teenyboppers also bought the Faces' records out of com-pletist fervor. 'What Rod got, they got', Gaff says of the Faces. 'Every-thing was shared totally equally'. Not only did Stewart not play solo gigs, but when he found himself with a hit requiring him to fulfill media promotional duties, he took the Faces along for the purpose. Many of those appearances, of course, involved lip-synching, or 'miming' as it was called in Stewart's native UK. As previously mentioned, *Top of the Pops*—then a national institution watched every week by a third of the country—played host to bizarre performances of 'Maggie May'. That Stewart mouthed the words while the Faces pretended to play instru-ments behind him regardless of the fact that only two of them (plus Stewart) were on the record was not hugely peculiar. On the second *TOTP* appearance, however, their friend the alternative-minded DJ John Peel sheepishly pretended to be rendering Ray Jackson's immortal mandolin part. The third appearance saw the band members swapping their instruments around (Jones on bass, Wood on keyboards, etc.). The latter prank may have alleviated suspicions of fraudulence, but too late for an infuriated Mick Waller, whose mother was called a liar by a neighbor when she told her that her son was Rod Stewart's drummer. It may be the case that Stewart instigated this policy of using the Faces for promotion as a way to help propel them up the ladder of public recognition. If so, it backfired, for however many people in the world were cognisant of the fact that the Faces were a band of more or less equals, there seemed an ever-greater number who assumed that they were merely Stewart's backing group.

Gaff doesn't buy this. 'The public had no problem', he says. 'They knew which was Rod Stewart and they knew who were the Faces. It was the Faces that didn't know who was Rod Stewart and who was the Faces'. One thing he does state, though, is that Stewart's huge success changed the dynamic within the band for the worse. 'All hell broke loose. The jealousies and the problems. That's when it all started. There was a lot of bitterness. It was never really aimed at Rod—it was aimed at everybody around him. Nobody could do anything right. I was in the firing line most of the time. It was a fucking nightmare'.

If the Faces were a little irritated at the way the vast majority of interviewers and fans wanted to speak only to their lead singer, it was as nothing compared to one fundamental, festering grievance. Some of the Faces—and some of the public—found it not just puzzling that Rod's albums always outshone Faces LPs but actively suspicious. 'Rod was making his solo album so the pressure was on him and I felt that all the Faces were left with was a bunch of riffs that we had to string into songs', says Jones. 'We made some good songs, don't get me wrong, but really there was more to choose from in Rod's repertoire'. When *Melody Maker* writer Mark Plummer suggested to Ronnie Lane in April 1971 that 'it would be nice if both Rod's and the Faces' own ideas could be fully combined', the bassist seemed on the brink of candor before appearing to clam up for discretion's sake. 'If all the good ideas on both Rod's solo albums and Faces' albums could be together it would be . . . ', he started. He limply concluded, 'Well there you go. That's the way things are and it's not of much importance'. McLagan also had issues about the subject, even if he maintained an equanimity about it. 'Look, if I was in a band and I also had a solo deal, obviously I'd save the best stuff for me', he reflects. 'Especially when he started to sell. Why would you put a good song on an album that isn't going to sell very well?' McLagan says there were most certainly discussions with Stewart about this. 'He never admitted it at the time, but it's a hard thing to admit'.

'Absolutely no way', says Gaff of that theory. 'If Rod had presented one of his good songs for a Faces album, they would have thrown it out anyway. There's no way they would have put 'Mandolin Wind' on their album, there's no way they would have put the stuff that Rod wanted to record. I'm sure the Faces saw themselves as the Rolling Stones, they saw themselves as rock 'n' roll. Rod saw the Faces a bit like that, too. Rod would never be that selfish'.

There were, though, instances of Stewart all but admitting to the theory that Gaff disputes. For example, in August 1973 he told *Melody Maker*, 'Mick Jagger said it recently, and it's true, that I've saved some of my best material for my own LPs'. However, he had a justification, one in fact that partway chimes with Gaff's comments. 'The band never got into the acoustic things I did, and I've always been a folkie at heart'. Adding a further complication, Stewart's oft-times collaborator Ronnie Wood told author John Pidgeon, 'That may have been going on in *his* head, but I didn't know about it. . . . If he used to say, "Oh no, let me have this Faces one for mine", I used to kick up and refuse'.

McLagan himself adds, 'For all of us slagging him off for saving his best stuff for his albums, the point is it helped the Faces no end. We toured anyway, but once he had a hit it reflected on us. . . . It was a wonderful thing to have hits whether they were ours or his. . . . It all reflected back. I was on those albums. I patted myself on the back too. . . . In some ways it worked against us of course, but it actually really helped the band'. Jones' point of view, though, is Stewart's solo success stopped the Faces fulfilling their potential. 'We would have had to have taken our recording a lot more seriously than we were at the time', he says. 'Obviously if Rod never had his solo stuff, we would have been concentrating on making the albums better than what they are, song-wise'.

Although Dee Harrington had been highly impressed when she saw the Faces live, she can see why their recorded output was less than over-whelming. 'It's quite difficult music to reproduce, when they ad-libbed so much and a lot [of it was] how they were that night on stage', she says. 'It was a party band'. However, she also notes, 'Their work ethic wasn't the same as his'. This impression was generated when she encountered Stewart returning unexpectedly from Faces recording sessions. 'I'd go, "Ohh, you're back early", and he said, "Well, they never turned up"'. On this, at least, she and Jones are in some kind of agreement. 'Woody and Mac would live through the night every night, and then they would go to sleep all day', says the drummer. 'Rod and I would turn up at the studio at four o'clock in the afternoon and nobody turned up until eight or nine. I would get fed up with that and so would Rod'.

Perhaps the Faces' cavalier attitude was down to the fact that, as the Small Faces, they'd already had one highly successful career and felt that they'd already put in the hours, whereas it was all fairly new to Stewart, notwithstanding his semi-success with Jeff Beck.

To some extent, though, the underwhelming nature of the Faces' catalogue wasn't that much of an issue at the time. Magazine reviewers might constantly refer to the aesthetic disparity between Stewart releases and Faces product, but from circa 1970 onwards the Faces were never perceived as anything less than one of the most significant artistes on the 'scene'. Partly this was because—contrary to Stewart's stated wishes—the public on one level barely differentiated between the Faces collectively and Stewart solo: they sort of seemed part of the same continuum. That continuum, moreover, was pervasive. In 1971, the Faces were a seriously hard-working band. When they weren't to be heard on radio sessions or seen on TV, they could be found at concert venues. On top of the Faces' live and promotional commitments, they released two albums. Those LPs framed Stewart's album that year, on which as ever the Faces variously appeared singly, in pairs and en bloc. 'We were just full-tilt the whole time', reflects McLagan. 'It was mad'. 'We were touring a lot and when we weren't touring we were in the studio', says Jones. 'We was busy. We were also a lot younger and enjoying every minute of it'. A not irrelevant factor in the exaggerated reputation of the Faces is that there was much goodwill towards them. Nineteen seventy-one also saw the Faces stipulate that their gigs be projected onto screens behind them on stage via closed circuit television to enable the audience at their increasingly large concert venues to be able to see them better. This innovation—standard at any medium-to-large-scale concert today—cost the group $10,000 a time. Another example of why the Faces were seen as a people's band, it was the kind of thing that resulted in what might be termed a tacit agreement—amongst both critics and the public—to perceive the Faces as a major act regardless of their actual artistic achievements.

At the same time, though, there was a real desire for the Faces to prove they were as good as Stewart, whether on the part of their fans, the media or the Faces members themselves. Speaking to Penny Valentine of *Sounds* in January 1972 about the making of the band's third album, Wood said that it was perceived by them as make-or-break. 'We felt that everything relied on this album—for the group's future', he said. 'Especially with Rod becoming such a ridiculous success. We had to come out with something good'. For many, they finally achieved that objective with *A Nod is as Good as a Wink . . . to a Blind Horse*, which appeared in November.

It's no coincidence that the album marked the first time that the Faces did not solely produce themselves. Having previously baulked at recruiting Glyn Johns, they now decided that his expertise was something for which they were prepared to pay. 'Once we got Glyn in, which was Ronnie Lane's idea, things turned around for the Faces', says McLagan, omitting to mention that it was he who had prevented them doing that on the first two albums. The album's songs still sometimes left something to be desired, but the new co-producer made an audible difference to their impact. Lengths were pruned by a median two minutes and instrumentation was buffed up, making for a sound more streamlined than many had felt possible for such a proudly raggedy-arsed aggregation.

Album opener 'Miss Judy's Farm' is a sort of X-rated version of Bob Dylan's 'Maggie's Farm', with a touch of 'Maggie May'. This Stewart/Wood composition constitutes the reminiscences of an eighteen-year-old whose body has had claims laid on it by the titular agriculturalist on the grounds that it's 'all part of your job'. An insurrection instigated by the disgruntled farm worker has to be put down by the National Guard, but that doesn't make the lyric feel any less a doodle. This purposeless aura is added to by the featureless boogie that accompanies the songwords. Even so, the music—unlike on the previous two Faces albums—at least now possesses sharp borders and a certain bite.

The downtempo Lane/McLagan track 'You're So Rude', sung by the bassist, is a tale of teenage lovers caught by the girls' parents *in flagrante delicto*. It's nothing special but comes from a far more sincere and likeable place than the opener. 'Love Lives Here' (Lane/Stewart/Wood) in a metaphor for a decaying love affair uses imagery from a phenomenon common in Britain at the time: the tearing down of slum housing for the purpose of building supposedly better homes that transpired to be buildings lacking in soul and opportunities for neighbourliness. Shimmering, cascading guitar lines and a passionate vocal from Stewart make for as sweet a listen as possible considering Wood's raspily intrusive guitar. The title of 'Last Orders Please' (Lane) is the cry that resounds around British pubs at ten-to-eleven at night as landlords prepare for 'chucking-out time'. Lane sings his own composition about two ex-lovers meeting by chance in a public setting, leaving the narrator ruminating on might-have-beens. Performed in a gently rolling style, it's not profound but is pleasant and thoughtful.

The Stewart/Wood 'Stay with Me', which closed side one, is exactly the type of song Faces fans wished they could have come up with more often. A decadent, growling-riffed anthem in classic Rolling Stones style, it veritably explodes from the speakers. Although there's no denying its nastiness (the groupie Stewart begs to stay is informed that, with a face like hers, she has nothing to laugh about and is instructed in no uncertain terms not to be there in the morning when he wakes), even in that sense this strutting creation suggests a band ready to take on the Stones on their own turf.

'Debris', another Lane song, is chockful of references readily comprehensible to the composer's compatriots but impenetrable to Americans. Its imagery is rooted in the Great Britain of the post–World War II period where, such was the devastation wrought on the UK by the Luftwaffe and such was the poverty of the country after the cessation of hostilities, many neighbourhood buildings were empty shells and remained so for decades: great fun for kids who wanted somewhere intriguing to play, but not exactly easy on the eye. Lane invokes this poor-but-happy world of his childhood in a song directed at his father. Once again, Wood's accompanying electric rhythm guitar—so loud that it's fluid—is, whatever its qualities, invasive. However, the melody is lovely, the other accompaniment simpatico and the sentiments affecting. Stewart rachets up the emotionality by singing harmony against Lane's lead vocal on the choruses.

In stark contrast to these Britishisms, 'Memphis, Tennessee' (or 'Memphis', as it's billed on the tracklisting) deals in the Americana with which UK rock was then suffused and would continue to be until the punk movement deemed it phony in around 1976. Being an extended jam on a rock standard, it feels like a refugee from a Stewart album. The song is chockful of the adroit colloquialisms and convincing domestic notes in which composer Chuck Berry specialised ('My uncle took the message and he wrote it on the wall'). Not only is it unusually slow-paced for him, it's also uncharacteristically sentimental, possessing a clever trick ending in which it's revealed that the loved one whom the narrator is pleading with a telephone operator to put him through to is not in fact his girlfriend, as we had inferred, but his young daughter. The Faces stay faithful to the plaintive mood of the 1959 original, although jolly it up a little in the instrumental passages. It's quite good but lacks the ebullient spaciousness of Stewart solo-album vamps.

The Wood/Stewart creation 'Too Bad' is like 'Stay with Me', a song about the rock 'n' roll lifestyle. (Insights into this privileged, debauched life were provided by the poster originally given away with the album which featured photographs of pills, capsules and underdressed young women whom it seems safe to assume are groupies.) The lyric complains that the band are barred from posh hotels because they don't have the right accents and old school ties. (The latter is a hallmark of British 'public schools'—i.e. private schools with long histories—and the phrase is often used as a shorthand for elitism.) The more nuanced reality, of course, is that the Faces were one of those bands not welcome at certain establishments because of their penchant for room wrecking—an adolescent, hedonistic rock-star tradition that takes no account of the feelings of the underprivileged types tasked with the clean-up afterwards. Which is not to say that—with its sprightly music and fist-pumping air of solidarity—the track isn't likable, even if Stewart is succumbing to his usual fault of casual rhyming schemes.

Closer 'That's All You Need' (Stewart/Wood) features a lyric about an IQ-obsessed violin virtuoso who unexpectedly turns up on the doorstep of his broke, countercultural sibling ('Late last night, reading my underground press') and is converted to the virtues of the narrator's more rough-hewn music. Unfortunately, the way this type of music is represented is yowling slide guitar from Wood. It's not the first time on the album that the guitarist has ruined a track with such harshly metallic work, and it's interesting that he was never allowed to be so overbearing on Stewart's albums. It's another reason why the Faces, even when at the top of their game as on this album, always had a tinge of boringness about them.

A Nod is as Good as a Wink . . . to a Blind Horse—named after a British expression amounting to 'I get it, say no more'—featured a front cover photograph of the Faces delighting a concert crowd, and a back cover on which the band were represented by uncannily accurate puppet caricatures, alongside a smiling horse with a tartan hide.

Of the 'come out with something good' objective that Wood articulated to *Sounds*' Penny Valentine, he said, 'With the help of Glyn Johns and a lot of concentration, I think we've done it. . . . It threw us together. We were thrown in at the deep end and we *had* to get results . . . With Glyn, this album took less time than any of the others — including Rod's — and it cost less, and we got better results'. Those familiar with Stewart's oeuvre so far might perceive that as wishful thinking. There was certainly some of the latter evident in the reviews.

Robert Christgau praised the album for 'Humor, detail, energy, warmth' and graded it 'A'. He later downgraded it to A−. One suspects that Christgau's original inflated grade was the consequence of the type of anxiety evident in the review by Dave Marsh in *Creem*. Early in his positive appraisal, Marsh asserted that the Faces had finally been able to deal with Rod Stewart as a member of the group: 'In the past, Stewart either laid out, or came in and dominated totally: the Faces had two separate identities, with Rod and without him, and the effect was to leave us with no real idea of who they were at all'. Ray Hollingworth's *Melody Maker* review—'At last the lads have got it all down on wax'—seems to find him obtaining as much relief as pleasure from the LP. Meanwhile, does Jon Tiven still agree with the final line of his orgasmic *Phonograph Record* review? It ran, 'The Faces have proved to me that they can save rock 'n' roll with their music, and not act as merely a backup band for an exceptional vocalist. Hot diggety doggie!'

Not everyone was kidding themselves. Jon Landau of *Rolling Stone* wrote, 'Rod Stewart has three solo albums out, all of them excellent. With the release of *A Nod Is as Good as a Wink* . . . the Faces, with Stewart singing lead, have three albums out, each of them duller than the one that preceded it. . . . It is apparent that when Stewart takes charge of his music he elevates the musicianship of everyone around him; when he submerges himself in the artistic group democracy of this particular band he only succeeds in bringing himself down to the level of the group's lowest common denominator'. He asserted that in contrast to the 'intensely personal and beautifully crafted' *Every Picture Tells a Story*, with *Nod* Stewart was participating 'in the making of [an album] almost completely devoid of personality, character, depth, or vision'. The Faces, he stated, 'can't sustain ideas, so their music tends to be filled with bits and pieces—a bright 30 seconds there, an exciting riff here—and then back into a basic track that is usually melodically undistinguished, unimaginatively arranged, and . . . a bore to listen to'. He had praise for Lane's three songs, finding 'charm, some real wit, and considerable style' in 'You're So Rude', 'Last Orders Please' and 'Debris', even if not great singing. 'He certainly bears watching in the future', he noted. However, he asserted that the gap in achievement between Stewart's albums and the Faces' was too great for it to go on. 'Glyn Johns was added as this album's co-producer in an attempt to break the mold of the last two albums. As a result, the new record certainly sounds good enough, but that seems to be about all that he was able to add to it'.

Landau perhaps went too far. After the smoke has cleared and the world has long forgotten just how much it ached for the Faces to prove they were as good as Stewart, it's clear that *A Nod is as Good as a Wink* can't be denied at least a quite-good status. Whatever the faults of the album, it contained some fine tracks, and was part of an incremental improvement that seemed to place that longed-for level-pegging with Stewart situation within reach. This latter perception was possibly bolstered by the fact that the previous Faces LP had been so recent: people may have subliminally adopted the attitude that they could view the aggregated best tracks off each as one release. This assessment of an upwards gradient was assisted by the fact that the album finally garnered the Faces hits on both singles and album charts. Its single 'Stay with Me' reached the US top 20 and in the UK climbed as high as number 6. The album reached number 6 when released in the US in November 1971. In the UK—where it appeared the following month—it made number 2. Or is that failure to just miss the top spot that seemed to come so easily to Stewart nowadays somehow emblematic?

AT THE BEGINNING OF 1972, Stewart once again acted as producer on one side of a John Baldry album whose other half was produced by Elton John. Perhaps it was only fair: both Baldry and Ray

Jackson were of the opinion that the Baldry LP *It Ain't Easy* was a blue-print for *Every Picture Tells a Story*, whether it be because of its largely identical personnel or the fact that Stewart found the confidence to officially produce alone on the latter for the first time. Baldry's follow-up, *Everything Stops for Tea*, featuring a cover illustration by Ronnie Wood, actually crept into what was this year renamed the *Billboard* Top LPs & Tape chart.

Stewart's own offering that year was *Never a Dull Moment*. On paper, it should have been as good as *Every Picture*: it's effectively the same album. The grid was by now being adhered to almost comically rigidly. The fact that it was the first Stewart album not to be an incremental improvement on its predecessor could hardly be held against it, as it was already clear that *Every Picture Tells a Story* was an extraordinary artistic high. However, it couldn't be denied that there were issues with the album and worrying portents about the artist's ability to sustain the quality of his output.

First track 'True Blue' is a song about a young man who has indulged his wanderlust but finds he misses his family as much as they miss him. By now, we are used to apparently autobiographical Stewart album openers. However, whereas 'Gasoline Alley' and 'Every Picture Tells a Story' conveyed a verisimilitude (even if a sometimes phony one), this composition strikes a false note with its very first line: 'Never be a millionaire'. Even those not cognisant of the specific fact that Stewart now lived in a thirty-two-room mansion would have known that the statement was preposterous. The album is pock-marked by such assertions of poverty and minimal prospects: the narrator of 'Italian Girls' states that at a motor show he attended he was dreaming of a flash car that would always be out of his financial reach; in 'You Wear It Well' the storyteller laments that he can't afford a long-distance phone call to his ex-girlfriend. Of course, Stewart could have been writing about his younger self, and there's a possibility that he's being mischievous. More-over, such hardship tableaux are always preferable to vistas of privilege, not least because they implicitly assert a sympathy for the disadvantaged. However, few can have listened to such lines without raising a meta-phorical eyebrow. This album finds Stewart at a crossroads, one where the known circumstances of his life and finances are audibly creating a tension with the nature of the art that had given him such riches in the first place. For some, the *Never a Dull Moment* LP will have created a feeling of melancholy, because it was obvious that there could be few, if any, more like it: Stewart was now too rich to pull off this kind of stuff anymore.

Not that that would have been at the absolute forefront of any listener's mind. Their first concern would have simply been whether the album was any good. It was—as indeed exemplified by 'True Blue', written by Stewart and Wood. It's a touching tale suffused with Stewart's perennial love of his class, family and life. Drumming is provided by Kenney Jones. Although he is settling into a stately even pedestrian approach rather less interesting than the blazing style he employed on Small Faces records (or indeed the previous album's '[I Know] I'm Losing You'), the track—like the rest of the album—has a real rough-hewn power, bulldozing pleasantly out of the speakers, assisted in no small measure by Wood's brazen, distorted guitar—an example of how solo Stewart harnessed his power, never letting it get out of hand like it did on Faces records. At the track's close, the narrator stops agonising and decides to make the journey home, the song moving into joyous double time as he does so.

Lane and McLagan also appear on the opener. By now, the public was cognisant that a track on a Stewart solo album played by the Faces was better than anything Stewart ever proffered for an actual Faces LP. However, the fact that the sleeve notes reveal that Glyn Johns engineered 'True Blue' takes this matter into a different dimension, because it reveals that it wasn't intended for a Stewart solo album at all but for *A Nod is as Good as a Wink*. Human nature being what it is, Stewart may have been justified in saving his best stuff for himself, but getting the Faces to play on a recording and then metaphorically sticking the tape under his coat was surely a moral step too far.

In 'Lost Paraguayos' (Stewart/Wood), the narrator declares his intention to leave behind his lover along with the chilly weather of his home country and head for the sunnier climes of South America. The music is a welter of delightfully cascading acoustic guitars. Some reviews of the album averred that, for all its qualities, Stewart was displaying no ambition to improve himself, but the fact that in its closing part this track is enriched with a brass section (players uncredited) rather contradicts that. The song's lyric is less delightful. Although the narrator doesn't explicitly reveal his lover to be underaged, he states that her 'ridiculous age' renders her unable to cross borders with him. Moreover, after telling her he wouldn't tell her a lie, he gives vent to a snicker.

Stewart's foray into the byways of Bob Dylan's canon this time out is 'Mama, You Been on My Mind'. A wistful musing on an ex-lover written by Dylan in 1964, it had since been recorded by, among others, Johnny Cash, Joan Baez, Judy Collins, the Kingston Trio and Linda Ronstadt. Distaff performers had tended to re-title it 'Daddy, You Been on My Mind', while the Kingston Trio, Doug Ashdown and Linda Ronstadt had sidestepped Oedipal awkwardness by replacing the first word with 'Babe' or 'Baby'.

Johnny Cash's 1965 version—the first one the public heard—was ridiculously jolly for such a heart-wracked song, even if the lyric is intended to convey a narrator deep in denial about the reason for his downcast state ('Maybe it's the weather or something like that'). Stewart injects the perfect amount of pathos. His musical assistance includes Spike Heatley on upright bass, someone credited only as 'Brian' on 'chest piano' i.e. accordion (Bobak: 'He was quite an elderly chap—he looked about forty'), and—in the first overt tone of country music in Stewart's art—Gordon Huntley on pedal steel guitar. An acoustic guitar is discreetly strummed, Waller maintains a pattering beat and Stewart is unusually husky on a recording that's simply exquisite.

The five-minute 'Italian Girls' (Stewart/Wood) is the longest track on a record whose running times boast unusual brevity for Rod. At the Turin Motor Show, a poor-boy narrator hooks up with a rich Italian girl who drives an envy-making Maserati as opposed to his shameful army-surplus jeep. The night of passion they share is all the more enjoyable because, her being a woman of the world, he doesn't have to tell her 'that I'd be gone with the morning sun'. Those conditioned by 'Stay with Me' to expect that to constitute the moral of the song are in for a surprise. The upbeat tone and uptempo music—including rollicking piano from Sears and some excellent thrumming bass from an uncredited player but possibly Lane, who appears on three other tracks—suddenly gives way to a stated desperation by the narrator to get back to his bella's floodlit villa. The trouble is, it's unconvincing, regardless of how many times Stewart insists that he misses the girl so bad and that she broke his heart. The switch from a rockin' first half into a broken-hearted second act—replete

with lachrymose guitars, mandolin and violin—has been utterly perfunctory and self-conscious. Stewart has always been a master of manipu-
lation—clearly casting one eye at the gallery as he emotes—but here one
becomes uncomfortably aware of the cold-blooded artifice behind his
recipe.

Jimi Hendrix composition 'Angel' had been an inclusion on *The Cry
of Love* (1971), the guitarist's first posthumous album, a record that surprised many in being more song leaning than guitar oriented. Although
a sweet enough composition, 'Angel' was never as transcendent as it
attempted to be, especially so in this iteration: Wood is a somewhat less
dexterous player than Hendrix. However, Stewart's version is pleasant
enough, helped by congas from Speedy Acquaye and a vocal judiciously
double-tracked in different pitches so that Stewart forms a mini choir
with himself.

For both Stewart and Harrington, the song had a massive sentimental
value, being Stewart's by-proxy tribute to her. Harrington recalls that in
concert, Stewart would announce, 'I'm singing a song for Dee. I recorded
it for her'. Whether or not it was for that reason, 'Angel' was hugely popular with Faces fans, becoming the band's signature song more than any of
their own compositions, and helped to inaugurate a gig tradition—now
commonplace but then rare—of the audience saving the artist the bother
of remembering the lyric.

Side two opened with 'Interludings', a guitar doodle of little over half
a minute that is the spiritual descendant of the previous album's 'Henry',
with the difference that it's written by Art Wood, one of Ronnie's two
brothers. A musician himself, Art was an alumnus of mid-1960s band
the Artwoods. (The original pressings of the album credited only 'Wood',
presumably before an aggrieved Art complained to Rod that his royalties
were going to Mrs. Wood's other already well-rewarded musician son.)
By this point in his career, Stewart knew that giving someone a track,
however brief, on one of his albums would confer on them a financial
bounty, so we can put 'Interludings' down to an act of generosity of little
actual importance to the listener, even if diverting enough.

The Stewart/Quittenton composition 'You Wear It Well' feels like a
companion piece to 'True Blue' in its humility, humanity and likeability.
It also resembles a bookend to 'Mama, You Been on My Mind' in consisting of thoughts addressed to an ex-lover. Stewart's is an epistolary song,

seeing the narrator, at a loose end on a stultifying day, reminiscing in a letter to a former girlfriend about their romance in tough circumstances: he recalls a cheap dress he bought for her that made her sit down and cry, causing him to feel like a millionaire. He then has to stop writing his missive because he's been informed it's time to get back to work. So far, so generic, even if the proletarian milieu is artfully communicated. When the lyric begins asking the ex if she remembers fine, idiosyncratic detail—basement parties, her brother's karate, all-day rock 'n' roll shows, homesick blues (possibly Bob Dylan's song 'Subterranean Homesick Blues') and radical views—it starts to feel like something from Stewart's genuine back pages. As well as that whiff of autobiography, 'You Wear It Well' has the power of universal truth, and furthermore a truth that's all the more resonant because it's one rarely acknowledged. In popular song, love is often depicted as a black-and-white proposition involving either utter adoration or bitter recrimination, but Stewart is exploring the far more realistic, if less dramatic, centre ground wherein romance has gone but mutual affection remains.

The melody follows straight, almost clichéd, lines, and the chorus is perfunctory, but the music is enjoyable, stately folk-inflected rock decorated with a fine fiddle solo. Like his lyric, Stewart's sober singing performance is miraculously devoid of ego, him once again proving he can dispense with attention-demanding vocal signatures to fully and unshowily inhabit the character he is drawing.

Following its non-inclusion on *Every Picture Tells a Story*, on this outing Stewart finally gets around to covering 'I'd Rather Go Blind'. Although the composition of the song was credited to Billy Foster and Ellington Jordan, original recording artist Etta James claimed that she wrote it with Jordan but attributed her share to her partner, Foster, for tax reasons. It was originally released as the B-side to James' 1967 single 'Tell Mama', which made number 23 on *Billboard*. It had subsequently been covered by Clarence Carter, Fugi, Spencer Wiggins and, most successfully, Chicken Shack. The latter (fronted by Christine Perfect, later Christine McVie) was a UK number 14 in 1969. The title is the pitiless statement of a narrator who knows instantly when she sees her lover talking to another woman that their love affair is over and that she will soon be helplessly watching them metaphorically walking away together. Stewart can't go wrong with the sultry melody and desolate lyric of this exquisite composition. As on James' version, a discrete brass section lifts the drama, although Wood is a coarser presence (if pleasantly so) than the subtle guitar sounds on the original.

'Twistin' the Night Away' had been a transatlantic top 10 for Sam Cooke in 1962. The succeeding years had seen versions by the Marvelettes, Bobby Rydell and Brian Poole and the Tremeloes, but covers had dropped off since the mid-1960s. Stewart resurrects the song to close *Never a Dull Moment*, making the formerly elegant number fit the raggedly powerful style of the album. It's fine enough if one doesn't listen to Cooke's smooth original beforehand, which has sweet brass accompaniment and drumming by Earl Palmer that is less leaden than Waller's, who is here below par. Meanwhile, some will have remembered a previous Stewart interview in which he stated that he would 'never touch' Cooke's material because it was 'sacred'. The fact that he had now moved beyond such humility seems, in retrospect, a harbinger of hubris to come.

John Craig once again came up with an elaborate double-gatefold sleeve. 'It was a little more playful with *Never a Dull Moment*', he says. 'I had found this old athlete's foot ad of this guy sitting in this chair and I basically just painted Rod in. This man flopped on this chair like he was totally bored: that whole never-a-dull-moment idea, the opposite of that'.

Stewart's recently changed circumstances were highlighted by the fact that one of the gatefold spreads featured before-and-after photos taken at a Faces gig: a picture of endless empty bleachers contrasting with in-concert shots when those benches were filled. As if to emphasise that, despite the newly found riches implied in the other spread, Stewart retained the tastes of the common man, the other spread showed a photo of a goalmouth at the ground of Hounslow Football Club. This time round, nobody could call Micky Waller's mum a liar: gathered in it were the album's personnel. Or at least most of them. The absence of McLagan and Jones from the picture was explained as 'decided to stay in bed', but McLagan says, 'He never told me and, the strange thing is, that was my hometown football ground. I was so pissed off when I realised. Just so upsetting'. Sears also didn't appear in the shot, as he'd had to fly to the States. The soccer ball in front of the group was captioned with his name. Meanwhile, an individual jocularly referred to only as 'Person' is Mercury's Tony Powell.

Never a Dull Moment was released in July 1972. Its playing time was rather ungenerous, its thirty-three minutes making it more than seven minutes shorter than its predecessor. The parsimoniousness is particularly objectionable considering that Stewart could have thrown on at least one more cut that wouldn't even have involved him going to the effort of writing: for the first time he hasn't included an extended jam on a standard. We also know that at least two extra tracks were available for inclusion: Stewart could have also chosen to include 'What's Made Milwaukee Famous (Has Made a Loser Out of Me)'. His competent cover of this maudlin country song about alcoholism, written by Glenn Sutton and made famous by Jerry Lee Lewis, was featured on the other side of his 1972 'Angel' single. Moreover, a completed Stewart/Quittenton song called 'Farewell' was held over for the next album. From Harrington's recollection, there would seem to have been even more cuts at the artist's disposal. 'He was always playing me stuff', she recalls. 'It was a couple of Elton John tracks that he'd recorded and at the end of it I said, "I think it's absolutely fantastic but I hate those Elton John songs". He wouldn't talk to me for two days. But two days later he went, "You're right. I'm not gonna use those tracks"'.

Of course, people tend not to notice being short-changed if they have been entertained: bad albums, whatever their duration, are the ones that seem the longest. This album was undeniably enjoyable. While its briefness was not a feature of the reviews, however, something that was was the fact that, for the first time, a Stewart LP seemed to represent not an incremental stylistic advance but simply more of the same. Yet it's an indication of the esteem in which Rod was then held by the cognoscenti that, on this score, people bent over backwards to make allowances for him.

The often-acerbic Robert Christgau, currently at *Newsday*, adjudged the album a masterpiece. 'Our greatest troubadour, he picks them as good as he writes them', he enthused. The issue of habitual modus operandi ossifying into formula was something he addressed only tangentially: 'Rod's consistency may eventually become tiresome, but this is his best yet'. In a separate column, he reflected, 'Because he's in love with the run of life, it would be a kind of contradiction for Stewart to attempt any grand esthetic advances. His consistency reflects his homely side, and so it's irrelevant to wonder whether his work is getting better until it really does get boring'.

Ken Barnes of *Phonograph Record* came out with something similar. 'He's rounded up roughly the same crew of musical cohorts and deployed them in the same general fashion, and the result . . . is a superb album. Only the songs have been changed, to protect the inner sense of individual integrity amongst the albums; but, actually, that's all you need . . . all that's required for another ace album is a new set of dynamics — and on *Never a Dull Moment* there's no letdown in this department'. He couldn't resist adding a variation of the lament that kept cropping up in Stewart reviews: 'It unfortunately again raises the dread specter of the Rod Stewart-solo and Rod Stewart-cum-Faces dichotomy (in that this album is vastly superior to *A Nod is as Good as a Wink* or its two predecessors)'.

The NME's Charles Shaar Murray also loved *Never a Dull Moment*. 'It features the usual Rod Stewart solo album studio band, which has with some justification been called the best studio band since the one Dylan assembled for *Highway 61 Revisited* and *Blonde on Blonde*', he wrote. 'This is an album which is going to give me a lot of listening time over the next few months, and I'm glad it's in the house'. His predictable addendum was, 'I just wish that, one day the Faces will make an album this good'.

There may have been an additional reason for reviewers to be indulgent about *Never a Dull Moment*'s water-treading. It came out at a remarkable juncture for UK rock. T. Rex's first post-stardom album *The Slider* appeared at the same time. Roxy Music's eponymous debut album and David Bowie's *The Rise and Fall of Ziggy Stardust and the Spiders from Mars* had been issued the previous month. Whatever the merits and demerits of those LPs, they all prided themselves on being arch, self-absorbed and postmodern. Stewart's effort must have seemed refreshingly unpretentious and soulful in comparison.

However, there was at least one reviewer who was able to push aside sentimentality and loyalty enough to provide a truly honest perspective on the album. In *Let It Rock*, Phil Hardy discussed the saviour-of-rock status his brilliance had garnered Stewart. 'Having "saved" rock once he can hardly expect to do it again', he said. 'Thus it's understandable that Rod hasn't chosen to compete for the crown this time out. But what is sad is that, the title notwithstanding, he's produced an LP that, "You Wear It Well", "Mama You Been on My Mind" and "True Blue" apart, is unexciting; not bad just unexciting. . . . His reworkings of other people's songs are solid enough but, in his own songs, his past seems to be slipping away, as though it is only available to him veiled by the mist of his superstar present'.

The public seemed to agree more with those reviews whose tenor was (to paraphrase 'You Wear It Well'), 'He's a little old-fashioned but that's alright'. 'You Wear It Well' was a UK chart topper, with 'Angel' making it to number 4. The latter success was quite surprising considering that second singles off albums was not yet a common tradition in Britain, whose denizens were apt to see milking long players as a rip-off. In the US, the same singles only achieved chart positions of 13 and 40 respectively, but the album made number 2, stayed there for three weeks, and was in the charts for a healthy twenty-one. The album also sustained a third US single, 'Twistin' the Night Away', which reached number 59. Moreover, Stewart's profile was kept at a healthy level by dint of the fact that this was the year 'Handbags and Gladrags' finally became a hit, reaching number 42.

PART OF THE REASON for *Never a Dull Moment*'s respectable American success was that, for a chunk of its chart life, the Faces were on tour.

The Faces weren't the only band playing in a US theatre near you in the summer of 1972. Also traversing America were the Rolling Stones. It didn't escape people's attention that the Faces' British origins, five-man format, hyperactive lead singer and riff-driven raggedy rock made them seem like a new Rolling Stones. However, for some, they weren't just a new variant but a superior one.

US music journalist Lester Bangs later recalled fellow American music writer Dave Marsh observing to him at the time, 'I'd take one Rod Stewart for five Mick Jaggers any day'. The Rolling Stones had long been the rock band that the young and the countercultural considered to be most on their side: bad-boy libertarians, people who had paid for their alternative values with prison sentences. Nine years on from their recording debut, that men-of-the-people image was fraying. A jet-setting lifestyle and tax exiledom from their home country were inevitable consequences of their popularity, and not even something fans would necessarily hold against them. However, there was a loftiness to the Stones these days. Whereas almost all other bands kept working simply because they needed to maintain revenue streams, they gigged sporadically. It had been three years, for instance, since the Stones had last toured the States. Their then-current album, *Exile on Main St.*, is now viewed by many as a masterpiece, but it didn't quite seem that way then. Its murky mix meant that it took many more listens to appreciate than their previous works. In addition, that murky mix came across to some as slovenliness, implicit in which was contempt for the consumer. So too did the scrappy freak-themed cover artwork, hand-scrawled sleeve annotation and vulgar catalogue number (COC 69100). Then there was the fact of Mick Jagger having recently and unexpectedly succumbed to convention by getting married, and furthermore doing so in an elaborate wedding in glittering St Tropez. The Stones had begun to seem less like the spirit of rebellion than figures of hauteur verging on sell-outs.

This was a marked contrast to the Faces. The latter might have been playing to houses of up to fourteen thousand people and averaging $75,000 per show (half a million dollars in today's money), but their one-of-the-boys aura remained intact. Stewart enjoyed the most kudos in this respect, and not merely because of the lead-singer-as-figurehead syndrome. He was likeable in interview, irreverent on stage and an ordinary Joe on record. As journalist Paul Nelson later said, 'Stewart was considered the Bruce Springsteen of his time: our least-affected, most down-to-earth rock star'.

What with the barnstorming year Stewart and the Faces had enjoyed in 1971, it at that point genuinely seemed that it was possible that the Stones might be eclipsed by their compatriots. 'We were outselling the Stones', notes Jones of Faces tickets.

Not much, it seemed, could go wrong for Rod Stewart and his colleagues.

5
I'M LOSING YOU

FOR ALL THEIR SUCCESS AND ACCLAIM, there were fissures forming beneath the Faces' blissful public exterior.

When Dave Marsh of *Creem* took in a Faces concert in Louisville in late summer 1972, he couldn't help noticing that Stewart seemed a rather weary figure. Speaking to him afterwards, his suspicions seemed confirmed. Already working on the follow-up to *Never a Dull Moment*, Stewart told him for a feature that appeared in August that year, 'There's too much work. . . . It's draining on the brain all the time. Fucking writing songs and getting them together. . . .There wasn't the pressure there before "Maggie May" or *Every Picture* that there is now. . . . If I could finish the album when I wanted to it'd be all right. . . . It's affecting me health. And there isn't any break, because we've got to start working on the group's album when this one's done'.

Tellingly, Harrington reveals that one of the attractions of being resident at Cranbourne Court was that it was 'out of London and away from band members'. Ronnie Wood was the only Face for whom the welcome mat was laid out ('They gelled very well. I think Rod could be just silly with Ronnie, and vice versa. They loved each other'). No one else in the Faces camp was made to feel welcome—even the spouse of the sole one who was. Harrington actually found Wood's wife Krissie turning up unannounced one day and declaring, 'Well, you clearly aren't going to invite us, so I thought I'd just come 'round'.

From Harrington's point of view, there was increasingly less reason for Stewart to desire the company of his bandmates. 'They were very unhappy about his huge success', she says. 'Why would you not want to be that successful? It's a contradiction. . . . Him being that successful enabled them to sell more records, play at bigger stadiums, and have a larger income. But they weren't happy with that. Ronnie Lane was very unhappy and would make quite unpleasant remarks that, "Oh, you look like an ageing queen". That upset me more than it upset Rod. I think Rod had prepared himself . . . for all of this to go down, because Ronnie Lane was so rude and so put out'.

With sessions for Stewart's fifth album completed, ones for the Faces' fourth album, *Ooh La La*, began in August 1972. Stewart was a dilettante presence. 'He really missed the first two weeks of recording', says McLagan. 'We cut loads of stuff and he'd come and he'd go, "Nah, don't like that". The track "Ooh La La", he said, "Nah, don't like it, it's the wrong key anyway". So we re-cut it and it was too high for Ronnie Lane and so he said, "Well, Woody, you sing it". . . . Glyn got really pissed off with Rod during *Ooh La La* because he wouldn't turn up and, when he did, he'd just be very offhand and didn't want to be there. . . . He wanted to get the best out of all of us, including Rod, but Rod wouldn't even turn up, and he'd be rattling his car keys soon after he got there'. Johns—again in the producer's seat—later observed of Stewart to John Tobler and Stuart Grundy, producers of the 1982 BBC radio series *The Record Producers*, 'I found him almost impossible to work with and I disliked him intensely . . . I don't think he really took much interest in the Faces. . . . He was far more interested in his solo career . . . I never felt his heart and soul was really in it . . . I always objected to the way it was "Rod Stewart and the Faces". They were as good as he was!'

Gaff describes as 'bullshit' the idea that Stewart began to take less interest in the Faces after the success of *Every Picture Tells a Story*. 'What he started to take less interest in was the fact that they could not accept that he was making all the money, giving them everything, and all they did was bitch and moan about everything all the time'.

The fourth Faces album actually preceded Stewart's new LP to the stores because legal complications held up the release of the latter. *Ooh La La* was issued in March 1973. That it had been fanfared by a good single, 'Cindy Incidentally', augured well for that equivalent-to-a-Rod-LP holy grail desired by so many rock critics and Faces fans. However, it started very unpromisingly indeed with 'Silicone Grown', written by Stewart and Wood. McLagan pounding dramatically away on piano does nothing to divert attention from the fact that it's just another piece of Faces rock ordinaire, plodding along to no effect, with the additional demerit of it being a boorish meditation on the then new phenomenon of breast implants.

'Cindy Incidentally' follows. A McLagan/Stewart composition, it finds a narrator imploring his partner to join him in his desire to move from their uninspiring neighbourhood. The band maintain a gentle chug, with Wood's continuous spikey guitar a nice accompaniment to a winding melody devised by McLagan after he'd tried playing 'Memphis' backwards. The lyric flows symbiotically with the music and contains nice internal rhymes, even if the external rhymes (as it were) display the laziness familiar from Stewart's solo albums.

'Flags and Banners' (written by Lane and Stewart, sung by the bassist) features a lyric that explores a surreal dream. Its unusualness makes it intriguing, but it's a brief wisp of a song and uncertain of its objective. Stewart and Wood both sing on 'My Fault', a McLagan/Stewart/Wood song of self-determination that could be read as being addressed to either a parent or a partner. It contains an astute observation in 'People don't change just overnight—it ain't natural' but is otherwise just another featureless Faces chug and another against which Stewart's voice strains uncomfortably.

Borstals were the equivalent of what Americans call reform schools and for McLagan, Stewart and Wood to write a song about an ex-inmate of such an institution played nicely into the Faces' laddish group image. Unfortunately, despite a breakneck tempo, things never get any more exciting than the klaxon that galvanisingly opens 'Borstal Boys'. Jones pounds an insistent tattoo and Stewart yells out actually quite legitimate complaints about the senseless brutality of Borstal regimes, but it all ends up feeling like much ado about nothing and one is quite relieved when it's over.

Vinyl side two opened with the instrumental 'Fly in the Ointment', credited to Jones, Lane, McLagan and Wood. It's a yet further step away from the brilliance of the instrumentals in which the Small Faces had specialised, a midtempo slice of anonymity clearly included to fill up space.

The rest of the side is dominated by Lane, who writes or co-writes the remaining four tracks. All are slowies out of keeping with the Faces'

Stonesalike image but, as the album's first side had unwittingly but comprehensively demonstrated that the Faces could never assume that mantle, this was not necessarily a bad thing. Almost all of the quartet is insubstantial, but all of the songs have a sweet tone to them and, in an unexpected way, infuse the album with that quintessential Faces concert warmth.

'If I'm on the Late Side' (Lane/Stewart, sung by Rod) is—as with so many songs in which Lane was involved—a vignette rather than a narrative and a snapshot of a sentiment as opposed to a fully fleshed idea. Inevitably it ends up feeling inconsequential, even if the generous, loving message is appealing and the melody attractive. The two Ronnies sing 'Glad and Sorry', whose line 'If I'm not smiling, I'm just thinking' demonstrates its winning but whimsical nature. McLagan plays a superb quavering piano motif, if one that gets slightly over-insistent. Wood's guitar solo is clean and thin in a way never heard from him before. The sentiment of the Lane-written, Stewart-sung 'Just Another Honky' is endearing, if one doesn't make the mistake of confusing art and artist. Lane's statement 'I don't own you' seems somewhat less noble and touching when taking into account the fact that he had recently and abruptly left his wife for another man's spouse.

Album-closer 'Ooh La La' presents the novelty of a Ronnie Wood lead vocal. Woody taking the drastic step of handling the singing himself, in the absence of Stewart's willingness to do so, turns out to be serendipitous, for his rough-hewn but expressive voice is superbly apt for a tale of a man giving bitter advice on love to his grandson, complete with a line that's a perfect distillation of regret: 'I wish that I knew what I know now when I was younger'. That this wonderful phrase could have come straight out of one of Stewart's own confessional creations makes his lack of interest in the song even more peculiar. Lane and Wood provide some great acoustic guitar-picking accompaniment.

And there—just as it gets truly interesting—the album comes to an end, a perfect illustration of the Faces' endless ability to frustrate all those desperate for them to fulfill their theoretical potential for greatness. To add insult to injury, the record is only half an hour long. That it's the first Faces album not to feature covers is hardly a mark of progress if it's achieved by shortchanging the public. If they were averse to beefing it up with a couple of oldies, the deficit could at least have been alleviated by including 'Skewiff (Mend the Fuse)', B-side of 'Cindy Incidentally'. Then again, the album was hardly crying out for another meandering instrumental. Moreover, many would not have wanted to listen to more of anything of whatever kind. The Faces were becoming predictable: the over-familiar boogie patterns, Wood's fat, slurred electric guitar, McLagan's blusteringly busy piano, Stewart's singing in a trebly range not his forte, songs that seemed to go nowhere . . .

Wood seemed to reveal another reason for the lack of power of Faces compositions when he told Ron Ross of *Circus* that most of the songs on *A Nod is as Good as a Wink* and *Ooh La La* originated in 'dressing room loons' when the band 'was full of adrenalin before we went onstage'. He added, 'We wanted to take the lyrical emphasis off things that were too personal. We didn't want too much on our personal love lives, for example'. Hardly the recipe for the blush-making compositional masterpieces in which solo Stewart specialised.

As noted, *Ooh La La* marked the point where the Rolling Stones comparisons were exposed as somewhat premature and overly optimistic. By this point in time, *Exile on Main St.* was beginning to belatedly be perceived as a classic. After four albums, the Faces had failed to live up to anything like that LP's kind of standard. Moreover, that they were incapable of matching even a below-par Rolling Stones album was definitively proven five months after the release of *Ooh La La* when *Goat's Head Soup* hit the stores. By common consensus, it was the worst Stones album since *The Rolling Stones No. 2* back in 1965, yet it was evident that the Faces could never in a million years attain the polish and poise of its best tracks like 'Angie' and 'Doo Doo Doo Doo Doo (Heartbreaker)'. Meanwhile, the effortlessly swaggering, decadent rock 'n' roll of the closing cut, 'Star Star', was precisely the sort of thing that the Faces transparently ached to be able to do.

Far more exertion seems to have been put into *Ooh La La*'s sleeve than its contents. Designed by Jim Ladwig and executed by John Craig, its front bore a tinted photograph of 1920s Italian music hall character Gastone. It featured the type of gimmick destined to ensure that mint copies of the original vinyl release are now virtually impossible to find: pressing down the top caused Gastone to make a funny face. More comedy was to be found in the gatefold spread: a shot of a can-can performer, with the Faces to be found at her feet delighting in that dance's trademark underwear-flashing ploy. The back cover takes a more sober tone, featuring thoughtful portraits of the band members.

In *Melody Maker* shortly after the album's release, Stewart did his bit for promotion by declaring it a 'stinking, rotten album'. His later comment to *Rolling Stone* that he actually said he thought the band were 'capable of doing a better album than we've done', adding that they had not found 'the right studios or the right formulas', was presumably meant as a mollifying gesture but actually served to widen the target of his ire to encompass the entire long-playing Faces catalogue to date. Yet Kenney Jones feels he may have had a point. The drummer says of the Faces' corpus, 'They're just sort of very loose and humble really. I was never really satisfied. I was always very conscious of the fact that I felt that we could have had a couple more commercial songs in there'. It should also be pointed out that McLagan had already poured cold water on the album's lead-off single (which, remember, he actually co-wrote) by remarking to the *NME*'s James Johnson of 'Cindy Incidentally', 'It doesn't really lead anywhere and I think it'd be nice if it did'. (It actually led to a UK no. 2.)

Considering all this, the album did surprisingly good business, being the band's first chart topper in their home country and making number 21 in the States. This may have been a consequence of the fact that, once again, a Faces album garnered reviews that were overly generous where they weren't actually deluded. 'When all the tumult and shouting have died, I think it'll go down in rock history as a goodie', unconvincingly declared Charles Shaar Murray of the *NME*. Some of his other comments gave him away: '*Ooh La La* is more satisfying than any of its predecessors' is hardly high praise, nor is 'as good as anything that the Faces have ever produced as a unit, and considerably better than most'. Dave Marsh of *Creem* also seemed to be trying to convince himself of the qualities of a record that he in his heart of hearts knew didn't amount to much. 'I'd say *Ooh La La* disappointed me if I hadn't listened to it more than I ever thought I would when it first arrived', he offered. 'This is still a frustrating record, made by a band that refuses to cut loose, but there is something valuable about it'. Once removed from the climate of the times, one would be hard-pressed to find anyone who considers *Ooh La La* of any particular significance. Robert Christgau (back at *Creem*) was already there. He wrote, 'I've been playing this album for weeks in the hope that it would eventually have its way with me, but my body is still untouched. Soul, too. Maybe Rod Stewart really does save his best songs for the solo albums'.

A COUPLE OF MONTHS AFTER *OOH LA LA*'S RELEASE, Stewart's voice could be heard on something considerably better than almost anything on that album. Not a new solo Stewart single, but an excavated Jeff Beck Group track. 'I've Been Drinking' had been the B-side of 'Love Is Blue', a 1968 single by that talent-oozing but tumultuous aggregation. An adaptation of 'Drinking Again' by Doris Tauber (music) and Johnny Mercer (lyrics), it's credited to Beck and Stewart (as 'Jeffrey Rod'). It's a tragic, mythmaking number typical of the band. Cannily re-released by producer and rights-holder Mickie Most—who ensured that the legend 'Vocal: Rod Stewart' was prominent on the reissue's label—it made number 27 in the UK.

It wasn't the only unauthorised chart action Stewart had recently enjoyed in his home country as a consequence of how bright his star currently shone. In late 1972, his voice was drifting across the British airwaves attached to a single released under the name Python Lee Jackson. 'In a Broken Dream' was a recording by an obscure Australian band that back in the late 1960s Stewart had dubbed vocals over in exchange for payment-in-kind. Although dug from the vaults purely to capitalise on his stardom, it deserved to be the top-3 hit it became. A haunting, surreal concoction, Stewart graced its poetic songwords with a committed performance that betrayed not a trace of mercenaryism (his prosaic remuneration had been carpeting for his car). Two further Stewart vocal tracks appeared on the subsequent double album of the same title.

AN INCIDENT GAFF DATES TO 1973 gives an indication of the tensions that were bubbling away in the Faces camp. He recalls, 'We were doing a huge tour of America. In the contract I had to put specifically that in any place, Madison Square Garden or anywhere else, Rod Stewart's name could not be put on the marquee. It would have to be "The Faces". I got a call from a promoter friend of mine. It could have been Detroit. He said, "Billy, you know we're not selling fucking tickets and I'm stuck with this clause? We're going to have half a house". I said,

"You're joking". He said, "Billy, I've got to put Rod's name up there. I've got to". I said, "Okay, do it, but would you do me a favour and get the bloody thing down before we arrive?" He forgot! It was possibly the worst night of my life—they went fucking berserk. But the gig sold out and Rod didn't mind'. From what he says, it sounds like this was the night that Gaff was vengefully locked out of his hotel room naked, with groupies looking on. Also from what he says, this incident would have been the handiwork of two specific Faces. 'Kenney Jones is a very, very nice guy. Woody too. The other two were total utter bullies of the highest order'.

The old Faces camaraderie was certainly nowhere to be seen in May 1973 when Lane and Stewart launched into a fistfight backstage at a Rhode Island gig. Such had once been the closeness of the Faces that they had felt comfortable enough to use as a band in-joke the phrase 'I'm leaving the group!' (Stock response: 'Bollocks, you cunt!') However, when just over a week after that incident Lane announced his departure, he wasn't playing for laughs. Additionally, the scuffle between Lane and McLagan onstage on the same evening Lane made his farewell declaration was not horseplay.

Lane fulfilled the remaining Faces live commitments before making his final exit in early June. He was soon releasing often lovely records of his own with his band Slim Chance (which name had been a contender for that of the Faces in the beginning). 'Ronnie Lane had to leave because all the songs he was writing, he could never do them live because we had a singer', says McLagan. 'It was rotten for Ronnie'. Other problems were Lane's disenchantment with playing in ever bigger and more impersonal venues, Wood now preferring to write with Stewart than with him, and the alleged fact that he relayed to a *Rolling Stone* journalist that 'the whole band was built around Rod, and Rod wasn't there 100 per cent'. Lane himself told the same magazine's Kurt Loder, 'Rod Stewart got so big-headed I couldn't take it anymore'.

Such sentiments would have come as a shock to people who felt that the personality that emerged from their speakers when they played Stewart records was of a humble, humane troubadour. 'He was a good actor', laughs Keith Altham. 'He could play that role when it suited him, when it was beneficial to him. In the Faces, he did that. As soon as it didn't suit him or he wanted to step out of it, he was off. Ronnie Lane was a victim.

You won't find many people that worked with Rod for any length of time that have got too much praise for him. And by a long time, I mean about two weeks. He was such a mean bastard. He was mean-spirited, as well'. As for the impression generally obtained of the Faces as one of the few bands who genuinely liked each other, he shrugs, 'There was a kind of superficial banter that was very apparent when you went to do interviews, but you'd get them on a one-to-one a few drinks later and you'd find out it was skin deep'.

Tetsu Yamauchi, formerly of Free, took over the vacant bass-player role. 'Tetsu gives us the musical kick up the arse we needed', averred Stewart to *Melody Maker's* Chris Welch in August 1973. However, he also admitted, 'He's not really a replacement for Ronnie Lane, because Ronnie was a character more than a bass player'. Something else he could have mentioned is that Lane was also a songwriter. Although a fine musician, Yamauchi had no composing skills. The sweetness and mellowness of Lane's compositions that had been a necessary leavening of the Faces' boogie inclinations was now gone forever. There was also no replacing the group spirit (already declining before Lane left) that gradually seeped from the Faces over the next couple of years.

Stewart later said that Lane 'was the engine of the group' and added, 'For me it all fell apart when Ronnie left'. Many people would concur with the last sentiment. Many—not least Lane—might consider it to be a bloody cheek. But, then, when he made those comments—2001— Stewart had long made his peace with the man with whom he had increasingly been at loggerheads during the Faces' lifespan, him helping pay Lane's considerable medical expenses after the latter developed multiple sclerosis in the mid-1970s. In what seems almost an act of penance, in 1998 Stewart finally got round to recording a version of 'Ooh La La', placing it on his covers album *When We Were the New Boys*.

Not only could Yamauchi not provide the songwriting input or onstage charisma of Lane, he also displayed a tendency to act like a cartoon version of a Faces member, throwing himself unreservedly into the boozing lifestyle for which the group had become famous without realising that to some extent it was an act: while it can't be denied that the Faces occupied time in the pub that could have more profitably been spent in the rehearsal hall or recording studio, they also knew how to pace themselves. An inebriated Yamauchi would sometimes have to be tied to an amplifier onstage to stop him falling over.

In July 1973, Yamauchi's first tour with the Faces was accompanied by the very first Rod Stewart compilation, *Sing It Again, Rod*. It came in a jacket, which Stewart designed himself, whose shape was as arresting, and almost as impractical for store rackers, as the Small Faces' circular *Ogdens' Nut Gone Flake* sleeve had been: a highball glass. Consisting as it did of the cream of Stewart's Mercury catalogue thus far, the album merited attention, even if the remixing of some tracks—done by Stewart—was not something destined to delight purists. His version of 'Pinball Wizard'—dating from his participation in a 1972 all-star London stage production and subsequent classical recording of the Who's *Tommy* album produced by old mate Lou Reizner—was included to tempt those who already possessed sufficient good taste to have bought everything else the set contained. (Stewart missed the chance to sing the song in the later Ken Russell *Tommy* movie because another old mate, Elton John, advised him against it, then took the job himself. 'What a bastard!' Stewart publicly reflected, although their friendship remained intact.)

'When Ronnie left, the Faces were then basically Rod's touring band because he wouldn't record', says McLagan. 'Because he had a solo career and didn't give a fuck for the Faces'. Yet although their career from hereon was a matter of a protracted, untidy and rancorous demise, and a complete absence of new albums, the Faces not only still gigged but managed to put out some fine singles tracks. One appeared on the B-side of a standalone Rod single, a cover of Goffin & King's 'Oh No Not My Baby', in August 1973, another UK top tenner. The sensual Stewart/Wood/McLagan-written 'Jodie' was credited as being by 'Rod & Faces' (with the addendum 'and a bottle of Campari'). At the end of the year came a Faces single proper in the shape of the uptempo, nicotine-suffused, low-life tableau 'Pool Hall Richard', which made the UK top 10.

Nowadays, 'Oh No Not My Baby' has settled into place as a so-so, deservedly lesser-known Stewart single, but it meant a lot to him at the time. 'It's a one-off', he enthused to Chris Welch of *Melody Maker*. 'And the first time I've used strings. It's one for the tartan hordes. . . . The faithful followers. . . . This is my first bona fide single since "You Wear It

Well". "Angel" was done without my consent and "Cindy Incidentally" was with the band. I've wanted to do this song for a couple of years. . . . The song was a hit for Maxine Brown in the Sixties and it's not been done again for some time. It was recorded in two days and I'm knocked out by the tartan cover on the sleeve. I don't know how it will do. . . . It's bound to be slated, as I've been the blue-eyed boy for too long!'

By this time, the distance between Stewart and the Faces had become more pronounced. He'd long been picked up at airports in a separate limousine simply because Mercury would provide him one, while Warner Bros. dispatched one for the Faces. Using the car his record company provided may have been a politic act, but these days he also had his own dressing room at venues. Yet, amazingly, Stewart still genuinely seems to have been thinking of himself first and foremost as a member of the Faces.

Lost in the folds of history are some extraordinary comments he made to more than one journalist in August 1973. Speaking to Chris Welch of *Melody Maker*, he said, 'My next solo LP will be my last, so it's got to be a classic'. His explanation for this eyebrow-raising determination to knock on the head one of the most successful solo careers of the era was, 'Recording takes so much time, and I've had virtually no social life for the last two or three years. I've been living and dying in the studios'. The retirement comment might sound like a passing whimsey, but Stewart said much the same thing that month to another UK music weekly, *Sounds*, and went into greater detail about the whys and wherefores. Speaking to Penny Valentine, he revealed that he'd had three aims when the Faces formed. 'One was to make the band successful, because rarely do you get a second chance to be at the top and I didn't think the Faces were going to get it in this country—but they have. I also wanted to make Woody a star . . . I've done that as well. He could be bigger, but he's well known in his own right now as a guitar player. And the third thing was to sell my own albums, which I've done'. He said it was precisely because he was now 'fairly complete' that his thoughts were turning to 'other things', although he also admitted, 'I'm never happy with what I've got. I always want something better'. To that end, 'From now on in we must combine albums. The band are suffering and I'm suffering with the situation. . . . We've got to channel all our energy in one direction to make really good albums'. Asserting that the best tracks from *Ooh La La* and

Never a Dull Moment would make a great album, he said, 'Right now I don't feel either my albums or the Faces albums are as good as they could be. So the next album is the last I'm going to make on my own and next year we start making them together. Rod Stewart/Faces albums'.

It's quite astonishing to read such comments from this end of history, when the narrative has long been established that Stewart's ever-ballooning ego was primarily responsible for the breakup of the Faces. If he was the selfish narcissist that people—including some of his Faces colleagues—claim, why did he come to a determination to resolve his dilemma of overwork by pooling artistic resources and sacrificing his own career? Then again, Stewart juxtaposed these communality-minded comments with ones of hard-nosed self-interest. 'I've always been worried about the band, but I've got to the point now where I think it's time to start thinking about myself a bit more', he mused to Valentine. 'I want to look after number one. I reckon I've done my fair share for the band'.

Asked if she thought Stewart was too loyal to the Faces by staying with them as long as he did, Dee Harrington says, 'Well, he's a non-confrontational person. At that time, I think he probably didn't want to let anybody down. It was a struggle. All of it was a struggle. In the end I think they just resented it too much—and why would you be making a good record under those circumstances?' What should also not be underestimated is the residual and sincere fondness Stewart had for his bandmates. Witness this quote he gave about them to *Melody Maker*'s Roy Hollingworth in September 1972: 'I could be laying half asleep, and mopin' by this pool, and I'd hear those lads comin', and there'd be a smile as wide as a half melon across me face'. In a culture much more macho than today's, men didn't often come out with such sentimental comments about other men.

The fact that the deeper one thinks about his contradictory comments in this period the more impossible it becomes to reconcile them leads one to the conclusion that, at this point in his life, Rod Stewart was rather mixed up and simply didn't know what he wanted to do.

6

LAST ORDERS PLEASE

JANUARY 1974 SAW THE RELEASE OF THE FACES' in-concert album *Coast to Coast: Overture and Beginners,* housed in a wraparound sleeve (converted from a poster designed by John Craig) depicting a fleet of airplanes.

An aural snapshot of the Faces in their live element was, one might imagine, precisely the type of thing that would help prove to doubters that the Faces were—as Glyn Johns thought—as good as Rod Stewart. It's somehow symptomatic of their current condition that, of all the live recordings that must have existed of them, this sloppy set of recordings was chosen for commercial release. According to Charles Shaar Murray in his review for the *NME,* though, it was an accurate reflection of the state of the group, who he declared had once been 'one of the most genuinely exciting bands in the country' but were now 'a painful travesty of their former selves'. Amazingly, the record was this bad despite Stewart having taken the trouble to overdub some vocals in the studio.

It appeared on Mercury, who ensured it was billed as by 'Rod Stewart/ Faces'. That it didn't come out via Warners provides a clue as to why it saw commercial release at all: it was designed by Stewart's management to bring to an end their client's contact with Mercury. It hardly seemed a courteous reward to the label that had always graciously overlooked the fact that the man signed to them was moonlighting. Moreover, as Mercury had secured for Stewart multiple number ones—including that famous 1971 double-double whammy—some might have assumed that the artist would have opted to sign a new deal with them rather than jump ship. 'He wasn't terribly fond of them', says Gaff of Stewart's feelings about Mercury. 'He loved Warner Bros. Warner Bros. did more to promote Rod Stewart than Mercury every did. . . . Warners were a far superior company. Oh Jesus, there's not a question. Warners were young, aggressive, fantastic people. You had Mo Austin and Joe Smith and they were dynamite and everybody that worked with them were dynamite. Mercury were Chicago, tired. . . . As much as I loved Irwin Steinberg, he did everything by computer. He had no ears at all. If it sold fifty records, oh that was worth an extra dollar in advertising, if it sold two hundred, it was worth a dollar fifty. That was the way he worked. Warners just went for broke on everything. If they felt good about it, they just went for it'. It should be pointed out that Stewart may actually have signed with Warners even before he'd achieved significant success at Mercury. In 1994, Gaff told Ray Coleman, 'Three or four years before Rod's contract expired with Mercury, he knew we were signed to Warner. But we didn't dare tell anybody. Only Rod and I and Mo Austin and Joe Smith knew'.

Far from being content with obtaining Stewart's future work, Warners also wanted the latest studio album Stewart had delivered to Mercury. They secured a court injunction temporarily preventing its release that claimed that said LP was theirs to release because, in their view, Stewart's Mercury contract had expired. It delayed the album for five months. When it appeared in October as *Smiler*, it bore a Mercury label. However, Stewart later averred that the company didn't promote the album properly in light of the fact that he would soon be departing. This may very well be true, but more plausible a reason for its poor commercial performance resides in the fact that it isn't very good.

The album starts with a canine cacophony. 'Micky had his dog in the studio', recalls Sears. 'We started off "Sweet Little Rock 'n' Roller". Just as the count-off started, Micky's dog started barking really loud. We kept that track. In fact, I think it added to the track. Right there, that's the spirit of things. If that had been the '80s or something, the producer would have had a fit and he would have banned the dog from the studio and we would have had to have done that take over'. Sadly, that instance of Stewart's usual off-the-cuff approach was about the only one on *Smiler*. Everything else felt strangely laboured. Moreover, while much else about the solo-Stewart modus operandi that had worked so well over the last few years was present, it was this time somehow not correct.

It would have been conceptually appropriate if the album had indeed been issued by Warners, for in retrospect it can be seen as confirming that Stewart had peaked artistically. Although superficially similar to its predecessors—the musicians were broadly the same and the grid/blueprint was still being adhered to—*Smiler* doesn't feel of a piece, timbre- or quality-wise, with his previous LPs and has far more in common with the music that he would proceed to make from hereon in.

The problems start with the grisly self-adoring title and grislier cover design. The latter features a photo of Stewart with his hands on his hips, throwing the camera a coy smile. For the first time on one of his record sleeves, he is not to be found in street clothes but is instead swathed in showbiz apparel, and pretty poncy apparel at that: material that is shiny, lacey, trailing, fluffy and plunging. The fact that this preening pic is set inside an ornamental metal frame is a piece of self-mythologising that is compounded by another in the frame being placed against a tartan backdrop. It looks cringe-makingly like the icky product of a man who has been told too many times in recent years that he is a legend and a sex symbol.

Music-wise, Sears smelt a change in the air. 'There were some really great moments in the studio with that album', he says, mentioning with particular fondness the evening that Paul and Linda McCartney came along to observe the recording of the song they'd donated. 'It was still very spontaneous in many ways'. However, he adds, 'Bringing in the Memphis Horns, perhaps there were signs that he was moving away from the more folk-based stuff. . . . There were signs when he was doing that album that he was perhaps getting frustrated or feeling like he wanted to move on to a different sound or start thinking about changing it somehow. I cannot really think of any specific thing. I just felt like it was losing some of that spontaneity, that magic that oddball, eccentric group of musicians managed to come up with together with Rod. Obviously, it happens to everybody. Nobody wants to stay the same'. Sears also notes that there was another missing element of spontaneity surrounding *Smiler*: 'The sessions were few and far between. The album took a long time to make'. This was the first Stewart album recorded outside his home country.

That he chose to lay down tracks far from Willesden in places like Frankfurt and Brussels is clearly not unrelated to Britain's high taxation rate and his own ballooning wealth.

For Mike Bobak, Stewart was for the first time finding that his formula approach was breaking down. 'He was just trying to re-create everything and I don't think it was really working as well. [He] was almost blaming me for the fact that he wasn't sounding the same as "Maggie May" and all that. I think he felt a lot of pressure. On one occasion he came in and he said, "God, I hate music now"'. The Memphis Horns, the brass section to be found on many classic records by the Bar-Kays, the Mar-Keys, and other Stax acts, proved no solution to Stewart's difficulties. Bobak: 'He did the first bit of the recording the way he usually did it, and then he plonked this lot on. I don't think it worked that well'.

The changes Bobak noticed in Stewart's character were most pronounced when he supervised his vocals on foreign trips. 'We used to go to hotels and stay in these studios and I used to cringe as he was shouting and screaming at all these hotel staff', the engineer recalls. 'Oh, it was awful listening to all this abuse he was throwing at everybody. He just thought he was God'. When it's suggested to Dee Harrington that this sounds like cocaine behaviour, she readily answers, 'It is. You're exactly right. Rod never screamed at anybody. He didn't even scream at me'. Both Stewart's non-confrontationalism and his disdain for drug use had gone by the wayside. 'He wouldn't let Ronnie Wood bring drugs into the house', says Harrington of his now previous self. 'He made him leave them outside the front door'. She feels that this changed because Stewart's strategy of wearing his fame and wealth lightly was beginning to fail him. 'He just dealt with it by being this ordinary guy, but slowly it started to change. All that work, and then there was criticism from the Faces and the unrest with Billy Gaff. So your whole kind of footing in life was changing. And he was changing. It was almost like it was a delayed reaction to being this famous. . . . It was quite a fraught time when Smiler was being recorded. . . . All that workload caught up on him and this was an easy way out. "Everyone else takes cocaine, so I might as well". . . . The cocaine was the beginning of the end for us, because I didn't do Class A drugs. He hadn't wanted me to. He didn't even want me to smoke a cigarette. . . . That changed our relationship, because he's not going to be with somebody who's straight, and I'm not going to be with some somebody who's stoned'.

For the first time since his debut, Stewart doesn't open a solo album with a piece of semi-autobiography. This might be reasonable enough, but opting for a cover of Chuck Berry's 'Sweet Little Rock 'n' Roller' is a strange lunge for cliché. As Berry was one of the original rock icons, known for sparkling lyrics that celebrated youth and its music (as well as, it must be admitted, slightly samey melodies), his iconic status was undisputed. By now, though, his stuff had been done to death. On his previous albums, Stewart had understood that the only way to make anyone want to listen to a song so well covered that it was now aural wallpaper was by stretching out the arrangement in order to facilitate some virtuoso musicianship. Here, he does the chestnut straight. The inevitable 'So what?' reaction from the listener is hardly likely to be assuaged by instrumentation that—McLagan's blurred-fingered piano work aside—is somewhat boring, especially the bludgeoning drumming.

Evidence that the old likeable and unaffected Stewart still exists is provided by the fact that he does another favour to a mate by giving him his own track, and hence publishing royalties out of all proportion to the effort involved. The half-minute keyboard instrumental 'Lochinvar' is credited to Pete Sears. 'He said he wanted a long interlude on something and I just went down and improvised that on the spot on a harpsichord', Sears explains. 'It was just supposed to be an interlude and there was absolutely no talk of calling it a name or anything like that'. Stewart then got wind of the fact that Sears had been made an offer to join the band that would become Jefferson Starship but flying over to the States to take it up was beyond his means. 'Jefferson Starship were offering to pay but I didn't want any commitments to anything. . . . So Rod said, "Well, we'll call it a song, give it a name and I'll give you a publishing advance, a couple of thousand pounds"'. Sears recalls an earlier incident of Stewart largesse when he was based in the States. 'I was playing with John Cipollina at the time with Copperhead. We were just practising and things were a bit tight money-wise'. Stewart was performing in San Francisco. 'I got an envelope from him that had a hundred dollars in it and it just said, "To help through subdued times". He had those instincts'.

That the album's Stewart/Quittenton collaboration is titled 'Farewell' turned out to be apposite, for the *Never a Dull Moment* holdover was the last song to see release that the two men wrote together. It's a half-fond, half-bitter kiss-off to both family members and a sweetheart from a narrator who—in the face of skepticism—has his sights set on stardom. Ray Jackson appears on mandolin and Family's Ric Grech on fiddle. It's not Stewart and Quittenton's best song but has some of the qualities—emotionality, humanity and a protagonist with a humble hinterland—that had seen the pair conjure classics that we cherish to this day.

In contrast to the generosity inherent in 'Lochinvar', 'Sailor' (Stewart/Wood) is the song on this set that can be said to be the measure of the man—or at least public persona—that Stewart is becoming, one somewhat less likable than the one we have known over the previous four albums. To a marching tempo we are treated to a not-exactly-remorseful account of jilting a bride at the altar. Fine songs have been written about similar subjects, but this one is boorish ('The bitch was cynical'), something compounded by him using a new gimmick—previously heard in equally dubious Stewart/Wood song 'Lost Paraguayos'—of emitting a snicker which he seems to think is adorable. What happened to the tenderfoot of two albums back who was ecstatic to be disabused of the notion that he didn't need anyone but himself? The music—pounding rhythm and shrill horns—is equally tiresome.

After the last outing's cover of 'Twistin' the Night Away', Stewart now tackles—as a Sam Cooke medley—both 'Bring It on Home to Me' and 'You Send Me'. 'Bring It on Home to Me'—an entreaty to a departed lover to return—suffers in comparison with both Cooke's suave 1962 original and the Animals' rumbling and more emotionally bitter 1965 hit version. However, the *Smiler* version is enjoyable enough, as is the snippet of 'You Send Me' (a slick paean to an object of desire and adoration that made play of a phrase trendy at the time of composition) grafted onto it like a conversation addendum. It's a smoothly rolling affair with a swooping string section and horns that for one of the few times on the album don't grate on the ear.

By now, Stewart was in the position of being offered first refusal on songs by superstars—or, rather, fellow superstars. This is demonstrated by the presence on this album of 'Let Me Be Your Car', written by

Elton John and Bernie Taupin, and 'Mine for Me', a composition by the McCartneys. Stewart was doing as much a favour to the writers by acquiescing to recording them as they were to him by giving him dibs. Actually, it could be argued that he got less out of the deal, because the songs were hardly masterpieces, or even appropriate to his musical style.

'Let Me Be Your Car'—a rather underdeveloped lover-automobile metaphor—presents an additional problem in the context of this album. While he has written numerous classics, Elton John has never been much good at rockin' out, meaning that this is an example of something of which *Smiler* has a surfeit: a track that imagines it's exciting but which is full of marching, horn-blasting bluster. Compounding that is the fact that at five minutes it's the longest song on the set by half a minute. The track, by the way, is the furthest away in personnel Stewart has yet come from either his Mercury studio group or the Faces: John plays piano, Andy Newmark drums and Willie Weeks bass.

Stewart provoked much ridicule for covering '(You Make Me Feel Like) A Natural Man', the song made famous by Aretha Franklin as '(You Make Me Feel Like) A Natural Woman'. Some even felt that Stewart assuming he could tackle it at all was as much a sign of his growing hubris as his increasing willingness to stamp over the once supposedly sacred ground of Sam Cooke. One is tempted to retort that it's an unfair complaint. After all, Franklin had, herself, taken Otis Redding's 'Respect' and instantly and indelibly turned a song intended for a male vocalist into an anthem of female emancipation. However, the Gerry Goffin/Carole King/Jerry Wexler composition feels quintessentially distaff, even if in a way difficult to define: it just seems odd coming from the mouth of a bloke. Opinions might differ on why, and the familiarity element does play a part: in the pause before Stewart enunciates the chorus's last word, we are anticipating 'woman' and almost startled to hear something else. For those who can get over that, Stewart's is a perfectly listenable rendition. He turns in a heartfelt vocal and the musical backing is not only lovely—a welter of cascading acoustic guitar and swelling horns—but isn't afflicted by the muffled production that affects most of the rest of the album.

The narrator of 'Dixie Toot' (Stewart/Wood) is a man from the Deep South who is determined to get himself a good time after a long period in the emotional doldrums. It's a mildly interesting exercise in assuming the persona of someone whose experiences lie outside the writers', but any fascination dissipates in an aimless middle section whose Dixieland brass—played by Chris Barber's Jazz Band—emphatically fails in its ambition to be joyous. Symptomatic of the album's substandard production is that a lovely choir part is buried in the mix. In another dubious Stewart first, his lyric drops the f-bomb.

'Hard Road' is a song by ex-Easybeats members Harry Vanda and George Young, who had gifted it to the man who had fronted that group, Stevie Wright, for his 1974 album of the same name, which Vanda, Young and Wright co-produced. A cry from the heart of a man who has chosen to plough his own furrow and is determined to stick to it regardless of the aggravations that go with it, in Wright's hands it was a powerful, if slightly one-dimensional, piece of rebel rock. Stewart's version is sluggish and irrelevantly adorned with pretty female vocals. Once again, production ineptitude makes things worse, with some exotic percussion frustratingly only half-discernible.

Stewart recorded for *Smiler* Cole Porter's 'Ev'ry Time We Say Goodbye' but it wasn't used, him presumably thinking that the time was not yet right for the idea—even in miniature—that he later triumphantly realised with the *Great American Songbook* series. The closest we get to it is 'I've Grown Accustomed to Her Face (Instrumental)', an Alan Jay Lerner/Frederick Loewe composition in the same non-rock vein that originates from the 1956 musical *My Fair Lady*. Played by Quittenton, it's a befuddling non sequitur. Why include it only as a minute-and-a-half vocal-less snatch? The only useful purpose it serves is one hardly intended by Stewart: its gentle strains provide a merciful release from the suffocating aural assault this album's music otherwise largely constitutes.

For the first time, Stewart's choice of a Bob Dylan song on a solo album is an obvious—by which is meant unimaginative—one. Relatively few had heard of the previous Dylan or Dylan-associated numbers Stewart had chosen to cover, but 'Girl from the North Country' had been one of the tracks on his second album, *The Freewheelin' Bob Dylan*, which was a well-known work because of its inclusion of the likes of signature songs like 'Blowin' in the Wind' and 'A Hard Rain's a-Gonna Fall'. Not only that, but it was hardly a track that displayed Dylan's originality of vision, him barely tweaking the lyric of a song as old as the hills. (Demonstrated by the fact that when Pete Townshend recorded a not-dissimilar version in 1982, he didn't attribute it to Dylan but stated it to be his own arrangement of a traditional.) When one puts out of mind the overarching pointlessness and laziness of the song choice, it can be acknowledged that Stewart's is quite a sweet rendition. However, it's rather worrying that such an old turkey provides one of the LP's few highlights.

Closing the set is the McCartneys' 'Mine for Me'. It's a song in the mold of Paul McCartney's post-Beatles work: pleasant, melodic, domestic and vaguely insubstantial. Bizarrely, it features Caribbean steel drums. Its main attribute in the context is that it's musically uncrowded.

All too often, *Smiler* is loud and exhausting, the spacious power of the previous albums replaced by a dense soundscape against which Stewart's voice strains for supremacy. For all the dramatic brass, backing choirs and songwriting contributions of heavyweights, more is less: regardless of clutter, the album just sounds empty. The maladroit production is inexplicable in that Stewart and Bobak—who had created such classy aural vistas hitherto—are once again at the controls. The mediocrity was all the more worrying at the time because it would seem this was all Stewart could muster after an extraordinarily long gap between releases in an era where an album per year was standard: it had been two and a quarter years since Stewart's last solo LP. Even taking into account the hold-ups caused by the legal shenanigans, the hiatus was eyebrow-raising: with the Faces not having released an album for more than eighteen months, it's not as if he was distracted. Nor could it be said that he'd been knuckling down to writing: the ratio of new Stewart creations to covers was actually lower than previously.

Other tracks were available that could have improved the album, as Stewart had 'overcut'. As well as the creditable 'Ev'ry Time We Say Goodbye', he recorded his own compositions 'So Tired', also known as 'Missed You', a slowie that is not stellar but at least reflective and sparely arranged; the soulful ballad 'You Put Something Better Inside Me' (written by Gerry Rafferty and Joe Egan); and the lovely 'Crying Laughing Loving Lying', a Labi Siffre song that is an exploration of relationship self-deception somewhat more subtle than 10cc's 'I'm Not in Love', which would be a huge hit the following year. Furthermore, the latter's acoustic guitars and fiddle make it one of the few things recorded at these sessions that resembled Stewart's usual sound.

Smiler's icky sleeve opened out to show a photographic panorama of musicians and studio staff, as well as various employees, friends, family and colleagues, with a key on the inner sleeve indicating who was who. (Both McLagan's and—somehow—Wood's names are misspelled by Stewart.) Waller is front and centre, along with his four-legged friend whose voice was the first one heard on the record.

Upon *Smiler*'s belated October 1974 appearance, Stewart was confronted with the novelty of reviews for a solo album that were actively unfavourable. Stephen Davis of *Rolling Stone* adjudged it a 'largely unmemorable' album and 'his weakest to date'. Robert Christgau, writing in *Village Voice*, gave it a shockingly low rating of C+ (albeit later revised upwards to B–). 'The elusiveness of this album's failure doesn't make it any less real—spiritual tone, energy, something like that', he said.

The negative reception to the LP and the decline in Stewart's standing was exacerbated by the crass promotional methods of his new PR man, the parodically named Tony Toon. Toon was simultaneously disheveled and flamboyant and was prone to refer to his prestigious client as 'she'. He gleefully planted stories in the national press about Stewart's glamorous, licentious lifestyle—true or untrue—that sought to further Stewart's fame but had little to do with why he had become famous in the first place, i.e. musical talent. 'Tony Toon was a nightmare', says Harrington. 'There was always a lot of rubbish in the papers. He felt he was doing his job, but he wasn't a great person. He wasn't very nice to me, because I knew what he was about. He would be trying to say, "Come on, darling— let's get Rod into bed together". I just thought, "You're really showing yourself now. This is who you really are"'.

'Yeah, I'm happy with it', Stewart told Chris Charlesworth of *Melody Maker* on the eve of *Smiler*'s release. 'I wouldn't be here if I wasn't. It'd have been scrapped by now'. Just under two years later, he was upfront with Barbara Charone of *Crawdaddy!* not only about its faults but also about the reasons for them. 'We all go through a drug period and that whole album was made through the nights putting a lot of "how's your father" away', he confessed. 'I lost all perspective. That's why *Smiler* was bad'. 'It's time to get back to the *Gasoline Alley* type of thing now', he said. 'I just know that I'll have given up listening to *Smiler* long before I ever forget about *Gasoline Alley*'. Depending

Rod Stewart in 1967 demonstrating the immaculately coiffed looks that garnered him the nickname "Rod the Mod." *Photofest*

The Jeff Beck Group was a band packed with talent. Ultimately, though, it achieved little. Left to right in this 1969 shot are Jeff Beck, Stewart, Micky Waller, and Ron Wood. *Photofest*

Three fifths of Stewart's colleagues in the Faces emerged from the band the Small Faces, seen here in 1966. Shown from left: Ian McLagan, Ronnie Lane, Kenney Jones, Steve Marriott. *Press Records/Photofest*

The UK cover of Stewart's first album *An Old Raincoat Won't Ever Let You Down*. The 1969 LP (known as *The Rod Stewart Album* in the US) was rather slight aesthetically but featured remarkable peaks.

The Faces seen in a picture from the photo session that produced the cover of their debut album, *First Step*. Left to right: Stewart, Jones, Wood, McLagan, Lane. *Photofest*

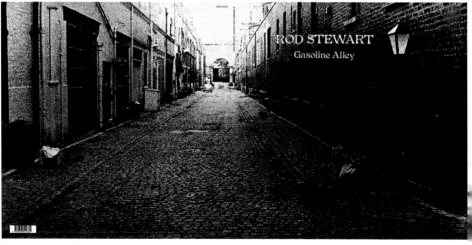

The evocative UK cover of Stewart's second long player *Gasoline Alley* (1970). It was this fine record that first suggested the artist had a great future.

Stewart with Dee Harrington, who shared his life for much of the first half of the seventies. *Trinity Mirror / Mirrorpix / Alamy Stock Photo*

Stewart shown collecting sales awards for his 1971 album *Every Picture Tells a Story*. However, its achievements went far beyond chart statistics: some are convinced that it is the greatest album ever made by any artist. *Penta Springs / Alamy Stock Photo*

The spoils of success: Stewart posing in the expansive grounds of his 32-room Windsor mansion Cranbourne Court, bought in 1971. *Trinity Mirror / Mirrorpix / Alamy Stock Photo*

More spoils: by the mid-seventies, Stewart's name could sell more than records, as demonstrated by this advert for Kickers shoes. *f8 archive / Alamy Stock Photo*

Never a Dull Moment (1972) was Stewart's fourth—and first post-superstardom—album. It lived up to its title— just. Critics liked it, but had to concede that he was beginning to repeat himself.

Tetsu Yamauchi (far right) was a competent bass player but no match in the Faces for the departed Ronnie Lane's personality and songwriting. *Photofest*

The regrettable jacket of Stewart's 1974 outing *Smiler* unwittingly communicated the hubris and decadence beginning to inform his music.

Actress Britt Ekland took over from Dee Harrington as the love of Stewart's life. She and Stewart are shown here in a mid-seventies picture with soccer legend Pelé. *Photofest*

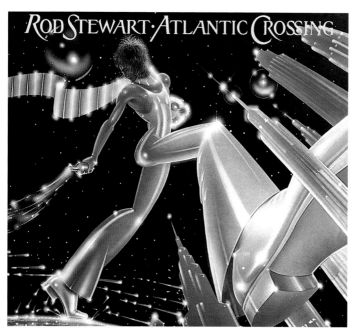

The flamboyant sleeve of Stewart's 1975 album *Atlantic Crossing*, his first to be made without either his old solo-album band or the Faces. After this, his music would never be the same again.

Stewart backstage at a Faces concert in 1975. Considering what would happen at the close of the year, it's tempting to speculate that he is asking his reflection whether he should remain in the band. *Trinity Mirror / Mirrorpix / Alamy Stock Photo*

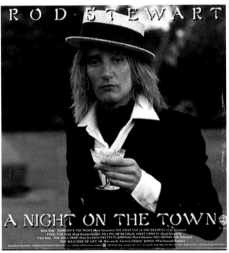

The cover of Stewart's 1976 album, *A Night on the Town*. The perceived decadence of such imagery made him a hate figure for punk rockers.

Rod Stewart performing on stage in Helsinki during his 1976 European tour alongside Jim Cregan. The guitarist would become Stewart's long-term friend and frequent songwriting foil. *Trinity Mirror / Mirrorpix / Alamy Stock Photo*

A variation on this picture was included in the booklet accompanying Stewart's 1977 album, *Foot Loose & Fancy Free*. The LP's intermittent brilliance was overlooked in an atmosphere in which Stewart's generation of artists were dismissed as over-the-hill. *Photofest*

Stewart in 1979. Around this time, his outlandish outfits, make-up, and sexualised stage moves saw him garner the sobriquet "male tart" and alienated large swathes of his previous "laddish" fanbase. *Fraser Gray / Alamy Stock Photo*

Stewart, pictured in the late seventies, when his love of "footie" seemed incongruous in the context of his increasingly feminine stage attire. *Photofest*

Rod Stewart pictured with first wife Alana Hamilton at London's Heathrow Airport in 1981. Colleague Jim Cregan attributes a dip in Stewart's professionalism to Hamilton. *Photofest*

Stewart on stage with Ronnie Wood in 2004. Aside from a bumpy period in the mid-seventies, "Woody" has been Stewart's lifelong mate. *Fox/Photofest*

Stewart's second and third wives shown together, Rachel Hunter (left) and Penny Lancaster (right). Stewart seems to have found stability with the latter. *Channel 5/Photofest*

Stewart becomes Sir Rod in 2016. He had come a long way from his Marxist youth. *PA Images / Alamy Stock Photo (Photographer: Gareth Fulller)*

on how weary you were with Rod's pronouncements, this was either a refreshing indication that he was prepared to criticise himself or a kick in the teeth to those members of the 'Tartan hordes' who had shelled out money for the album.

In the UK, a double–A-sided single was released of 'Farewell' and 'Bring It on Home to Me/You Send Me'. It made number 7. The album achieved the top spot but stayed in the charts for twenty weeks compared to the thirty-six racked up by *Never a Dull Moment* and forty-five by *Every Picture Tells a Story*. The album did reasonably well Stateside (no. 13) but the mediocre chart performance there of its single ('Mine for Me', which only climbed as high as no. 91) seemed to be confirming the suspicions raised by the underperformance of the *Sing It Again, Rod* compilation (no. 31, compared to pole position in the UK) that Stewart's US superstardom was over.

Smiler was at least superior to Wood's 1974 solo debut *I've Got My Own Album to Do*. Nobody would have taken if off the turntable in disgust but equally nobody would care if they never heard it again, a charge that could be levelled against all the rest of Woody's subsequent sporadic catalogue. Wood arranged some London gigs in July to promote the debut. It is perhaps significant that he was joined onstage by Keith Richards. Kenney Jones also released a solo record that year, issuing in October the single 'Ready or Not', a Jackson Browne cover.

Perhaps all this solo activity was a good idea, for Stewart's latest public comments seemed to suggest that his quotes from August 1973 about wanting to merge his and the Faces' recording careers into one were indeed a passing fancy. 'We've tried it in the studio four times and it's never really worked out', Stewart lamented in the *NME* in August 1974. 'My albums have always been better than Faces albums, always'. (Ironically, this was for the first time a challengeable assertion—whatever its faults, *Ooh La La* was a less wearisome listening experience than *Smiler*.) He further stated, 'We won't make another Faces album. I think we'll just cut singles from now on', although he added comments that made it clear that he had not discussed this matter with the other members. He was now even contemplating hitting the stage on his own. 'I dream about a solo concert of my own some day', he told *Melody Maker*'s Chris Charlesworth in August 1974. 'There's gotta be a chance of it happening with all the people that appear on my albums. I've asked them and they all say I ought to do it some day. Mmmmm, lovely acoustic guitars behind me'.

Yet despite the paucity of their product, the declining stage ability alleged by the likes of Charles Shaar Murray, and their internal fissures, the Faces actually worked a lot in 1974. There was an Australasian and Far East tour in January (Yamauchi was greeted like a superstar in his native Japan and proved a handy aide in a hotel ruckus when it transpired he was a Kendo black belt), British gigs in February, the UK Buxton festival in July—where the Faces' appearance fee was so large that they decided to indulge themselves by hiring the Memphis Horns to decorate their sound—three US festivals in August, a fifteen-week European tour from September onwards and a British tour in November–December which was reputed to be the most financially successful UK sojourn of the year (even if that reputation was partly brought about by their camp's media briefings).

The Faces had no new group product to promote when the UK tour kicked off on 15 November, but they did at least give their fans a wonderful early Christmas present in the shape of the single—credited to 'Rod Stewart and the Faces'—'You Can Make Me Dance Sing or Anything (Even Take the Dog for a Walk, Mend a Fuse, Fold Away the Ironing Board, or Any Other Domestic Short Comings)'. The elongated title might have been typical Faces humour but there was nothing bog-standard about the recording (whose composition was credited to all five current Faces). On this release, for the first time ever, the Faces' sound was widescreen and polished. There is no producer credited but, whoever is responsible, the high production values only enhanced an already lively and tender piece of soul-pop. The smoldering Stewart/Wood-written flip 'As Long as You Tell Him' is also high quality, albeit afflicted by cookie-tin drumming. The record (which made a UK no. 12) indicated that, though Lane was no longer present, this new incarnation of the Faces most definitely had potential. Tragically, it would prove to be the final Faces release. Just at the moment of their greatest triumph, the band was stumbling to a spiteful end.

7

IT'S ALL OVER NOW

AT THE START OF 1975, the Faces embarked on a five-week, coast-to-coast tour of the United States. The cash they racked up from sold-out arenas enabled them to put aside not only their personal differences but the fall-out from the resentment at the string section and additional guitarist Stewart had insisted on.

It was during this time that Stewart met Swedish actress Britt Ekland. The two would become one of the golden couples of the 1970s. However, that status could only be facilitated by Stewart sloughing off the woman with whom he'd shared his life over the past three years. 'He's always very gentlemanly to the women he's with', says Jim Cregan. 'He doesn't treat them badly at all. But doesn't mean to say he's going to stay with them either. . . . He was not very good at confronting girls and saying, "Look, it's over". He would just be seen out and around the town with somebody else'. Harrington contends that it was she who finished with Stewart, but perhaps part of Stewart's guile involved him manipulating his departing partners into believing that they were the split instigators.

Harrington had met Stewart when he was about to make a transition from moderately successful recording artist to household name. With that new status came additional benefits for Stewart. A man whose long chin, big nose and mouth mole had seemed to rule him out of sex-symbol status was suddenly a pin-up on the bedroom walls of millions of teenaged girls. Most of those fans could never dream of getting any closer to Stewart than the front row of a concert venue. Some, though, had the wherewithal and cunning to turn fantasy into reality. 'I just used to say that every woman in the world wants to sleep with my boyfriend', says Harrington. 'The minute I met him, that started to happen'. She recalls the bedlam backstage at the Long Beach Arena concert where she first saw Stewart strut his stuff on stage. 'Trying to get to his dressing room was near-on impossible. I can see him way down in the dressing room saying to these guys, "No, her, *her*. Get *her*". So I already knew this thing before "Maggie May"'. Harrington quickly became cognisant of the fact that being the significant other in the life of a figure like Stewart made her both an irritating obstacle and an object of hate. 'When we would go to functions together, whether it was music business or whatever, we would be pinned up against the wall and they would all the time try and push me out of the way, push me away, push me away. . . . It was just such a shock. I never said anything because he would always handle it very well, but from the beginning it was there. These women — *and* men — wanted him. . . . It sometimes was a very hard time. But he was used to it. . . . We'd walk into the hotel room and the phone would be ringing and it was one of the groupies. They were like a gang, they were like a band in themselves. They just knew when all the rock people were coming to town so that they could get to see them, get into bed with them. That was their existence'.

Stewart wanted Harrington by his side as much as possible. 'I used to go to the studio and sit in with Rod whilst he was doing vocals and recording', she recalls. 'I think he just didn't like being on his own'. She also says, 'He was wanting me involved in going on tour or being at gigs, whereas he didn't like any of that beforehand'. Initially, she was happy to oblige. 'They'd only do short tours. They did like ten-day tours and I did go on the earlier ones'. However, the purchase of Cranbourne Court militated against the practice: 'I had this bloody great house to deal with'. Stewart's desire to have Harrington by his side and his *sangfroid* as people threw themselves at him in front of the love of his life, however, did not mean that he didn't avail himself of opportunities for dalliances. Harrington says, 'We did love each other quite passionately' and that Stewart is 'a very sensitive person'. However, she was always realistic about the fact that Stewart saw no contradiction in both being committed to a relationship and having bits on the side. 'If you are with a rock star and you've got a problem about groupies, then you need to get out', she shrugs.

Not that Stewart was a swinger. 'Jagger always had a little bit of a thing for me', says Harrington. 'I was a blonde, Marianne-Faithfull type of person. He was married to Bianca at the time. . . . We went to a Stones do and he said to us, "How about us swapping our women tonight?" He was serious. Rod got me out of that place so quickly. . . . He was quite appalled that that could have been brought up. . . . He's got this slightly old-fashioned thing with women: quite gentlemanly and quite posses-sive. Even though he had all these other women available. It's a funny combination'.

Her and Stewart's relationship might be loving but was also up-and-down, pocked by several walkouts on Harrington's part in which she went back to her parents' house. 'Because I couldn't cope. It wasn't necessarily his fault. He would be very upset and he would get Micky Waller to ring me up and go, "If Rod rings you up, will you speak to him?" I'd go, "Of course, Micky". He would often ring people up and go, "She's left me" and they'd go, "I'm sure she's gonna come back". It wasn't like I'd left him because I hated him. Looking back, I was very young as a person and I was having to deal with a lot. I was having to deal with his life, and that was huge'.

Stewart's dalliances didn't even much bother Harrington when she had to read in the newspapers that he'd been stepping out with some beauty or even when she found herself answering the telephone in bed to one with Stewart lying beside her. 'I'm the one he comes home to, aren't I?' she reasoned to the *Daily Mail*. That philosophical attitude changed in March 1975 when she actually encountered Stewart in the company of one of his paramours. As the Faces prepared to play the LA Forum, Stewart placed a call to Cranbourne Court. 'He wanted me to fly to LA', Harrington recalls. 'He said, "Can you get on the next plane, please?" I said, "Well, I can't come on the next plane. I've got all these things that I've organised tomorrow". "Oh, I don't like being in LA without you". I said, "I'll come the next day". "Oh, alright". But he didn't like that, because that's rejection. What's more important than being with me, type of thing. Don't forget, we're taking cocaine now, and we're in a stress situation because of all the years that have gone before and what's happening. So our relationship was strained. I got on the plane the next day and then he inferred when I got there that there must have been somebody else that I wanted to be with. This is where his possessiveness [said], "You're not making me a priority".

'Tony Toon was there. Rod went off and Tony came in and said, "Oh, Rod's gone down to meet so-and-so". I think it was Bobby Womack. I went, "Okay, anyway, it'll give me time to unpack". He hired me this Mercedes sports car so that "You can go and visit your friends". So Tony and I go down to the garage to get the car and we're driving along the Strip. We're coming to the Troubadour and I can see Rod getting out of a limousine with who I thought was Krissie Wood, because I knew Krissie was in town. So I parked the car and I ran into the Troubadour entrance. It was Britt Ekland'. Swedish-born actress Ekland was famous for roles in the likes of *Get Carter*, *The Wicker Man* and *The Man with the Golden Gun*, as well as for having been previously married to Peter Sellers. Harrington cared little about such stuff in that moment and, in fact, isn't even sure if she recognised Stewart's companion. 'I said, "What are you doing?"' she recalls. 'He said, "It works both ways". So I turn, came out, I got in the car and came back and said, "Tony, book my flight tomorrow". It was almost like somebody handed me this here's-your-out card'.

Harrington had been going through a personal crisis pretty much simultaneous with Stewart's. 'I had this whole, "Who am I?" [feeling]. I had to have a purpose . . . I hadn't grown as a person because I'd been in the Rod Stewart world. It was almost like my development had been put on hold. I was like a child. I hadn't grown or developed into any work ethic'. With no career and no means of support, Harrington's life became hard for a while. 'It had become difficult to be Rod Stewart's woman, and it became very difficult to be Rod Stewart's ex-woman', she says. 'But I [founded] my antique clothes shops to work in that I adored . . . I owned two shops. The first was in North End Road called Razzmatazz and the second one was the New Kings Road called Dee Harrington Clothes. They both sold '20s and '30s clothes and specialised in wedding dresses made from antique lace and new silk made to measure. . . . And then I became a manager in the music industry, and worked for ten years, and was involved in 400 million units. There was an upside to this'. She also points out that she and Stewart remain friends and have even subsequently had a professional relationship. 'I managed Simon Climie and Climie Fisher and Rod's recorded a couple of Simon's songs'.

Asked if, back in 1975, Stewart had wanted out of their relationship as well, Harrington says, 'I don't think he would have chosen that, no'. If this is true, Stewart recovered from the disappointment quickly and comprehensively. Within literally days, the newspapers were reporting that he and Ekland were an item. That they then became a staple of those newspapers was something helped in no small part by the indefatigable/desperate efforts of Tony Toon. The public perception of them was often as a shallow pair of jetsetters whose relationship was as gushily meaningless as that of teenagers in the first flush of love, but Ekland had two children from previous relationships and Stewart became a willing stepfather to them.

Did Harrington regret having the relationship with Stewart in the first place? 'Oh God, no. That was a real great journey. And let me tell you, [what] I learnt about people in those first years with him has held me in good stead throughout my life. Because with Rod, you attract all the worst people in the world as well as the great ones'.

THE US TOUR INTERRUPTED SOME FACES SESSIONS at AIR Studios in London. They went so well that, for the first time, Jones found himself enthused about a burgeoning Faces album. But when sessions recommenced in the Power Plant in Los Angeles, the discipline that had given the Faces a good groove back in London gave way to decadent LA methods. The record never appeared, partly because Wood began working on his second solo album, *Now Look*, released in June 1975 and partly because Stewart decided not to return to 'Blighty'.

The sessions were finally released on the 2004 Faces box set, *Five Guys Walk into a Bar* (one track had appeared on previous Faces compilation *Nice Boys When They're Asleep*). It's difficult to adjudge whether the cuts bear out Jones' feelings. Three of them are covers. While the decision to tackle the eccentric Beach Boys number 'Gettin' Hungry' indicates a band thinking laterally, renditions of hoary old chestnuts like 'Hi Heel Sneakers' and 'Everybody Needs Somebody to Love' smack, for a band at this stage of their career, of lack of imagination and inspiration. However, the plaintive McLagan-Stewart-Wood track 'Open to Ideas' is high quality and the McLagan-written 'Rock Me' pretty good.

When in April Stewart departed to America, it wasn't merely to record a new solo album: he was planning to apply for US citizenship.

In Britain, people in his income bracket were paying 83 per cent in tax. 'The government thinks they'll tax us bastards right up to the hilt because we won't leave', he told *Melody Maker*'s Chris Charlesworth in summer 1974. 'It's so bloody unfair. They're thinking of a wealth tax now and that's bloody criminal. That's like, for a young man, paying your death duties before you die. . . . It's just not worth living in England any more. I'm all for paying taxes . . . I'll pay my dues, but I've got one shot at the big ball for all my life. I can't do anything else but sing and maybe play a bit of football'. The latter this-could-all-end-tomorrow comments are representative of the belief among musicians in the 1970s, and indeed for a long while thereafter. Back then, there was no nostalgia circuit. Apart from a very small minority of people like Elvis Presley, who were artists so big that they had ceased to be mere mortals subject to career tribulations, music stars were hot for a few years and then became tainted with the 'unclean' stigma of has-been.

While his relocation could be viewed as a sensible move financially, Stewart would shortly be afflicted by homesickness (with no satellite TV, it was impossible to watch British soccer) and irritating inconveniences (when stranded at London's Heathrow Airport in 1975, Stewart had to cosset himself in the international VIP lounge because stepping onto British soil—which other parts of the airport constituted—would have made him liable for 100 per cent more in tax payments to the Inland Revenue). It also put him into the same rarified bracket as the Rolling Stones and the other established acts to whom the Faces had once been seen as a refreshing down-to-earth antidote. Charles Shaar Murray, writing in the *New Musical Express* in May 1976, put his finger on the problem it caused Stewart spiritually and hence artistically. Citing what he felt to be the difference between a tax exile and an expatriate, he placed the now States-based John Lennon in the latter bracket, Stewart in the less admirable former. 'It has more to do with the way that someone carries themselves than the reasons that sent him away', he asserted. 'Stewart sounds to have lost touch with his background without having established any real temporary root system; artistically as well as politically and geographically, he is in limbo. . . . Lennon determined from the outset that if he was gonna live in America he was . . . gonna righteously live there and involve himself as fully in American cultural, social and political life as anybody else on his block; without denying his Englishness he was simultaneously going to do his damnedest to be a good American'. The unmoored, unengaged Stewart increasingly had nothing to write about except himself in the now—and how many songs can you write about being well rewarded, well laid and well fed?

Stewart, incidentally, insisted that if tax was the only motivation for his move, he would have simply relocated to the low-tax island of Jersey in the English Channel. He insisted that heading for the States was partly because he had needed new musicians around him. It was certainly the case that, preparing his next work, he jettisoned his usual colleagues, even dispensing with Wood and Quittenton as songwriting collaborators.

The usually saintly Kenney Jones was infuriated by Stewart's relocation, complaining to the press that he considered Rod a 'friend who has gone astray'. By July, the Faces had not worked for four months and Jones claimed that he had lost £80,000 (£700,000 in today's coinage) because Rod's absence had meant the cancellation of a planned series of Faces stadium gigs. 'Those English gigs he talked about were never really on, because Woody was doing the Stones tour and he knew that', Stewart retorted in a Chris Welch *Melody Maker* interview the following month.

Indeed. While Stewart was preparing what would become the album *Atlantic Crossing*, Wood went on tour with the band with whom the Faces had so often been compared. The acrimonious departure of Mick Taylor from the Rolling Stones in late 1974 had left a hole that had still not been plugged. Wood had been one of several guitarists who had played on Stones sessions in the first few months of 1975 and would eventually appear on two tracks on the resultant album *Black and Blue* (released somewhat belatedly in April 1976). The guitarist was publicly insistent that the American Stones trek in which he took part in June through August was just a matter of someone helping out his mates until they acquired a proper replacement. However, Wood couldn't have denied to anybody who put it to him that it had given him the opportunity to play in the band he had always fantasised about being a member of. (In fact, he would later find he could have back in 1969, the last time a similar vacancy had existed. A telephoned offer to join from Stones roadie Ian Stewart made to the Bermondsey rehearsal space being used by the Faces was rebuffed on his behalf, and without his knowledge, by Lane.) The

Stones' tour was extended beyond its original dates, about which Stewart added his own grievance, pointing out that this had cut into rehearsal time for the new Faces tour and necessitated the cancellation of three Miami dates at a cost of £20,000. Wood also took part in a short December European Stones tour.

As was now the norm, the Faces were conducting a less than fraternal dialogue through the press in the run up to their next tour. McLagan was caustically observing that Stewart was treating the Faces like his backing band, summoning the group to Miami for rehearsals and insisting that a string section accompany them in concert to help play *Atlantic Crossing*'s lush songs such as 'Sailing'. The Faces were not amused to find that they were required to share this additional expense, even though it was a Stewart solo album the orchestra was helping to promote. McLagan noted that the Faces planned on going into the studio in November and that 'if Rod isn't going to sing on the numbers, we'll do them ourselves'. Stewart meanwhile was telling *Creem* that it was time the Faces got more disciplined and stopped treating live work as though it was party time. This reservation about drink-related sloppiness was neither unreasonable nor even new in the Faces camp, but there was a certain imperiousness in Stewart's tone when he declared, 'If it doesn't work out in rehearsal then we just won't tour. If it doesn't sound how I want it to sound, that's it. I want it to sound like something new, like the record I've made'.

STEWART WAS LATER HEARD TO OBSERVE of the multiple alterations in his life on several fronts at this juncture, 'I think it's good for everyone to do that now and then. A change of atmosphere, a change of environment. You can't keep on with the same person or the same music all your life'.

Atlantic Crossing was quite ostentatiously a new Stewart record for a new Stewart era. Not only did its title allude to his continental relocation but it was his first solo album for Warner Bros., his first to be informed by his relationship with Ekland and the first to not feature any of his colleagues from either the Faces or his old solo band. Moreover, it marked the point at which Stewart left behind his frequently rustic, folk-inflected sound of the first half of the 1970s and replaced it with the glossy stadium anthems that would become his new stock in trade.

That Warners were aiming for a serious return on their investment was illustrated by the fact that his new album would see him for the first time supervised by a producer (Lou Reizner's contributions to his first two albums by common consensus being titular). Tom Dowd was a legendary figure in production, his name already attached to classic records by Otis Redding, the Young Rascals, Cream, Dusty Springfield, Derek and the Dominos and the Allman Brothers Band. Dowd, as was his wont, did his homework on Stewart, familiarising himself with his keys and his range before flying out to California to meet him.

The two discussed whether Stewart would use the Faces on the new album, with Dowd recalling Stewart saying he wasn't sure if he was going to record with them again. It so happened that the Faces were recording at that point, and Stewart and Dowd spent an hour listening to them from the control booth of the studio. Dowd concluded that the Faces displayed glaring weaknesses, not possessing the depth of knowledge or roots to change their style of playing in order to facilitate the kind of record Stewart wanted to make.

While Stewart may not have relayed this exact exchange to McLagan, he did apprise him of the fact that things would be changing. 'He said, "I'm going to cut my next record in America, in LA. Do you have any suggestions for musicians?"' McLagan recalls. 'I said, "Yeah, Booker T and the MG's, Steve Cropper, all that"'. Not only were the MG's responsible for classic singles like 'Green Onions', 'Hang 'em High', and 'Time Is Tight', but they were known to the cognoscenti as the house band behind countless timeless Stax records. Dowd told Barney Hoskyns of *Mojo* in 1995, 'Rod had dreams about Otis Redding and Arthur Conley, and he asked me about Wilson Pickett and Aretha Franklin. Like a lot of English artists, he knew what he was talking about'. Dowd was one up on Stewart, though, for he had actually worked with the people responsible for some of his favourite records. The MG's, meanwhile, were friends of his. Dowd suggested Stewart use two or three different rhythm sections to prevent all the songs sounding the same.

There was no room for any musicians with whom Stewart had previously collaborated, including his closest friend. Tellingly, Stewart had given another reason to Barbara Charone of *Crawdaddy!* for the poor quality of *Smiler*. 'The combination of Quittenton/Waller/Wood/Mac was wearing pretty thin', he said. 'My writing had narrowed down'. A few months after the release of *Atlantic Crossing*, Stewart was telling Charone, 'I *thought* it was going to be strange making the album without Woody, but it wasn't . . . I must have had blinkers on these last five years. I must have been mad using the same musicians over and over again'.

There was one existing fixture of Stewart's solo career that he did want on board for his new direction, but he turned him down. Martin Quittenton was invited by Stewart to work on new songs with him while he toured with the Faces, but the hell-raising road life for which the band were famous was something the sober-minded Quittenton decided he didn't want to be part of. 'Martin didn't want to go down the *road*', notes an amused Harrington. 'Martin was not cut from the same bit of cloth'. Quittenton never heard from Stewart again.

Quittenton failed to capitalise on the fact that he co-wrote one of the most enduring rock anthems of all time. 'Maggie May' was the highlight of a songwriting career that was severely truncated. 'Martin was a complete and utter worrier', says Gaff. 'He worried about everything'. Quittenton actually worried himself into hospital, where he wound up in the late 1970s after having a breakdown. There, movie-style, he fell in love with his nurse, Dorothy, and the two later married. When Ewbank and Hildred tracked him down for their 2003 Stewart biography, they found Quittenton and his wife running a wildlife sanctuary on their fifteen-acre property in Anglesey, Wales. It was funded completely by his royalties from the handful of songs he'd co-written with Stewart.

Stewart failed to respond when Quittenton sent him a couple of new songs following his recovery. In moving out of Stewart's orbit, he had turned into the sort of supplicant which Stewart's camp tends, possibly by necessity, to deftly deflect. 'Rod was very fair to me down to the last letter', Quittenton told Ewbank and Hildred, 'but I do wake up at night sometimes wondering what I will do when the royalties stop'. Such issues ceased to worry him in 2015, when he passed away a week before his seventieth birthday. According to a 2021 *Daily Mail* interview with his widow, this was the culmination of the anorexia and bulimia with which he had long been afflicted. She also claimed, though, that Quittenton was happy in his reclusive life, in which playing guitar happened only for recreational purposes in a private setting and that he was also content with a frugal existence. 'We kept a bit to live on, but the vast majority went to animal charities', she said.

Atlantic Crossing was recorded in New York, Miami, Memphis, Los Angeles and Alabama across a cumulative three weeks. Sessions at Muscle Shoals Sound, Alabama, were arranged in order for Stewart and Dowd to avail themselves of the services of its renowned rhythm section. There, Stewart got two surprises. The first was that the crack sessioners at the legendary studio weren't, as he had always assumed about people with so much evident soul, black. The second was the ease involved in conveying his ideas to them. 'Barry Beckett, the big piano player down there . . . he'd listen to the song, and write it down in figures', Stewart revealed to Welch. 'They don't write music in the traditional way, they put four, four, dash, dash, two, two, dash, dash . . . and they say: "Is that how you want it?" and play it back to you'. Once it had been ascertained this was indeed how the artist wanted it, the peculiar transcription method was photocopied and handed out to the band. This Muscle Shoals invention was something the singer found refreshing after a lifetime of it-goes-like-this discussions with musical colleagues, ones he described as 'a real headache'.

Less happy for Stewart was the fact that Alabama was a dry state. Because of such privation, Stewart's vocal on 'Sailing' was, by his own admission, one of the few he had rendered without any alcohol in his system at all.

As well as his old collaborators, Stewart also dispensed with traditional rock concepts about pacing. 'I remember saying to him once, "Can't you just put all the fast stuff on one side and put all the slow stuff on the other side so that I don't have to skip tracks and turn the fucking thing round?"' says Gaff. 'I never liked him doing rock 'n' roll. That's a personal thing, that's nothing to do with whether it was good, bad or indifferent. I like the Stones for rock 'n' roll'. *Atlantic Crossing* was divided not between sides one and two but a 'fast side' and a 'slow side'.

The former got underway with 'Three Time Loser', a Stewart-penned tale of a man thrice stricken with venereal disease that at one point Rod was hoping would be released as an American single. Despite its supposedly daring subject matter (hyped up in interviews), it's a slight song, but does work up an impressive groove and is good, if vulgar, fun (the narrator is 'jacking off' to *Playboy*).

'Alright for an Hour', written by Stewart and Jesse Ed Davis, is a kiss-off to a demanding rich woman by a gas attendant narrator with wanderlust.

Musically, it's Stewart's first foray into reggae. It doesn't cut it: a percolating bass part should have been mixed higher and the drumming made a bit more nimble. Long before its four-plus minutes are up, we're looking forward to the end. For his part, Stewart was so enamored with Davis that he took him on tour with the Faces that year.

'All in the Name of Rock 'n' Roll' is another Stewart solo composition, this one examining the sort of rock-tour carnage of which Quittenton was so wary. It's awful. As it struggles to overcome its own torpor, a guitar riff recurs monotonously, horns blast ineffectually somewhere in the distance and a guitarist grinds out an utterly flat solo. This goes on for five minutes until it all ends so abruptly and untidily that the listener can't help thinking that an exasperated observer had switched off the power.

Such is the blustering mediocrity of that track, that the listener can hardly object when the album's concept is temporarily abandoned to enable a ballad to hove into view: 'Drift Away' may not be fast but it is at least easier on the ears. Written by Mentor Williams, it was a 1973 US top 5 hit for Dobie Gray. It's an anthem for popular music that is unusual in achieving the objective of making the listener understand the virtue of the form the narrator extols. Stewart's version has a hint of reggae that's somewhat more successful than the more overt stylings in that direction in 'Alright for an Hour'.

The strutting 'Stone Cold Sober' is a collaboration between Stewart and Steve Cropper that doesn't rise above the merely competent. There's a little too much of the wrenching but static guitar style and only just discernible horns that characterise this album. The retained applause of those present in the studio is a hubristic touch.

The album's slow side is much more successful.

Danny Whitten was a guitarist in Neil Young's early 1970s backing band, Crazy Horse, which subsequently became a group in its own right. He was fired because of his heroin use, although his story was more complicated than the usual tale of rock-musician self-indulgence, as he relied on the drug to mitigate the effects of his rheumatoid arthritis. Whitten shone on Crazy Horse's powerful 1971 eponymous first album, not least because of his ballad of romantic abandonment 'I Don't Want to Talk about It'. Tragically, his talent was lost to the world by the following year, a death that had all but been predicted by Young in his song 'The Needle and the Damage Done'.

'I Don't Want to Talk about It' has now been endlessly covered, but in 1975, Stewart was one of the first to see its virtues. An exquisite lovelorn number with slightly mysterious imagery, it was tailor-made for one of his sensitive readings. His aching vocal (done live) is set against churning acoustic guitars, a discrete string section and a tasteful electric guitar solo. It's when the strings are allowed to soar towards the end of the four-and-three-quarters-minute running time that for the first time we get a feeling of music beyond the parameters of Stewart's usual cohorts.

After lyricist Gerry Goffin stopped writing with his musical foil Carole King following their divorce, he worked with a variety of collaborators, one of whom was Barry Goldberg, with whom he devised 'It's Not the Spotlight', which featured on his 1973 solo album *It Ain't Exactly Entertainment*. As this song was written so close to the point of Goffin's split from King, it's difficult not to conclude that it's about her. The narrator speaks of a light that shone in his ex-lover's eyes and onto him, one far more iridescent than spotlights, flashbulbs, moonlight, sunlight or even 'the streetlights of some old street of dreams'. As often with popular song, of course, what originated as personal and specific became general and universal by virtue of the interpretations of others with no insight into its background, whether they be the interpretations of artists covering it or consumers listening to it. By the time Stewart included the song on *Atlantic Crossing*, 'It's Not the Spotlight' had already been covered by the Bobby Blue Bland and Ted Neeley, as well as Goldberg himself. This surprising amount of interest in a slightly bland album track was no doubt a consequence of Goffin retaining the vast inroads into publishers' and managers' attentions common to freelance songsmiths.

All of the versions that had succeeded it had actually improved on Goffin's template, especially Bland's soulful rendition. Stewart's is, if not the best of them, then certainly nudging that status, him benefitting from a rich mellow arrangement against which he is happy to sing his heart out.

One of the big ironies about *Atlantic Crossing* is the fact that, although Stewart jettisoned his old colleagues to achieve his soul ambitions, by his own admission the only soul number on the album is his version of the Isley Brothers hit 'This Old Heart of Mine' (written by the songwriting team with the wonderfully symmetrical credit format, Holland/

Dozier/Holland). A double irony is that the track doesn't really work. That he and his producer take the option of slowing down the melody is legitimate, but this tilt for greater drama is undermined by overegging of the pudding: we don't also need the syrupy strings, burbles of electric guitar, cooing female backing vocals, cocktail-lounge saxophone work, and four-minute-plus playing time. It's pleasant enough but also close to 'cheesy-listening' parody.

Stewart's only compositional contribution on the slow side is 'Still Love You'. If some might feel that the echo on his voice is unnecessary embellishment for a man whose singing hardly needs assistance to convey emotion, it's compensated for by the fact that the track is a return to the humility, tenderness and proletarian landscapes that had lately seemed to be disappearing from his songwriting. Even the phrase 'I would not change a thing if I could do it all over again' pleasantly reminds us of more than one line from his back pages, and indeed of the whole early Rod Stewart worldview. Then again, is another epistolary song not repeating himself? And is talk of humble horizons (albeit here in retrospect) not the kind of thing *Never a Dull Moment* suggested he should now steer clear of? There's also a false note, his talk of a room over a drugstore and an unreliable Chevy van—rather than a 'bedsit' and a 'Commer'—being received, stylised American imagery rather than the stuff of personal experience. Dee Harrington, though, feels there is at least a whiff of the latter in the track. 'I would pick up on things and think, "Mm, okay, I think that's a bit close to the whatsit"', she says of Stewart product released after their split. She thinks this song is about her. 'We probably still loved each other'.

The set closes with the sleek, anthemic 'Sailing', a homesickness anthem first released in 1972 by the Sutherland Bros. Band. Its presence is the closest Stewart ever got to a plan he spoke vaguely of at the time to record a chunk of an album with the Sutherland Brothers and Quiver, a British ensemble who were then making a name for themselves and would secure their first hit ('Arms of Mary') the following year. Peculiarly, even though it's a Gavin Sutherland composition, 'Sailing' feels vaguely like a successor to 'Flying', the Lane/Stewart/Wood-written track heard on the first Faces album. Stewart's version of 'Sailing' both slows it down and enhances it. It's graced with cascading acoustic guitar, gliding organ and a grandeur-granting Arif Mardin string arrangement. It also develops the original's incremental build of instrumentation and emotion. As with so many of Stewart's own songs, Sutherland's ambitions for elegance are slightly spoilt by a lazy approach to rhyming.

Once again, Stewart had more tracks than could fit on the album: a superb, impassioned version of the Bee Gees' 'To Love Somebody', a competent rendition of Allen Toussaint's clipped, soulful 'Holy Cow' (first released by Lee Dorsey) and an odd interpretation of Otis Blackwell/Winfield Scott's Elvis hit 'Return to Sender' decorated with a roller-rink organ part and a chirpy tone. The inclusion of these outtakes could have improved their album, albeit at the further expense of the fast/slow-side conceit. (A version of the traditional Scottish 'Skye Boat Song' with a drum and pipe band is no loss. It was later released as a single—under the name the Atlantic Crossing Drum & Pipe Band—on Riva, a company run by Billy Gaff, and 30 per cent owned by Stewart, that was both a record label—it would issue Stewart's product in the UK over the next seven years—and a song publisher.)

While there was nothing necessarily wrong in Stewart seeking to explore territories beyond the rustic and Celtic flavours that had imbued his previous solo albums, the sad fact is that what has replaced his old sound is in almost every sense inferior. Too often, *Atlantic Crossing* is flat, sterile and overdone. Moreover, while *Atlantic Crossing* contains two tracks that have become Stewart signature songs, both are from outside sources. None of the Stewart originals are top rank. Although it must be admitted that two of his greatest ever songs—'Mandolin Wind' and 'You're in My Heart (The Final Acclaim)'—are exclusively his, it also has to be stated that Stewart would never again forge a composing partnership as fruitful as those he'd enjoyed with Quittenton or Wood.

Rolling Stone gave Paul Nelson the task of reviewing *Atlantic Crossing*. That he was a long-term champion of Stewart was something almost painfully evident in his opening paragraph: 'To a lot of people, Rod Stewart onstage in midstrut—hair flying, handy with brandy, and partial to the broad smile and easy wink—offers as good a definition of the full flash of rock & roll as one is likely to get. . . . Even as we envy his outgoing, big-winner's style, we revel in the knowledge he provides via self-mockery that he can lose as often and as badly as we do. That, I think, is a large part of his magic: He touches all of the places in the rock & roll heart'. Quite a set up to a review that could only reach the tepid conclusion, 'If *Atlantic*

Crossing isn't Rod Stewart's best record—and it isn't—it at least comes within hailing distance of earlier masterpieces'. Six years later, Nelson co-authored with Lester Bangs a book on Stewart written from the glum perspectives of disillusioned ex-fans. In it, Nelson wrote, '*Smiler* and *Atlantic Crossing* should have been the tip-offs, I suppose, yet they didn't sound like such terrible turning points then. Perhaps we were still blinded by the beauty of *Gasoline Alley* and *Every Picture Tells a Story* or by the singer's genuinely likeable personality'.

Melody Maker's Chris Welch came across more as Stewart's public relations man than a journalist as he mused, 'Rod Stewart cannot . . . expect the kind of tender mercy accorded a bright new talent. He will be analysed. Stern chaps with tape recorders and inky notebooks will be busy scrutinising. And in the rush to judgement we might hear such cries as: "Past his best", or even "bilge". . . . Well speaking as a man who has publicly admitted to liking Paul McCartney's last album and thus flew in the face of prevailing opinion, I rather like Mr. Stewart's latest'. He did at least put aside the partiality long enough to mention something about Stewart that other reviewers had picked up on: Dowd not always playing to his client's raspy strengths: 'He almost takes a back-seat role'.

On the surface, Bud Scoppa of *Circus* seemed enthusiastic, starting his review with the observation, 'Happily, that horny, rank, exuberant rascal who romped through Rod Stewart's masterpieces *Gasoline Alley*, *Every Picture Tells a Story*, and *Never a Dull Moment* has returned'. He ended it with, 'I'm . . . more than pleased to find that the best rock & roll singer of the '70s still has it'. However, that he was wishing these sentiments to be true rather than convinced they were seemed to be betrayed by some of his other, somewhat more lukewarm comments: 'Even if *Atlantic Crossing* is only half-great (and I'm not yet willing to accept that qualified a judgment), that's still substantially better than last year's badly flawed *Smiler*. . . . A less rigid sequencing might have made the album seem stronger, but I'm nearly certain the slow side, too, will eventually reveal some unexpected treasures'.

John Morthland of *Creem* had a clearer-eyed perspective. He averred that *Atlantic Crossing* showed Stewart 'trying to get a firm footing on some new ground, succeeding stupendously a couple times but more often falling a little short'. He continued, 'Stewart albums used to hold a new surprise on virtually every song', claiming that 'shifting tempos, short, punchy solos, and dramatic silences' were as much a Rod solo-album signature as his own voice, but 'on this album, the rockers all steamroll straight ahead, and the ballads are all drawn out to uniformly slow tempos'. He concluded, 'If two great songs and eight near-misses don't add up to a failure, neither can it be considered very satisfying'.

That Robert Christgau didn't kid himself about the aesthetic position he felt Stewart now occupied is perhaps demonstrated by the fact that he never revised the grade of B+ he gave the album in *Village Voice*. 'After *Smiler* I was convinced that his talent, always hard to pin down, had vanished; now it seems that he'll be breathing life into 10 songs a year in perpetuity', he reflected. 'But granted that confidence we can also agree that good Stewart too often satisfies without calling us back for more'.

Atlantic Crossing was released in August 1975 housed in a wrap-around illustrated jacket in which Stewart was stylishly depicted by Peter Lloyd taking a giant stride across the titular ocean, trailing in his steps to the States spilt champagne and the flowing scarf accessory to a silken costume. The album made number 9 on *Billboard*. Its singles fared considerably less impressively, 'Sailing' climbing to number 58 and 'This Old Heart of Mine' making it only so far as number 83.

If *Atlantic Crossing* didn't do as well in Stewart's new country of residence as he and Warners had hoped, it was a huge success in the 'Rest of the World', especially—quasi-paradoxically—in the country the sleeve almost made a virtue of him leaving behind. *Atlantic Crossing* entered the UK chart at number 1. It cumulatively occupied that position for seven weeks and racked up a cumulative ninety 'weeks on chart'. 'This Old Heart of Mine' was a UK number 4. 'Sailing' became a UK smash twice over, climbing to number 1 in 1975 and then making the top 10 again the following year when it was used in a TV documentary series about aircraft carrier *HMS Ark Royal*. Possibly just as gratifying to a soccer nut like Stewart is the fact that the song became a football-terrace anthem. Attending a Scotland game with his father, Stewart came back from the toilets to find his dad crying: the 'Tartan Army' had been belting out 'Sailing' while he was away. To this day, the fans of London soccer club Millwall—notorious for their prosaic play and the viciousness of some of their fans—sing to the 'Sailing' melody the lament, 'No one likes us/We don't care'. Even then, Britain was not finished with *Atlantic Crossing*. In 1977, Stewart had another number-1 single in his home country with a double–A-sided 45 that paired 'I Don't Want to Talk About It' with 'First Cut Is the Deepest', the latter a track off his latest album, *A Night on the Town*. Although British charts didn't quantify which side of a double-A generated sales, the belated exposure given 'I Don't Want to Talk About It' can't exactly have done any harm to its parent album.

For Stewart, his new methods conferred a benefit perhaps just as important as any sales figures. 'I've got a new lease on me confidence now', he said to *Creem*'s Barbara Charone in 1975. 'You're talking to a new man. . . . All the fun has come back into recording for me at last. I've never liked going into the studio and now I can't wait to go back'. Stewart went further than those comments in his promotional efforts for the album, coming out with remarks that might be considered to be put-downs of his usual colleagues. For instance, he noted, 'The musicianship is a lot more polished, which is what I wanted, and at last I've found a rhythm section I can really get into'.

Yet Stewart still had enough loyalty to the Faces to tour with them. Furthermore, being back in the bosom of his longtime friends and col-leagues seemed to perk up his spirits and to enhance his lately lowered opinions of them. As the tour got underway, he noted publicly that the Faces were sounding tighter. As it progressed, he was doing something that had been frequent in the band's early days but which had latterly become rarer: singing their praises to the press. 'It dawned on me last night how good everybody in the group is', he enthused.

For Bobak, it would seem such talk was cheap and false. '"Maggie May" eclipsed the Faces and then there were huge rows', he says. 'They certainly had a few rows about it at the end. I did something at Olympic with them and then we went into the pub next door and there was a huge row and I think they broke up a few days after that. I think the Faces were pissed off that he put what they were playing on his album'. Bobak's memories seem a little mashed-up here—by 1975, Stewart was well past the point of wanting to include anything that the Faces had recorded on one of his releases—but it seems reasonable to at least accept the validity of his firsthand impressionistic recollection: that a poison began invading the Faces *esprit de corps* because of the life-changing hit record that he had helped shape, and that it developed into a fatal dose when the career it shaped became Stewart's overwhelming priority.

Meanwhile, rumours that Wood was a Rolling Stone–elect rumbled in the music press throughout 1975. In the issue of *Rolling Stone* cover–dated 6 November 1975—Tom Nolan quoted the guitarist as saying, 'They do talk to me about it, yeah. Keith does. He'll say, "Ball's in your court. Can't go on with both groups forever you know". With Mac, it's like, "Do what you want. But—what we gonna do when. . . ." So if I was thinking of leaving I'd be forced to say, "Oh I won't be around then". The thing is, both groups know I'm not leading 'em on a merry journey. I'm just trying to fit in both categories, as long as it remains comfortable. . . . The Faces know that I'm with 'em, you know? And the Stones know I'm always there when I've got that time off . . . I've always thought of meself as a member of the Faces for the duration. I don't want to make the choice, particularly. . . . It's only the people who talk about it who make me think of it. Otherwise I wouldn't . . . I could very easily say, ah well, fuck that, I'll just run off with the Faces—Stones rather, I mean. Getting the groups muddled up now. But I feel a loyalty to the Faces that's very strong'. Reading such comments makes it understandable that Jones later said that Wood had been playing both ends against the middle.

The same might be said of Stewart. Right up to the finish, he was alternating between sniping at the Faces and sentimentally singing their praises. He even went so far as to proclaim to *Rolling Stone*'s Tom Nolan in November 1975, 'I'll be as bold as to say that even if Woody does leave—and he should make up his mind sooner or later, though I think genuinely he does want to tour with both bands—even if he did join them, I think I would stay with the band. . . . I'd miss him. Christ. But I've realised how good the others are'. In the same interview, he said, 'I'd be willing to have a go at a Faces album. . . . We could create something really good. But someone's got to take the helm. I'd give anything to produce it. Or even get Tom Dowd or somebody in to produce it for us'.

All of this talk came to nothing, and the hopes for a long-awaited post-Lane Faces studio album lay forever unfulfilled, because in December 1975, Stewart dropped a bombshell—and gave his former colleagues quite a Christmas gift—when he publicly announced he was no longer a Face. For good measure, he allowed Tony Toon to lay the blame elsewhere with the statement, 'Rod feels he can no longer work in a situation where the group's lead guitarist Ron Wood seems to be permanently "on loan" to the Rolling Stones'. At a London press conference that month, Stewart pointedly announced that he would be forming a new band that would back him at a concert in London's Wembley Stadium on 26 June.

McLagan himself later suggested that Stewart had made the announcement because he'd received a tip-off that Wood had finally made up his mind to defect to the Stones and wanted to trump his announcement. Yet when Wood was interviewed by Barbara Charone in the 24 January 1976 issue of *Sounds*, he was suggesting that him joining the Stones was still not a done deal: 'The job is there if I want it. None of the Stones wanted to press too hard about me leaving the Faces so they didn't mention it much. Then Rod came out with that *amazing* statement. . . . They've all eased up a bit and thought "oh well, looks like you'll be in a vacant position". So it's up to me to decide in the next few months. I won't wait very long. You'll know one way or the other within a month'. Yet, perhaps revealingly, Wood also said that Stewart's comments were irritating because 'had he played his cards right and hung on for a bit longer, Rod could have put the blame on me'. Gaff said, 'I have been told Ron Wood is 98% certain of joining the Rolling Stones. Of course, Jagger is denying it because they are probably in the middle of negotiations'. The following month, it was formally announced that Wood was Mick Taylor's permanent replacement.

Complicating matters yet further, though, in June 1976 Stewart told Barbara Charone of *Sounds*, 'The Faces breaking up had nothing to do with Woody playing with the Stones. Ian McLagan and I couldn't get on any longer . . . I wanted to take the band further than a five-piece. . . . Mac wanted to keep it as a five-piece on the bare boards. We had endless arguments'. However, deep-seated misgivings about the band as a whole were evident in an interview Stewart gave the *NME* the same month, where he said, 'The looseness that the Faces were known for . . . just became too loose. . . . It was such an unprofessional band. I mean, how many times can you get away with being an hour and a half late at a gig for 15,000? You can't go on doing that, year in and year out'. He was still able to concede, 'They made me what I am, to an extent. I owe those guys a lot. . . . They were a great band, a great bunch of lads through all their mistakes and all the things we did wrong. I don't regret the six years I was with them. I hope they feel the same. But I hope they're also mature enough to realise that it was getting bad'.

'The tragedy is, with hindsight, we never needed to split up', says Jones. 'All we needed to do was do nothing for a bit and then come back together and do the Faces for a bit. There's enough to go round in the business, but everyone gets greedy. Look at Genesis—they're the classic at that. Everyone goes [and] does their own separate things and come together as one again. Why kill something when it doesn't need to be killed?'

Gaff sounds less heartbroken by events. 'The trouble with the Faces, Rod was the identity . . . McLagan sat at a piano, he didn't fucking do very much. It was the Woody and Rod Show, with Kenney pulling up the rear. As much as I respected Ronnie Lane in his own right, he was a bit out of his depth there. *He* was the one that should have been the folk singer. . . . Basically Lane and McLagan were kind of left out, so there was a bit of a mishmash and a bit of a conflict. I don't think it ever really worked musically. When they had to do Rod's stuff on stage, the sets got better. Rod and Ronnie Wood, they were the gellers. It worked okay, but it never *really* worked. It was neither one thing or the other. It was a watered-down Rod, it was a watered-down Faces. There was times when they did one of Rod's ballads it was great, but I don't think it worked until Rod went solo. . . . If Rod hadn't broken when he broke, I'm not sure how long they would have gone on. I think Rod was so generous that he went on with them. I knew deep down he hated every minute of it, like I did'.

8
DEBRIS

ROD STEWART'S NEXT SOLO ALBUM, then, was his first since his debut not to be recorded against the psychological background of being a member of the Faces.

That difference aside, by all rights the record might have been expected to be an action replay of *Atlantic Crossing*. Dowd was retained as producer for sessions at Cherokee Recording Studios, Hollywood, and several of the same musicians were employed from the previous LP. Yet despite the crossover in personnel, *A Night on the Town* has much more depth, texture and variety of tone than its predecessor.

Famous names littering the credits—in addition to those also heard on the previous LP—include bassist Lee Sklar, guitarist Joe Walsh and drummer Andy Newmark. This stellar lineup is termed by the sleeve notes the 'Garage Band'. As with the last Stewart album, vinyl sides are divided between 'fast' and 'slow', with the uptempo tracks this time being placed on side two. Also as with *Atlantic Crossing*, Stewart cheats when it comes to the speed designations. Another similarity is that the fast side is palpably weaker than the slow side.

Stewart-written side-one opener 'Tonight's the Night (Gonna Be Alright)' immediately augers well. Its lovely sighing intro of tinkling acoustic guitar, warbling organ, and drum patter is a top-notch production flourish. It leads into one of Stewart's most seductive vocals. To an elegantly swinging rhythm and gliding strings, he sets about putting a woman at her ease prior to suggesting that they should retire for the night. It's undoubtedly a song about sex but on a different plane to anthems of horniness. Even an innuendo is classy: 'Spread your wings and let me come inside' he suggests to a companion he has likened to an angel.

'The First Cut Is the Deepest' is a composition by British pop-folkie Cat Stevens that asserts that the heartaches of romance are more painful when compounded by lack of experience. It was first recorded by Pat 'PP' Arnold, an African American vocalist who relocated to Britain in the 1960s. Her 1967 single has an intermittently marching beat, a rich backing that includes brass and strings, and a nigh-operatic vocal delivery. It was quickly covered in Jamaica by Norma Frazer in a reggae arrangement before Stevens' own version appeared at the end of the year. By 1976, it had been covered several more times, including versions by Love Affair, Lou Reizner and Keith Hampshire. It seems unlikely that Stewart was familiar with the song through the latter, even if Hampshire's somewhat epic arrangement secured a 1973 Canadian number 1. Stewart's old champion and producer Reizner is a candidate for Rod's introduction to it, but so is PP Arnold, with whom Stewart was once romantically involved.

That Stewart's version was recorded—aside from the strings—at Muscle Shoals suggests it's a holdover from the *Atlantic Crossing* sessions. Oddly, and thankfully, it doesn't sound of a piece with that often-antiseptic album, being a rich and musty rendition. Despite some busy drumming and a quasi-aggressive electric guitar solo, it's quite low-key. Stewart perfectly conjures the vulnerability of heartbreak in the aftermath of young love and a tremulous determination to not let it be the end of the world ('If you want, I'll try to love again').

Stewart's rarified lifestyle is reflected in his composition 'Fool for You', an epistolary breakup song that is the polar opposite of 'You Wear It Well' and its hard-times backdrop. He states that he gets depressed when he reads about his ex on the arm of somebody else 'in all the national press'. Landmarks and trademarks mentioned include Paris, Rome, St Tropez, Chanel and Cartier. It's of course perfectly legitimate to explore such environs in song—and more honest than continuing to trade in poor-boy narratives—but a composition peppered with such milieux is hardly something to which average people can relate and is therefore less powerful than his previous stripe of material, and that's leaving aside the resentment that talk of privilege often engenders. For all that, a love song is a love song, and like the best love songs 'Fool for You' has some poignancy. The narrator tells his ex that he'll have feelings for her forever, even as he admits, 'Pride won't let me stay'. The backing is verging on middle-of-the-road but is also pleasing in its delicate slickness.

'He's always felt comfortable with gay people', says Dee Harrington of Stewart. This is amply demonstrated by the fact that Stewart was voluntarily surrounded by homosexuals in his life, including John Baldry, Elton John, Billy Gaff, Gaff's assistant Mike Gill, Faces publicist and author of Stewart's 1977 authorized biography Peter Burton, and Tony Toon. However, while this fact was known of within the industry, it wasn't something of which the public was then broadly cognisant. Much of the public would have looked askance at Stewart had they known. In the mid-1970s, expressing sympathy for, or even tolerance of, gays could get somebody tainted with the stigma of being a—in the parlance of Stewart's homeland—'poof' or 'bender'. Moreover, even men who simply wore their hair long—which most rock musicians then did—were, even by this point in history, still suspected by a large section of the population of being 'that way'. Revelations in the tabloids that Stewart had a sensual preference for women's underwear provided another reason for suspicion. It was therefore an act of bravery for Stewart to write and release 'The Killing of Georgie (Part I and II)', the six-and-a-half-minute song that closes A Night on the Town's slow side.

In this story song, the narrator uses his memories of the titular character as a framing device to describe Georgie's journey of coming out, rejection by family, acceptance by Manhattan's gay scene and accidental killing by a street gang who—it's implied—are infuriated by the sight of him arm-in-arm with another man. The North Londoner depicts New York in convincing fine detail, from Greyhound buses to Broadway hypes, to old queens blowing a fuse at Georgie's flamboyance and popularity. He is also unshowily open-minded: the narrator telling George he is pleased that he has found love was, in 1976—to a greater or lesser degree—shocking for the majority of people in both Britain and the United States, where gay relationships may have been tolerated by the law but were widely viewed as being in no way as legitimate or genuine as heterosexual ones. That conversation with George is one of several passages that are rather moving. Others include the relating of the lack of understanding of George's parents, George expounding his live-for-today philosophy and the narrator's concluding gentle-but-defiant statement, 'Georgie was a friend of mine'.

The percolating music—which includes classical harp—is smooth without being bland. The pace is stately, with its verses rotating with a whistling motif and female vocalists cooing a doo-doo-doo chorus. Structurally, the track is reminiscent of an opera, a first scene-setting part giving way to a middle section where the killing takes place and Stewart's vocal becomes accordingly breathless, culminating in a chant-like two-minute requiem. One could argue that Lou Reed's 'Walk on the Wild Side', the Beatles' 'Don't Let Me Down' and Bob Dylan's 'Simple Twist of Fate' can all be discerned in the melody or structure, but if plagiarism is involved, it's never distracting.

Stewart has never been given enough credit for either releasing this song or issuing it as a single. The assumption that will have been made by many who heard it that it constituted a coded message about himself could have had an adverse effect on his career. Anybody doubting this danger is referred to the catastrophic drop in the sales of Elton John records at the end of that decade, following his public statement that he was bisexual.

The Fast Side begins with 'The Balltrap' (Stewart). A scabrous and racy lyric describes a love-hate, on-off romantic relationship to a clipped, syncopated backing, with a brass section flaring in the choruses. It's earthy stuff (the title refers to a state of testicular imprisonment) but nonetheless toe-tapping. However, as the narrator tells his lover that rumours of her prostituting herself and being seen on the arm of a black man make him conclude he'd rather that she be hanged or paralysed, we are struck that such mean-spiritedness is a quite extraordinary contrast to the overarching sensitivity of the slow side. On some level, Stewart himself knew this. He mused of such songs to Barbara Charone of *Sounds* in June 1976, 'It must be some sort of insecurity. . . . I must get someone to look inside my brainbox'.

'Pretty Flamingo' is a passionate but elegant tribute to an unattainable beauty. In 1966, Manfred Mann pipped Gene Pitney to the post in issuing the first version after their producer played them a demo by writer Mark Barkan. Recorded over the protests of vocalist Paul Jones, who thought it too sweet and white for this rhythm and blues combo, it proceeded to become the band's second UK chart-topper and a US top-30 entry. A host of acts covered it in the 1960s, including the Everly Brothers, Mel Tormé, Gerry and the Pacemakers and the Sandpipers, but the song had been dormant during the 1970s.

Stewart's version is less wistful than the original, speeding up the tempo slightly and boasting an odd introduction similar to a soccer-terrace handclap rhythm. However, its instrumental passages—featuring trombones and flute—give it a lusher and more elegant air than any previous interpretation. Stewart's vocal is his usual high-grade work, although his dog-like barks make his narrator come across as more predatory than worshipful.

Gib Guilbeau's 'Big Bayou' was first recorded by Swampwater, one of a spate of late 1960s bands who could be posited as country-rock pioneers. Released on their eponymous 1971 debut album, it expresses a determination to return home that's not uncommon among country boys who decamp to the city for professional reasons but dislike what they find there. A similar sentiment, of course, was expressed in 'Country Comfort', although that was manufactured by Englishmen deploying received American imagery. Swampwater's enjoyable template was big and loud and almost innocent. Since then, it had been recorded by Larry Murray, the Dillards and—less predictably—a certain Mr. Ronnie Wood, who included a version on *Now Look*. Paradoxically, Woody's take eschewed any countryisms, being blaring, sinewy rock. Stewart executes a cross between the approach taken by his old mucker and the more rustic predecessors insofar as the 4/4 rhythm is juxtaposed with a fiddle (albeit only just discernible). Confusingly, it also features a strident brass section. The track is as much a hodgepodge-cum-mess as that sounds. It's also the first one on this album whose end comes as a relief.

The writing of 'The Wild Side of Life' is credited to Arlie Carter and William Warren, but it has a long, tangled history. The melody was already so old as to be public domain and had been used in 'I'm Thinking Tonight of My Blue Eyes' (the Carter Family) and 'The Great Speckled Bird' (Roy Acuff). Carter and Warren wrote a new lyric for it, but some have suggested that 'The Wild Side of Life' was itself an adaptation of 'The Prisoner's Song', written by Guy Massey and released by Vernon Dalhart as far back as 1924. The 1951 Carter/Warren song is, in any case, somewhat racier than any antecedent, being the bitter reflections of a man whose estranged partner has become a barfly and a quasi-prostitute.

A feminist answer song called 'It Wasn't God Who Made Honky Tonk Angels' by J. D. Miller, who used the same melody, became a huge hit the next year for Kitty Wells.

As with the previous track, Stewart makes us sort of wonder why he's decided to tackle the song by the fact of him barely acknowledging any country provenance, him employing a stomping rock beat, a barrage of electric guitars and smears of brass work. On a different note, his yelps of excitement seem unearned, although it's sometimes difficult to assess the quality of performance because of thin, blurry production, reminiscent of the worst parts of *Atlantic Crossing*.

The side's uptempo concept is dispensed with for slow closer 'Trade Winds', a philosophical rumination across five minutes. Written by Ralph MacDonald and William Salter, it had hitherto been exclusively the preserve of distaff artists like the Three Degrees, Roberta Flack, Esther Marrow and Stewart's old collaborator Maggie Bell. The song strives vainly for profundity, but its compassion is opaque and scattershot, its message about modern troubled youth casting around for meaning in life risibly stranded between 'All You Need Is Love' and 'Fings Ain't Wot They Used to Be'. Stewart can't turn such material into anything more substantial regardless of his formidable pipes, which are here heard to smoother, more note-sustaining effect than ever before. His call-and-response with velvet-throated backing vocalists (or, rather, response-and-call, him repeating their lines) is pretty. However, the cocktail lounge saxophone work only adds to the air of a bourgeois protest song.

A Night on the Town was released in June 1976. On the card inner sleeve, Stewart looks every inch the rock star, posed with arms folded, wolf-tooth neckband resting on his bare, wet chest. The outer sleeve opts for a somewhat different look, him sporting a boater, blazer and cravat as he clings to a champagne glass, making him resemble an aristocrat attending a garden party held on his own grounds. He is seen in a similar get-up on the other side in a pastiche of a Renoir painting.

John Morthland of *Creem* raved, 'This is as brilliant an album as any Rod Stewart has made. . . . After the perfunctory *Smiler* and the near-miss *Atlantic Crossing*, *A Night on the Town* comes as a partial surprise and a complete thrill. . . . Stewart is able to remain both aristocrat and every-man, the smalltime kid who made it out, learned some valuable lessons along the way, and isn't afraid to look back and remember'. *Phonograph Record*'s Bud Scoppa concluded, 'Without changing any of the crucial elements of the *Atlantic Crossing* production, he's managed to substantially change the chemistry. . . . The ambience is much closer to that of his classic Mercury albums than to his recent work, and through that surprising atmospheric shift, Rod has set the scene for compelling performances of the best group of romantic and confessional songs he's come up with since . . . *Moment*'.

In *Sounds*, Barbara Charone was also ecstatic. 'Rod Stewart sounds hungry again. This album is a total surprise and a wonderful treat. . . . *A Night on the Town* is the great album Rod Stewart needed to maintain his top position in the rock hierarchy. The rockers are his absolute best while the ballads are the most emotional he's done in years . . . Rod Stewart may well be the Sam Cooke of the Seventies yet'. *Rolling Stone*'s Dave Marsh was one of several critics who gushingly professed his adoration of the artist before even beginning to address his latest product, talking of Stewart as someone with whom he had an 'almost mystical rapport'. He wrote, 'A *Night on the Town* is among Stewart's most splendid efforts' and exulted in Stewart's 'working-class eloquence, a belief in the simplest truths that won't let him get caught up in the canonisation of mere punks and gangsters'.

One of the closest things to a pan came from *Melody Maker*'s Chris Welch, who was mystifyingly less impressed with this outing than he had been with *Atlantic Crossing*. 'Rod needs, perhaps, the iron boot of poverty and an empty belly to bring fire to his vocal cords', he wrote. 'That is the first impression from the "slow side" where he sings in oddly restrained fashion. . . . Side two . . . is much better, with the dread strings shown the door and the boys in the band awake at the wheel. . . . An album that improves with further listening, but not a world shaking sizzler of the type we demand daily'.

The one product of the *Night on the Town* sessions that resembled Mercury-era Stewart (an era that it could now be recognised was tonally and musically in the definitive past) was 'Rosie'. This Stewart composition was used as the B-side of the 'Killing of Georgie' single. Proletarian (the narrator speaks of rescuing the titular girl from morning blues and eight-hour days by gaming the welfare system) and folkie (it features prominent mandolin), it could have come — smokey saxophone aside — straight off *Gasoline Alley*. It would have made a good inclusion on *A Night on the Town* but would also have stuck out like a sore thumb—or perhaps like a down-and-out at the kind of posh 'do' its sleeve depicted. Tellingly, from now on, Stewart would largely restrict poverty tableaux in his songs to explicitly nostalgic pieces.

That 'Georgie' single—the second from the LP in the UK—was a number 2. Its predecessor 'Tonight's the Night' got as high as number 5 despite a ban by *Top of the Pops* (but, contradictorily, not BBC radio) for its sexual suggestiveness. The album was a chart-topper and lodged in the top 10 for eighteen consecutive weeks. In the States, the album completed Stewart's commercial rehabilitation in a country that had lately seemed to be losing interest in him. It made number 2, while its singles all did either respectably ('First Cut Is the Deepest' making no. 21; 'The Killing of Georgie' no. 30) or spectacularly ('Tonight's the Night' topped the *Billboard* Hot 100 for eight weeks).

In his June 1976 interview with Barbara Charone, Stewart cut an altogether more affable and happy figure than the tetchy one exuding 'eerie smugness' she had encountered a year before, although he did frankly still sound a little pleased with himself. 'Britt brought something out in me that I didn't think was there—self-esteem', he said. 'Before, I didn't think I was particularly good at anything. I just felt like I was filling a need for the public. . . . Confidence is the biggest change. I know I've got a nice body now. I know I've got a good voice and I know I'm good onstage, but I was never too sure. Now I don't feel self-conscious at all. I don't have to drink to do anything now. . . . It just comes naturally. Before what I was doing was never natural'.

IN APRIL 1977, IN A JOINT *CIRCUS* REVIEW of two compilations— *The Best of Rod Stewart Vol. 2* and *Snakes and Ladders: The Best of the Faces*—Lester Bangs said, 'His original output grows slighter (in both senses) with each successive album . . . Stewart's last three solo LPs suggest that his compositional inspiration is drying up—perhaps, as his recent interviews suggest, because of the increasing distance his personal life puts him at from the people and places that constitute his roots and the wellsprings of his subject matter'. Suggesting that he didn't look very happy on the cover of *A Night on the Town*, Bangs mooted, 'He probably won't ever be one of the lads again'.

In retrospect, Bangs can be seen to be groping his way towards an opinion on Stewart and a reassessment of the generally well-received *A Night on the Town* that would become the consensus once people were able to achieve 20/20 hindsight through the prism of the punk revolution. That revolution began to burn in the mid-1970s. In Tony Palmer's celebrated 1976 TV history of popular music, *All You Need Is Love*, Bangs, then the editor of esteemed rock magazine *Creem*, was to be found lamenting how moribund rock currently was. In a December 1975 *NME* feature, Charles Shaar Murray scathingly wrote, 'Maybe the time has come to sacrifice a few of the old gods . . . who have become either too preoccupied by the circumstances of their godhood, or too debilitated by the stresses and strains of said godhood to be able to remember or act upon the memory of why we made 'em gods in the first place . . . the ones who're too busy hiding out from taxmen, romancing movie stars, and getting their blood changed to do records and tours and get the crumbling remnants of their music out to the people who save up for the albums and queue three days to get tickets to see 'em on stage. . . . These people have consciously divorced themselves from us to the point that what they have to say to us don't matter any more. What Mick Jagger thinks about anything is no longer relevant. What Rod Stewart thinks isn't relevant'. Even one of those gods, Ronnie Lane, was expressing similar sentiments, telling Chris Welch in *Melody Maker* in January 1976, 'When we started the Faces it was just for a loon. And then they had to turn it into something else. All the rock bands turned into the very thing they were supposed to be kicking against. It all became an industry, and that's what really nauses me'. Throughout 1976, such sentiments would take firmer hold amongst musicians a generation younger than Lane.

Harrington for one was shocked at Stewart's new milieu. 'He left everything he loved', she says. 'His family, he left me, he left his home. He left football. . . . And he's with these people who are film people. . . . They were so not him. It was a shock to think that he would be so different'. Talking to the *NME*'s Tony Stewart in June 1976, Stewart was adamant that his life in his new domicile in Hollywood, and the riches that went with it, had not brought about a change in his approach to his art. Stewart (Tony) raised the issue of the substitution of his 'Jack the Lad' persona (a brash, cocky, proletarian young man) of earlier days for the Showbiz Joe of now. 'How can you maintain that image for the rest of your life?' Stewart responded. 'And who wants to, come to that? Not that I was ashamed of it, but the person's improved, the music's improved and I'm also six years older. Obviously I wanna earn some money, I don't wanna be broke. . . . When I read these things: "Oh. Rod's gone to Hollywood and it's spoilt the music and he's no longer hungry". . . it's such bullshit! I live such a humble life there . . . I had that huge house down at Windsor in 17 acres with 20-odd bedrooms. But no one criticised me then, right? . . . I don't even live in Beverly Hills, I live in Holmby Hills, which is a poor neighbor. . . . How can I ever change? I'm working class. I always will be . . . I don't think the person's been spoilt. . . . That certain style of life might come in the fact that I now go to Saville Row to buy a suit and I don't go to Take Six . . . I will drive a Lamborghini as opposed to a Mini Cooper or whatever. Materialistic things . . . but I'm sure most people would do the same. Most Jack the Lads would anyway. . . . All I can say is that it hasn't affected my song writing so far. Perhaps in a year's time it may do. But as it is, I haven't been wealthy enough, long enough, for it to spoil what I'm doing'.

It might be said that punks were already begging to differ, were it not for the fact that punks were not the begging kind. The punk revolution that had been fermenting in the UK fully took hold in December 1976 when the Sex Pistols—de facto leaders of the movement—become household names through a profane appearance on an early evening television show that made front-page headlines. While in a pre-internet age the contempt felt by the London four-piece and their multitudinous followers in what had been termed the punk rock movement had not yet fully crossed the Atlantic, Bangs and his fellow influential scribes were beginning to become aware of it and would soon be as much in thrall to it as the Sex Pistols' fans, which latter category included not just consumers but musical groups who had either formed or reshaped themselves in their honour.

That, throughout 1976, the Sex Pistols made waves on the lower levels of the UK gig circuit via a *raison d'être* that was explicitly to provide an antidote to the increasing remoteness and pretension of established rock stars would not have counted for much had the Pistols not been both a band of incendiary power and the type of act never before seen in rock history. With his bizarre staring eyes and sinister, wheezing singing style, front man Johnny Rotten was a riveting stage presence. He also wrote quite remarkably scabrous and twisted songwords, seething with both class hatred and self-loathing. Those lyrics were realist, anti-glamour and determinedly English. Almost uniquely, the Sex Pistols did not mythologise romantically faraway places but instead dealt with the issues of their own backyard, however unprepossessing it was (not only is the UK perennially unglamorous in its spiritual modesty and meteo-rological gloominess, but it was then going through much in the way of social crises). They broke with tradition in another way too: they were the first artists since Elvis had kicked off the whole rock revolution to not venerate their elders. Early on, they busted a taboo by publicly dismissing the Rolling Stones—for a decade the exemplars of the counterculture and its libertarian ethos—as 'establishment'. The Stones, though, got off lightly compared to Stewart, who had attracted their particular ire. Contemporaneous reviews might have been good but the retrospective view of A *Night on the Town* shortly became that it showed a man lost to malign forces, and it's difficult to calculate just how damaging this was to Stewart's public perception. It was precisely the wrong point in history for decadent imagery like its boater-blazer-and-Bollinger sleeve. Nor was it merely him 'poncing about' like an aristocrat that made A *Night on the Town* seem to a certain societal subsection to encapsulate everything that was wrong with rock. The overarching lack of rawness to the music, Britt Ekland's spoken-word French emoting in 'Tonight's the Night', and the hint of racism in 'Balltrap' also served to underline that Stewart—along with so many other artists of his generation—was engaged in a process of turning soft and/or decadent and/or disagreeable. Moreover, the fact that Stewart and Ekland were in the papers as often as movie star couple Richard Burton and Elizabeth Taylor in their heyday was a soap opera that was the opposite of rock 'n' roll edginess.

Yet it should be emphasised that none of this affected Stewart's sales. His UK singles chart action in 1976 was plentiful. On top of the high placings of 'Tonight's the Night' and 'The Killing of Georgie', 'Maggie May' re-entered the charts and made number 31, and he nudged the top 10 with a version of Lennon/McCartney's 'Get Back'. The latter origi-nated with the soundtrack of *All This and World War II*, a feature film that fatuously matched Second World War footage with cover versions of Beatles songs. Stewart's 'Get Back' proved that such was his stature that he could even carve out a piece of success from what was otherwise a commercial and critical catastrophe. Moreover, the fact that for all its sales triumphs A *Night on the Town* had not generated a number 1 was finally rectified—technically—with 'I Don't Want to Talk about It/First Cut Is the Deepest'.

Around the same time as the release of the latter disc, the Sex Pistols released a follow-up to their stunning November 1976 debut single, 'Anarchy in the UK'. 'God Save the Queen' was issued in May 1977 to tie in with the celebrations surrounding Elizabeth II's Silver Jubilee, although it was hardly a tribute to the monarch's twenty-five years on the throne, rhyming as it did the title line with the phrase, 'She ain't no human being'. This broadside broke one of Britain's last taboos. These days, the Royal Family has been greatly demystified to the British people. Back then, and particularly in the midst of the national anniversary celebrations, few publicly questioned the divinity of the monarchy. No less shocking than Rotten's sneered contempt was the publicity art for the single: photos of the Queen with her eyes and mouth torn away and replaced by untidy ransom-note lettering spelling out the name of the band and the record's title.

To the mainstream media's vociferously expressed disgust, the record soared up the various UK charts, despite receiving no airplay on almost all radio stations, and made number 1 in most of them in Silver Jubilee week. Strangely, and conveniently, it stalled at number 2 in the British Market Research Bureau chart—the most important, as it was the one used by both BBC's Radio One (then the UK's only national pop radio station) and *Top of the Pops*. It later emerged that BMRB, under instructions from the British Phonographic Institute, had not counted the sales of the record in Virgin retail outlets that week—the stores where sales were the briskest because the Pistols were signed to the affiliated Virgin music label.

And who was the beneficiary of this intrigue? Step forward Mr. Roderick Stewart, whose single milking both his previous two albums accordingly remained in pole position for a fourth and final week. The last thing Stewart needed at this point was to be involved, however unwittingly, in an establishment conspiracy to keep the young usurpers off the top of the charts.

Some might imagine that Stewart would hardly be inclined to care that punks had another reason to hate him, nor about the increasingly disobliging remarks that music critics felt emboldened to make now that somebody had mentioned the elephant in the room of rock-aristocracy mediocrity and mendacity. It's easy for music critics to get an inflated sense of their own importance. The declining interest of the cognoscenti certainly wasn't important to the ever-increasing numbers buying Stewart product. However, it can't be denied that not too long previously, and quite possibly still, those people's opinions and approval were important to him and it's unlikely that someone who—as do most in his profession—considered himself a no-bullshit, raw rocker would have been untouched by the type of rebukes and brickbats that until lately had been so rare. On his 1977/1978 tour, he was fulminating about the punks to his old friend and champion Paul Nelson, in an interview that was printed in Nelson's 1981 book on him. 'What the fuck!' he said. 'I make records. You don't have to buy them if you don't want them'. Praising Pete Townshend for saying that it was up to the punks to knock him off his perch, he said, 'He's served his fucking dues. These cunts haven't'.

Perhaps Stewart was a bit bewildered. After all, whether one liked his current output or not, it couldn't be denied that he was trying hard with it, unlike the Rolling Stones, who had been audibly treading water with their wares since circa 1973. Perhaps he was also smarting over the lukewarm critical reception to his November 1977 offering, *Foot Loose & Fancy Free*, which was the first Stewart album not to be given any kind of benefit of doubt.

9

YOU GOT A NERVE

AS NOTED, AN ELEMENT OF REVIEWS OF ROD STEWART albums from 1974 to 1976 had been obsequious confessionals about how his music had always spoken to the relevant journalist's soul. They had become recognisable as the preamble to a free pass, leading to mealy-mouthed and self-deluding appraisals of *Smiler* and *Atlantic Crossing* and to the weaker parts of *A Night on the Town*.

In their reviews of *Foot Loose & Fancy Free*, such critics now seemed to be embarrassed by their previous behaviour and were admitting that they'd been in denial about the drop in quality Stewart's art had suffered in recent years. Rather than being angry with themselves, they seemed to channel their fury in Stewart's direction. With the most exquisite irony, they overcompensated. The *Foot Loose* reviews barely noticed or acknowledged some superb songs and a genuine advancement in Stewart's songcraft.

Following the mix-and-match approach to the last two albums that saw an assortment of musicians called into service as and when required or available, Stewart now opted to put together a new permanent band. Interestingly, Kenney Jones was meant to be part of it. 'Rod and I got together and I was help[ing] start the new band with him', Jones recalls. 'Billy Peek and Gary Grainger and Phil Chen and me on drums. We did a few rehearsals and stuff, and then we were going to go to America. Rod and I were having a crack, got along really well together, drumming-wise and as mates . . . Rod said, "Oh, Kenney, I haven't heard you play like that". I said, "When I'm playing in the Faces, I play Faces stuff. I do a lot of sessions where I do whatever I want to do". He loved what I was playing'. However, Jones says, 'It was only when they came round to collect my kit I got cold feet . . . I thought, "I don't want to be seen like I've sold out the Faces' legacy or appear to be in a backing band". I just got put off by it. I went, "No, this doesn't feel right". . . . So I went and got my kit back from the airport and I phoned him up and said, "Look, no, I can't do this"'.

American Carmine Appice took the vacant drum stool and his compatriot John Barlow Jarvis—who'd played on A *Night on the Town*—was retained on keyboards to line up alongside Grainger and Peek (an English and American guitarist respectively) and Jamaican bassist Chen. There was yet another guitarist—as well as another Briton—added in the shape of Jim Cregan, whose smiling visage had become familiar to music-TV viewers through his exhilarating acoustic break in Steve Harley & Cockney Rebel's 1975 UK number 1 'Make Me Smile (Come Up and See Me)'. 'That guitar solo did me a lot of good', reflects Cregan. This aggregation—formally named as the 'Rod Stewart Band' on their second album (*Blondes Have More Fun*) and the 'Rod Stewart Group' on their third (*Foolish Behaviour*)—would essentially be around for the next three LPs, a distinct and reputation-making/breaking era in Stewart's career and life.

It was a multi-talented aggregation. A disproportionate number of band members possessed vocal abilities that enabled smooth decorative harmonies. Members would also be Stewart's songwriting foils in various configurations, leading to a gradual increase in the original material on his product. 'I was very happy in Cockney Rebel and we were doing really well', notes Cregan. 'The main reason that I joined the Stewart band was because the first question I asked him was "Would there be any songwriting?" There was no songwriting in Cockney Rebel at the time because that was Harley's gig'. Despite Stewart's willingness to collaborate, though, all of the Rod Stewart Band/Group's lyrics were Stewart's and Cregan adds, 'He would quite often have a hand in the melody'.

'He liked the Fleetwood Mac idea of having three guitar players', Cregan explains of the line-up. 'Gary was a very strong, forceful Joe Walsh/Pete Townshend–style guitar player. He knew he wanted Gary as one of the foundations of the band. And then he thought he needed somebody a little bit more adaptable, because that particular style would only go so far. He needed somebody who could play all the other kinds of shit: finger picking, acoustic guitars, and those Steve Cropper kinds of things that I can easily do. . . . The variety of things I'd been asked to do in different bands had made me a bit of an all-rounder. I could play a bit of a country, I could play a bit of jazz. That wasn't Gary's thing . . . Billy Peek, who played for sixteen years with Chuck Berry, was a wonderful, wonderful rock player in the traditional sense. . . . We weren't all three guitar players on every record. Billy Peek played the rock tunes, mainly . . . Gary took plenty of guitar solos and so did Billy. It was shared out amongst whoever could cover that style best, whatever the song was'.

Of Phil Chen, Cregan says, 'A master. A wonderful, wonderful bass player'. Chen also brought exotic possibilities to the band's palette: 'He was a Chinese Jamaican and he was a wonderful reggae player'. He describes Jarvis as 'classically trained, brilliant. By far the best musician in the band in terms of background'.

Yet although dazzlingly able, the Rod Stewart Band/Group were for some a little too slick. Greil Marcus' assertion that they were 'hacks incapable of playing a note that had not already been bled dry' is overstating the case, but there's an element of truth in it. Cregan adjudges the too-smooth criticism 'a lot of bollocks'. He says, 'We were really fairly loose. We could really rock. I didn't think of us as tidy. We'd be jamming, we'd be having fun. It wasn't nailed down too tight'. Yet Cregan isn't blind to the faults of the ensemble. 'Sadly, Kenney wasn't playing drums. Carmine Appice is not really a band drummer. He's too flamboyant and fairly unsteady. He wants to show off too much. . . . We could have had a drummer that could play various styles. Carmine just played Carmine and you were stuck with that'.

It being the case that Stewart had latterly been doing perfectly well with hired hands, and furthermore had suffered a lot of tribulations with the last fixed group he'd been in, some might have wondered why he would form a new one. Cregan confirms it was because Stewart missed the *esprit de corps* of the Faces. 'He did. Absolutely. That was made clear to us right from the beginning: that he wanted us to be a band that did the gigs, wrote the songs, played on the records and made the videos. If you look at the "Hot Legs" video, that's all the boys there. That idea was pretty good. . . . On tour, we travelled in the same plane, we stayed at the same hotels. It was a real band. It had a great band vibe'. The members received no record royalties aside from songwriting dues. 'We weren't signed to the label', Cregan reasons. 'Rod was signed to the label. We were session musicians. We'd get paid good double-scale sessions for the time we put in, and sometimes we'd be making [a] record for months, so that worked out fairly well'. However, in other areas they had remuneration way above and beyond what was normal. Stewart decided to make their status touring shareholders. Cregan: 'We did the whole rehearsals and setup of the band on borrowed money, which we paid back on the first tour, and then we went into profit. Went on for a few years and paid very nicely, thank you. And that was a very good move on Rod's part and quite generous. We felt responsible for what the performances were like because the ticket sales were all, in the main, that we were making'.

And how was Stewart as a boss? Cregan: 'Oh, fabulous. Absolutely wonderful. Couldn't ask for better. He was funny. He was generous. He was thoughtful. We hardly ever had any disagreements. We might disagree over a musical point of view. Because his name was on the record, we would have to defer to him at the end, but we'd argue about stuff and say, "Well, actually I think this is much better like this". It was all done very gently. There was never any acrimonious stuff. . . . Most of the time, he'd be in a good mood. I never tiptoed round him. I never had to'.

With Tom Dowd once again producing, the album was recorded at the studios Mantra Sound (Toronto) and Cherokee and Wally Heider (both Los Angeles). The original intention was to make a double album, but oncoming tour dates stymied that ambition. Additional musicians included saxophonist Phil Kenzie, acoustic guitarist Fred Tackett, keyboardist Nicky Hopkins (actually engaged on the very modern string synthesizer), violinist Richard Greene and percussionists Paulinho Da Costa and Tommy Vig.

'Wouldn't have got much change out of three or four months', says Cregan of the recording time. This doesn't include rehearsals, which took place in Stewart's garage. 'We didn't annoy the neighbours, as it turned out', says Cregan. 'Gregory Peck was his next-door neighbour and was quoted as saying, "I quite like it". This went until we had enough songs, then we would overcut. . . . We would cut twenty songs in order to come out with twelve'. Cregan says that Stewart gave no indication of any particular direction he wanted to go in, either on this album or any immediately succeeding one. 'We just would go in, whatever songs came out, came out. We'd just do whatever we felt like. . . . If he had a master plan, he never shared it with anybody. His beloved Faces was like that. Kind of chaotic. He didn't mind that at all. Later on, he's become far more—shall we say—professional in sorting out what he wants to do'.

Foot Loose & Fancy Free's opener 'Hot Legs' (written by Stewart and Grainger) epitomises both the strengths and weakness of the Rod Stewart Band/Group. This midtempo track works up a good groove, but it's one that can feel a little secondhand, industrial and loveless. Lyric-wise the song is the lament of a working man (ahem) who is worried that he'll be too worn out come morning to concentrate on his day job because of the titular, willowy female. We can accept that it's not meant to be profound, but the enjoyable brainlessness tips over into something more disagreeable when he throws in the line 'in the morning make sure you're gone'. Stewart once hived off such tedious commitment-phobia-as-virtue to Faces albums (cf. 'Stay with Me'), but since *Smiler*, he's obviously more than happy to place it on his own product.

'You're Insane' (Stewart/Chen) is a similarly funky and salivating concoction, although less complimentary, with the narrator inveighing against the female subject's alcohol and drug intake, sadomasochistic-sex proclivities, vulgarity, makeup, fashion sense, foolishness, outdated flower-power philosophy and even inability to play a musical instrument. Throwing in the caveat 'There's no substitute for love' doesn't quite make it an 'Every Picture Tells a Story'–level redemption tale.

The credits state that Stewart wrote 'You're in My Heart (The Final Acclaim)' on his own. 'No, he didn't', laughs Cregan. 'We're sitting in the back garden at his house. He said, "Play me a descending chord sequence". He sang over it. That was very early on in our working relationship and, when it came to who wrote it, he said, "Well, actually, it was me that asked you to play the descending chord sequence". I said, "Yes, it was, but there's loads of descending chord sequences. It was that particular chord sequence that prompted you to write the melody that you wrote over it". . . . If somebody writes the chords that prompts the

melody, you usually split that half and half. But he stood his ground. . . .
Now, he did have the melody for the chorus, so really most of that song
is his. . . . [But] if you listen to it, there's a nice diminished chord there's
no possible way in the world that Rod knew how to play. I'd been in the
band about eight months and I wasn't comfortable enough with Rod to
say, "No, actually, I think you should give me this". But that never happened again'.

Either way, in the midst of the hard-tooled music and vitriolic and
licentious sentiments we've experienced so far, the song's sensitivity, lyri-
cism and acoustic strains are completely unexpected. (The unexpected-
ness has little to do with this being the record's 'fast' side—by now we're
used to these descriptions being meaningless.) They're also mercifully
welcome. The track feels like a blast of fresh air in a dank cellar. Moreover, with its confessional nature, vulnerability and prominent use of
fiddle, it almost feels custom-designed to convince the older Stewart fans
that he hasn't lost his bearings, talent or warmth. The fiddle could even
be said to be a development of that trademark Mercury sound, as it actually interacts with the vocal instead of only coming to life when Stewart
takes a break from singing.

Musically, the track is technically flawless, but not in a way that com-
promises the soulfulness. Burbling keyboards, brushed drums and cooing backing vocals—as well as that snaking violin—create a creamy bed
for Stewart's songwords, with electric guitar introduced as the recording
moves into an anthemic end section.

It doesn't matter much—the track takes on the universality that all
great love songs do—but 'You're in My Heart' is clearly about Britt
Ekland, from whom Stewart had recently had an acrimonious parting.
Remarkably, there's no evident vindictiveness. Spiritually, the track
is warm and likeable from the opening verse, in which the narrator
recalls not knowing what day it was when the subject walked into the
room and confesses that initially the attraction was purely physical.
Despite the latter line, for the first time on the album, sex is not the
be-all-and-end-all.

That Stewart is not the callow young man of a few years previously
is evident in a new eloquence. Lines like, 'You're a rhapsody, a comedy'
would have been beyond the bloke who clearly didn't really understand
the phrase 'Every picture tells a story', as would an assertion that his partner

is characterised by lace, fineness, beauty and elegance. There's something else. Stewart had written several classic songs before, but almost all of them had faults for which the listener had to make allowances: a cavalier attitude towards rhyming schemes and disdain for choruses. Suddenly, and miraculously, he has acquired something approaching a meticulousness about both. Because the song is tidily structured and because its rhymes are tight and whipcrack-smart, its lyric's generosity of spirit is correspondingly more delightful. Only an attempted match-up of 'play' and 'me' grates in its laziness.

No sooner does Stewart give the impression of evolution than he appears to regress into the primordial mud. 'Born Loose' (Stewart/Grainger/Cregan) is another sweaty rocker that celebrates sex and disdains relationships (this one depressingly puts its cards on the table with the first line: 'Don't you count on me to be here when the sun goes down'). The narrator further asserts that responsibility and fidelity have never meant a thing to him. Meanwhile, Stewart is cheerfully joining in the late-1970s' newly permissive-cum-sleazy vibe: profanities—once absent from his product—are piling up; this one adds a 'piss' to the 'pussy' and 'shit' already heard here. Yet it can't be denied that, like the opening two tracks, 'Born Loose' has a certain shady, syncopated entertainment factor, not least because of some appropriately greasy mouth harp from John Mayall.

Vanilla Fudge were a somewhat bizarre late-1960s aggregation who specialised in slow but bombastic remakes of well-known songs. Most famously, they turned 'You Keep Me Hangin' On' (Holland/Dozier/Holland) from a quintessential Motown pop number into a hard rock freak out. It reached number 6 in the States and number 18 in the UK in 1967, the year after the Supremes' original made the American top spot and the British top 10. That Stewart's version takes after the Fudge's interpretation is rather odd considering that, by 1977, the Vanilla Fudge approach was considered as much a relic of the psychedelic era as beads, peace signs and headbands. However, the Fudge's drummer had been one Carmine Appice. 'It was Carmine's idea', confirms Cregan of the song's presence on *Foot Loose & Fancy Free*.

It opened side two. (Had it been transposed with 'You're in My Heart', the 'fast' and 'slow' side-designations would have been accurate.) Stewart's version's seven-and-a-half-minute length beats the

Fudge's, but it's not that long in the context of this album, where the four-and-a-half-minute playing time of 'You're in My Heart' is easily the most modest. It's quite good, with some impressive instrumental passages, but—as it had been reimagined in this way before—at the same time quite pointless.

After it was written by Homer Banks, Carl Hampton and Raymond Jackson, '(If Loving You Is Wrong) I Don't Want to Be Right' took some time to see the light of day, because its sentiments were rather daring for early-1970s popular music. The anguished story of a married man and father conducting an illicit affair, it failed to find an outlet until Luther Ingram heard a shelved recording by girl group the Emotions. Once the dam was broken, though, its late-night melancholy and we're-all-adults/life's-not-a-rehearsal realism-cum-moral ambiguity saw it quickly spawn a spate of cover versions. By 1974, there'd been a dozen, with more to come, including renditions by David Ruffin, Isaac Hayes, Tom Jones, Bobby Bland and Millie Jackson. If one can get past the overarching fact that we're listening to the self-pity of an adulterer, and the further problematic issue that this song would seem to have spoken to Stewart at this point in his life for a tellingly specific reason (Stewart's infidelity ruptured the relationship with Ekland, as he admitted in interviews), Stewart's version is highly enjoyable. Cregan says, 'We did that up in Canada. . . . Hasn't it got a beautiful orchestral intro? John Jarvis wrote that'. (Steve Cropper's presence on guitar suggests that it's also in part a recording excavated from the can.) Ultra-smooth piano runs, Del Newman's sweeping strings, a sultry saxophone and electric guitar flecks frame a Stewart vocal given echo to provide an extra atmosphere to the narrator's tortured declarations to his mistress ('I'll see you when I can').

It's back to originals with a brace of Stewart/Grainger collaborations. The vindictiveness of 'You Got a Nerve' is the diametric opposite to the generosity of spirit of 'You're in My Heart'. An elongated, simmering put-down of a faithless lover, it sees Stewart explain in fine detail across the course of five minutes why he doesn't want her back. The backing is vaguely Eastern sounding, with a guitar tuned to resemble a sitar. The track is grimly compelling, the listener hypnotised by the dark ambience and even darker sentiments (the narrator gloatingly speaks of the pleasure it gives him 'to know that you're bleeding inside').

The six-minute closer 'I Was Only Joking' brings us back to the humanity, likeability and partly acoustic timbre provided by 'You're in My Heart (The Final Acclaim)'. It's another dissection of a relationship breakup, but this time around Stewart admits that the fault is his. In fact, the song is an epic *mea culpa,* him looking back on his mistakes across the course of his life, and doing so with that knack for convincing fine detail and winning humour that has always been his strength—but now with the added bonus of spot-on rhymes.

Recalling the flashy fashions he and his teenage mates adopted to attract females, the narrator amusingly concedes, 'My dad said we looked ridic-u-luss'. In later verses, he provides his own critiques of his actions, musing that he had collected lovers like butterflies to no apparent benefit and—in a meta moment—noting that the morality of detailing his romantic tribulations in songs like this is open to question. As in 'You're in My Heart', he seems to be using elements of his pre–*Atlantic Crossing* sound with almost Pavlovian intent: there is a folk-rock ambience that includes a guitar part uncannily reminiscent of a mandolin. Some of the elements of this ultra-smooth concoction, though, are things of which his old band would have been incapable and maybe even unwilling, including the very skillful but very main-stream electric guitar solo.

First pressings of *Foot Loose & Fancy Free* came with a deluxe booklet insert each of whose pages featured the musician lineup of an album cut accompanied by a line from the relevant song and an illustration designed to resemble either an old trashy paperback cover or comic book panel. Compared to *A Night on the Town,* the jacket's front cover was fairly restrained, finding Stewart gazing at the camera on a hazy sunny day, while the back of the jacket showed him quietly walking his dog on a misty morning. Those looking for signs of decadence, though, would have noted that he sported a dangling earring and that his ever-more stylised 'barnet' was now dyed blonde.

Stewart told *Record Mirror*'s Rosalind Russell, 'I think it's the best album I've ever made'. He said to Tony Stewart of the *NME,* 'If I haven't got the best rock 'n' roll band in the world, then I don't know who has'. It's easy to see why he would believe such things. The album was slicker—more professional, if you like—than anything to which he'd previously attached his name, and the importance of that fact to him personally shouldn't be underestimated after his enduring half a decade of Faces shambolicness and underachievement. There were definite forward steps in evidence. The suspicion had grown in recent years that by this point he was aiming his records less at discerning rock consumers than at an undemanding housewife market, but the album's lyrically risqué slabs of hard rock hardly suggest that. Meanwhile, whatever one's opinions on the Supremes-by-way-of-Vanilla-Fudge cover, it can't be denied that it's adventurous: purely and simply, progressive rock. More importantly, he is making real strides in his songcraft, finally addressing weaknesses that had always threatened to spoil even the high-quality likes of 'Every Picture Tells a Story' and 'Maggie May'. Moreover, in his best moments he is doing this while retaining his humanity, humility and tenderness, or at least his convincing pretence at humanity, humility and tenderness. 'You're in My Heart (The Final Acclaim)' and 'I Was Only Joking' are quite simply heartrending masterpieces.

None of these merits were widely acknowledged. The tragedy of Stewart at the juncture of this album's release is that his personal and artistic development and some great songs were made irrelevant by the critical prerequisites of the times. To be fair, they were also obscured by genuine demerits: lyrics that, where they weren't demonstrating his uncommon sensitivity and humanity, were increasingly vulgar, sex obsessed and self-aggrandising; music that prioritised rigid flash over grit and suppleness. Meanwhile, the decorative depictions of women in his songs, the album booklet and the promotional film for 'Hot Legs' had come to seem passe and offensive to anyone *au fait* with the androgyny and female assertiveness of the punk moment: the news didn't seem to have reached Rod that women weren't only located in *Playboy* and on catwalks these days but could be found in music groups. The long hair of Stewart's colleagues that was to be seen in the album's booklet was something else that looked prehistoric in the context of the pointedly short-haired New Wavers. Such stuff might sound fairly trivial, but they were big issues at that juncture to those who believed that the time had come for a day of reckoning for a music industry that had grown fat, complacent and out of touch.

The review by Joe McEwen in *Rolling Stone* provides an illustration of the climate of the era, one-part genuine outrage to one-part *gestalt* posturing. 'There's something to be said for the New Wave rebellion

against . . . "old meat"', he wrote. 'Even if this reaction is mostly con-
fined to England, it seems very healthy. There are a lot of kids in England who don't care what kind of fashionably gauche trinkets decorate
Rod Stewart's high-class, Hollywood home . . . Stewart has lost touch
with them, not only musically but culturally as well. And for Rod Stewart this dilemma seems particularly complex. After all, it wasn't too long
ago that Stewart . . . was digging graves for a living and feeling a little
testy himself'. While he acknowledged that it was to Stewart's credit that
he declined to return to Muscle Shoals and sessioners and was trying
to go back to rock 'n' roll, McEwen opined, 'There's just one problem:
the record falls flat. Part of the trouble is the band, which sounds stiff
and not particularly inspired'. He also had caveats that were not about
what was in the grooves but the ether. He stated that 'Hot Legs' 'might
have worked five years ago but now sounds only lecherous and silly' and
noted of a sort-of New Wave artist's latest tour, 'You can bet Graham
Parker isn't lugging around 64,000 pounds of equipment, a seamstress,
a masseuse, a tour photographer and a makeup "girl"'. He concluded
of the album, 'It's sure hard to care much about "Hot Legs" with Elvis
Costello and the Sex Pistols around'.

While McEwen was summing up the opinions of a highly influential group, it was also a numerically small one. These days, the people
who bought Rod Stewart records tended not to be the type who also
purchased Rolling Stone or New Musical Express, and the sociopolitical
concerns that informed those periodicals' appraisals of his product were
destined never to impinge on their consciousnesses, let alone sway their
buying decisions. In the UK, 'You're in My Heart' b/w 'You Got a Nerve'
was released as a single and made number 3. The double-A-sided 'Hot
Legs/I Was Only Joking' made number 5. The album was a number 3.
It climbed one higher in the States, where 'You're in My Heart' made
number 4, 'Hot Legs' b/w 'You're Insane' number 28 and an edited 'I Was
Only Joking' b/w 'Born Loose' number 22.

Stewart in fact was having another bumper year in Britain, which
continued to evince little resentment at the fact that he had abandoned
its shores. The Best of Rod Stewart, which recycled his hits for yet another
compilation album, made the top 3 and scored 105 Weeks on Chart.
'Ole Ola (Mulher Brasileira)', a single credited to Rod Stewart and the
Scottish World Cup Squad, overcame its monotony, four-minute-plus

length, nonsensical title and absurd over-optimism about the prospects of Scotland in the titular tournament (which took place in Argentina, not Brazil) to make number 4.

Perhaps all this was hard to swallow for those who felt that it offended against the ideal that commercial success should be commensurate with artistic quality. Leaving aside the fact that aesthetic achievement is subjective, the turn that Stewart's music and public image took next is something that neither his staunchest fans nor fiercest critics could ever have predicted.

10

FOOLISH BEHAVIOUR

IN EARLY 1978 CAME AN AMUSING FOOTNOTE in the Rod Stewart story.

A single by vocalist Bonnie Tyler called 'It's a Heartache' was a UK number 4 and a US number 3. That Tyler's husky vocal style made her seem a female equivalent of Stewart was not that remarkable (see Maggie Bell). What was eyebrow-raising was the fact that writers Ronnie Scott and Steve Wolf had—intentionally or not—perfectly captured the wracked emotional pattern and melodic style of current Stewart ballads. Moreover, the recording's tune and even guitar solo bears some resemblance to those of 'Sailing'. Tyler completes the eerie effect by imitating Stewart's phrasing. It all made for a concoction that caused people hearing it for the first time to exclaim things along the lines of, 'oo's this—Rod Stewart's sister or summing?' Stewart much later covered the song on *Still the Same . . . Great Rock Classics of Our Time* (2006), which some might suggest was an exercise in bringing sand to the desert.

Meanwhile, Stewart had a new beau. Alana Hamilton, whom he met in March 1978, was a blonde beauty, but was otherwise very different to his previous lady friends, particularly the milieu in which she operated, one that can be imagined from the fact that she was a former wife of perma-tanned actor George Hamilton.

'Not a great woman', says Cregan of Hamilton. 'Not at all. . . . Trying to find love true love in Hollywood—no. Not really. Almost impossible'. He considers her effect on Stewart to be deleterious. 'Britt Ekland definitely introduced him to the Hollywood movie-star set. And then Alana. . . . She moved him very strongly into the Hollywood set . . . I guess if you're a guy from Archway and you've been making some music, [then] suddenly you're really seriously a Hollywood A-lister—that could easily go to your head. He was suddenly just reveling in the fact that he was rubbing shoulders with . . . name anybody around at that time. She was connected'.

Cregan and his colleagues might possibly have considered all this none of their business were it not for the fact that it was impinging on Stewart's work. 'When he first started going out with Alana, they were trying to outdo each other for staying up late and being fabulous and all that stuff', Cregan recalls. 'He was all over the place in the press and he'd be seen at this or that. So he was not working as hard [at] his music as we were'. Stewart even started committing the professional sin that had so infuriated him about the Faces. Cregan: 'He'd come late to rehearsals, which was not like him. He didn't think it was alright to be kept waiting a couple of hours, so he didn't do it to us. He started to do it then'.

Whether related or not, the spiritual and philosophical devolution described by parts of *Foot Loose & Fancy Free* continued in spades. *Foot Loose* was followed in November 1978 by *Blondes Have More Fun*. Even more than the low spots of its predecessor, it was an LP that described the mindset of someone who prioritises sex over love and who has dispensed with reflection and maturity for the pursuit of a man-child lifestyle involving the lack of responsibility and hedonism that people ten years younger are actually beginning to grow out of. None of this is to say that it didn't create some good music, but it was disconcerting and dismaying for his long-term fans—or, as they increasingly were, ex-fans. After all, such was the sensitivity and generosity of the material on Stewart's Mercury albums that he had seemed mature for his age, often even like a wise old man.

Recording at Smoke Tree and Cherokee Studios was, once again, overseen by Tom Dowd. The same lineup of musicians as on *Foot Loose* return except for the fact that this time keyboards are handled by Duane Hitchings and Nicky Hopkins. 'John Jarvis left, he wasn't fired', says Cregan. 'It wasn't really his cup of tea touring the world in a rock band. He was a very sweet human being and I don't think that was quite what he felt he ought to be doing. We used to wind him up, too. A journalist came out on the road, a girl who was not particularly attractive. She fancied John and we told John he had to sleep with her, had to take one for the team. He was absolutely horrified. . . . He became a very successful session player and writer down in Nashville and made a good career for himself'.

The album opens with 'Da Ya Think I'm Sexy?' (yes, it's 'Da', not 'Do'). The song's composition is a tangled tale. It was originally credited to Stewart and Appice. However, Appice's friend—and credited album keyboardist—Duane Hitchings has belatedly been added to the credit, although Stewart has admitted unconscious plagiarism of both a Jorge Ben Jor melody ('Taj Mahal') and very conscious plagiarism of a Bobby Womack riff ('[If You Want My Love] Put Something Down on It'). With regards to the latter nick, Stewart wrote, 'The rules are that you can lift a line from an arrangement—as distinct from a melody line—without infringing copyright. So you can't touch me for that'; with regards to the former, he donated his royalties to UNICEF in recompense.

Royalties aside—it became a monster hit single—some might assume that not many would actually want their name attached to 'Da Ya Think I'm Sexy?' It was a recording that only served to make Stewart's disenfranchised original fanbase hate him all the more because it saw him embrace disco, a highly fashionable dance-oriented musical form that many of them considered to be as shallow and trashy as they felt he had become. Moreover, his take on the genre took disco into trashier realms still.

The record, of course, was a shameless piece of bandwagon jumping, but Stewart was only one of many to hitch a ride on the disco gravy train, and some of them had more street cred than him. Said people included such unlikely artists as Ian Dury and the Blockheads ('Hit Me with Your Rhythm Stick'), Blondie ('Heart of Glass') and the Rolling Stones ('Miss You'). 'It's a rip off of "Miss You"', says Ian McLagan, who played electric piano on the latter song. 'He's admitted that to me'. While not disputing the importance of 'Miss You'—a huge hit single—to Stewart's song, Cregan prefers to use the term 'inspired in part by'.

While mammon may have lain behind Stewart's release, a venture into new territory is by definition also motivated by adventurism, and Stewart deserves kudos for not sticking with the terrain he knew—not least because he makes such a good fist of it. Cregan credits Phil Chen:

'That particular bass pattern, when he played that, the whole song just seemed to fall into place. I was doing my Nile Rodgers impersonations'. Stewart and his crew expertly purvey disco's four-on-the-floor drumbeat, clipped guitar approach, and throbbing bass style. A soaring synth riff and a howling sax line decorate the five-and-a-half-minute proceedings, which feature several atmospheric respites.

Lyric-wise there's a strange disconnect between choruses and verses. The chorus and its (almost) title line are vainglorious, juvenile, icky and concerned with physical pleasure, but the verses are unshowy and moving, revolving around a couple's mutual quest to find an intimacy deeper than sex in the heart of the pitiless big city. It's full of pleasingly convincing domestic detail ('He says, "I'm sorry, but I'm out of milk and coffee"'). This dichotomy is a microcosm of Stewart's recent recording persona—sometimes mature and tender, sometimes juvenile and narcissistic—with the difference that he usually splits those different parts of himself between separate songs.

Ironically, the following track is actually what people mistakenly expect 'Da Ya Think I'm Sexy?' to be from its title. 'Dirty Weekend' (Stewart/Grainger) starts with one of Stewart's 'lovable' snickers and proceeds to regale us with the less than salubrious story of a couple checking into a hotel under an assumed name. A decade earlier, the Stones' 'Let's Spend the Night Together' was genuinely daring, as was to some extent the revelation in Stewart's 1969 song 'Cindy's Lament' that he and Cindy had had sex. With censorious shackles and pre-marital celibacy now largely a thing of history, Stewart has to up the ante with lack of principles (the narrator is having it off with his best friend's girl), drug references (the couple spice things up with quaaludes, supplied by the woman's mother's doctor) and crudeness ('I'm gonna rock you 'til your pussy's sore'). The musical accompaniment is even more unprepossessing, all thudding rhythm and grinding guitars. Mercifully, the two-and-a-half-minute track is as short as it's ugly.

'Ain't Love a Bitch' (Stewart/Grainger)—in spite of its title—boasts gentle, melodious and sprightly tones that come as a relief after the aural and moral assault we've just experienced. Stewart has now been a public figure long enough to be able to be self-referential and self-mythologising. His whistlestop tour of his romantic history refers to a woman who, when he was seventeen, took his virginity and made a first-class fool out of him.

'Oh Maggie, if you're still out there the rest is history' he appends. In his detailing of the vicissitudes of romance, he admits that some of his suffering has stemmed from the fact that he can't grow up—something we could have told him after having had to endure the previous track.

'The Best Days of My Life' is a gorgeous return to the old-style vulnerable, humble, and grateful Stewart love anthem, complete with a reference to the narrator's poverty ('Ain't got money but we sure got laughs'). Written by Stewart and Cregan, its music is comprised of winding acoustic guitar, fluttering flute, burbling keyboards, pattering percussion and classical strings. The only problem is that there's something indefinably off about it, something that strikes a false note. Perhaps it's our knowledge of Stewart's less than exemplary behaviour in his private life, or the fact that the very slick instrumentation and production makes us feel we're being manipulated. Maybe such cynicism is unfair, but we nonetheless can't help wishing that he'd written the song—the exact same one—five or six years before (and done it in that old semi-rustic style for good measure).

Side closer 'Is That the Thanks I Get?' (Stewart/Cregan) takes us fully back to the present day and the artist's current glittering lifestyle, knowledge of which seemed to be another thing complicating our view of the previous track. It's clearly another composition inspired by Britt, if not necessarily completely autobiographical, but this one is less generous than 'You're in My Heart'. The narrator might be entitled to complain about his ex's lawyers, detectives and private eyes, but when he says, 'You didn't give me one chance to explain', we're reminded that it was Stewart's infidelity that created that situation (which he also seems to be exaggerating) of recompense-seeking recrimination. The midtempo music is impressively glossy but, as is frequently the case with Stewart's backing these days, we are left wondering whether the fact of there not being a note out of place is such a good thing.

Vinyl side two opened with the Stewart/Grainger creation 'Attractive Female Wanted'. That this song of loneliness is not cut from quite the same cloth as 'You Wear It Well' is evident from the first line ('I'm tired of buying *Penthouse*, *Oui*, and *Hustler*') and the last few (in which the narrator implores *Playboy* publisher Hugh Hefner to send him one of his bunnies). The staccato melody, undulating sax work and decorative harmonies all please to a degree, but can't exactly make the track loveable.

'Blondes (Have More Fun)' (Stewart/Cregan) is a slinky 1950s shuffle. It's also possibly the most genuinely autobiographical song Stewart has written up to this point, if depressingly so. Rather than using a nostalgia trip as a jumping-off point for a declaration of love's redemptive power (cf. 'Every Picture Tells a Story'), his focus here is determinedly below the belt as he tells us—as if we hadn't guessed already—that his preference in women is for the statuesque and the fair-haired. It sees Stewart displaying two of the classic signs of hubris by referring to himself in the third person and via a pet name ('God knows, Rodder just needs to ball'). That there's no poverty claiming is not a refreshing honesty: we're taken on a tour of a world of casting couches, limousines, bodyguards and face-lifts that—try as he might—Rod can't make sound like fun.

In complete contrast, 'Last Summer' (Stewart/Chen) is a piece of breezy, sweet and gentle soul-pop that tilts for a feeling of innocence. The gauche narrator informs us of how endlessly unsuccessful he is with women ('Love always seems to let me down'), while Gary Herbig's flute dips and darts. Amidst all the surrounding decadence, it's difficult to know how to listen to this. Are we being had if we take it at face value? More to the point, is this what Rod Stewart's art has come to: something that it's not able to consume without making mental reference to past albums, past conduct, and present company? Okay, the problem might be with us rather than him but, in any case, should music be this difficult?

Thank God for the safe ground of an uncomplicated cover version. 'Standing in the Shadows of Love' was another classic from that once-prolific Motown songwriting partnership of Lamont Dozier and Brian and Eddie Holland. After its first release in 1966 by the Four Tops in a recording that became a transatlantic top 10, the poetic plea for mercy from an abandoned lover had been the recipient of a surprisingly low number of cover versions. However, the likes of Tommy Boyce and Bobby Hart, the Jackson 5 and Barry White had had a go. Stewart decides to disco-fy the song (and drop the 'g' of its first word), with the rhythm section doing pretty much what they do on 'Da Ya Think I'm Sexy?', even if the virtuoso guitar is pure rock. Despite Cregan's reservations about him, Appice excels himself in an instrumental midsection. With crushing predictability, though, the track turns out to not be such a safe ground after all: Stewart amends a line to read, 'Didn't I screw you right?'

The album closes on a wholly unexpected note. 'Scarred and Scared' (Stewart/Grainger) is the five-minute lament of a man who has, in unexplained circumstances, killed a teenaged boy and is now resigned to his fate, which he has determined will not be the humiliation of legal retribution but instead death by his own hand. He is fearful of the shame he will bring on his parents, and apprehensive of the judgment of his maker. He admits to an unknown addressee that he is scarred and scared, but implores them not to let on to his son that he was anything but 'big and strong' in his moment of crisis. Cascading acoustic lines and a harmonica (presumably from Stewart himself) complete the pathos, even if unnecessary string ornamentation threatens to undermine it. It all makes for a creation that, no less than 'Mandolin Wind', sees Stewart convincingly inhabit the persona of someone whose experiences lie completely beyond his own frame of reference. While we can treat our reaction of, 'It's great—but where is this coming from?' as effectively a compliment, we have another response that's not quite that, namely: what connection does this have to the flash and trash, and bump and grind, of much of what precedes it? It can, these days, truly be exhausting trying to keep up with Stewart's mercurial mind and morality.

The album was released in a cover that made old fans groan with contempt—and no doubt newer devotees groan with something else. The black-clad, blonde-tressed Stewart is seen cavorting with females in leopard-print clothing, a black-haired one on the front and a blonde one (Alana) on the back.

In the critical community, Rosalind Russell of *Record Mirror* was one of the LP's few fans, adjudging it '100 per cent better' than *Foot Loose & Fancy Free* and 'his best album since *Gasoline Alley*'. She wrote, 'He's got back to basics, back to love songs—be they broken hearted, or out and out lust. And the arrangements have changed accordingly. He's ditched a lot of the schmaltz and honed down the sound, making it less like a Hollywood film score and more like rock and roll'.

More representative of the verdict of music scribes was the demolition by Peter Silverton in *Sounds*, who was disgusted by the big-hootered Stewart presenting himself as a glamour puss on the cover and dismissed the contents as 'a very competent if uninspired rock album' whose theme was 'bloated egos with lots of money get to see more of the world'. *Rolling Stone*'s Janet Maslin was more eloquent but just as scathing. She wrote,

'Never before has he attacked such uncertain material with so little gusto or levity — for once, his trademarked "Whooo!" carries no conviction. And never has he offered an album that's actively disagreeable to listen to. . . . The artist's boastfulness, which accounts for what little vitality the LP has, takes a truly ugly turn when it's accompanied by self-pity. . . . In his earlier writing, Stewart's fearlessness was his hallmark quality, the note that made him instantly authentic and understandable: inside the adventurer in "Every Picture Tells a Story" was someone who didn't altogether like what he saw in the mirror . . . *Blondes Have More Fun* is every bit as uncertain as Stewart's premier albums, but as he trades in his doubts for bombast, he eclipses his most likable side. And the hot air is none too effective on its own'.

The contempt of the old Stewart fans (many of them in the music press) and the adoration of the newer devotees (almost none of them in the music press) delineated a gap that was now at its widest. Although those who had loved the humanitarianism and sensitivity of his Mercury albums and the frayed, friendly ambience of Faces shows increasingly gave up on him, they were more than replaced. The fact that there seemed to be a significant overlap with his new audience and lovers of records by, say, Barry Manilow is something that, if it occurred to Stewart, didn't seem to bother him. Nor did the fact that his male fans were not only increasingly fewer in number but were widely suspected of being habitues of singles bars. Rod's ever-expanding fanbase—utterly unperturbed by, and largely unaware of, the critical disdain—lapped up both the album (a UK no. 3 and a three-week US chart-topper) and its lead-off single. With those who didn't buy it, said single created a perfect storm of contempt: for the record itself, for the way Stewart performed it and for disco music *per se*.

'Sexy?' was released as a single in the UK in September 1978. It climbed to number 1 in his native Britain in December and made the top in the States the following February (the same day, in fact, as its parent album). It was unintentionally part of a phalanx that achieved world domination. In the UK, the first five number 1 singles of 1979 were all disco records, including the Village People's 'YMCA', Gloria Gaynor's 'I Will Survive', Ian Dury's 'Hit Me with Your Rhythm Stick' and Blondie's 'Heart of Glass'. Over in the States, disco's supremacy was even more extraordinary. For fully half of 1979, disco records were sitting at the top of the *Billboard* Hot 100. 'I Will Survive' and 'Heart of Glass' got to number 1 in the States like they did in the UK. Amii Stewart scaled the summit with a disco-fied–cum–space age recalibration of the old soul number 'Knock on Wood'. Anita Ward proffered the jingle-ish 'Ring My Bell', and Donna Summer made number 1 with both the pumping, horny 'Hot Stuff' and prostitute's anthem 'Bad Girls'. Barbra Streisand shamelessly hitched up with Summer for 'No More Tears (Enough Is Enough)', the latter's third US number 1 of the year. Michael Jackson's bandwagon-jumping chart-topper was 'Don't Stop 'til You Get Enough'.

Disco was a love-it-or-hate-it proposition. Its hooks and slogans made it infernally catchy but it was sharp-edged and relentless: disco soundscapes were not habitually softened with acoustic instruments or leavened with respites. As such, it was difficult to tolerate in anything more than short bursts (i.e. it wasn't album music but consigned to the currently looked-down-on world of singles). Some had other problems with disco. The endless penchant of disco producers for using classical strings, however stylishly or rhythmically, seemed somehow inimical to the unkempt spirit of rock. Moreover, while some thought disco socially progressive for the way the white, male dominance of 1970s rock didn't apply in a medium where women and minorities were highly visible, the pitiless admission policies of New York's Studio 54 and other dance venues were felt in some quarters to be predicated on their own forms of prejudice. Moreover, many rock fans thought disco reactionary by default because it embraced apolitical hedonism. Into this raging debate stepped Stewart and 'Da Ya Think I'm Sexy?'. The record's title played into the ballooning twin public perceptions of Stewart as slimy and pathetic and disco as a music for people who were obsessed with themselves.

'"Do you think I'm sexy?" does not appear in the song at all', points out Cregan. 'It's, "If you want my body and you think I'm sexy"'. That was Billy Gaff came up with that idea, and the misspelling of it'. Maybe so, but presumably the way Stewart performed the song in concert was his own idea and not done under any form of duress. Stewart's new younger-and-dumber-by-the-day recording persona was these days reflected quite overtly in his appearance and stage behaviour. To his peroxided hair he added mascara, leopard-skin leggings, and crop tops. On stage, he would get the lighting crew to shine a spotlight on his backside and, as his

drummer maintained a sultry beat, provocatively and for extended peri-
ods thrust his hips left and right. It could only lead the public to assume
that the song title was a question he was coquettishly asking them. It's difficult to convey how unusual—for which read 'embarrassing'—this was
at the time. Mick Jagger had pioneered an androgynous-cum-effeminate
stage style in the early 1970s. Stewart's new schtick took it a large stride
further, creating an image one critic referred to as a 'male tart'. Yet in Jagger's case it made some sort of sense. The Rolling Stones having always
been social provocateurs, challenging assumptions about gender identity and stage presentation was a natural extension of what they were
about. In the context of Stewart's image as an apolitical ordinary bloke
and football devotee, his new persona simply seemed apropos of nothing—except self-adoration. That's even leaving aside the fact that Jagger had the looks to bring off his schtick. The juxtaposition of Stewart's
schnoz and his stripper moves simply put one in mind of a *Foot Loose*
song title: 'You Got a Nerve'. For much of the world at this point, Stewart
was a wretch and a joke.

The thought must have flashed across the minds of some that the
only reason he had dispensed with the Faces is because, if he had acted
this way around them, they would have taken the piss. Dee Harrington
agrees that he would never have dared wiggle in front of his former band.
She also, to some degree, extends that absence of healthy mockery in
Stewart's life to the entire unpretentious British nation: 'Don't forget,
he'd left here. He was there, and they quite like some of that'.

Cregan denies that Stewart's colleagues were mortified. 'It was so
much fun, we didn't give a shit. It was all tongue-in-cheek. He doesn't
take himself seriously at all. That wiggling his bum is all a bit of a laugh
to him. I think in some cases he's been a little bit maligned and maybe
misunderstood, but that's part of the job—for people to not understand
what you're doing. Because I know him so well, I don't feel betrayed,
as some of those guys might about the old bluesman that he was in his
early days'. He adds, 'He was always a bit of a peacock, wasn't he? The
backcombed hair, and he always liked beautiful clothes. So it was kind
of on its way. He just maybe took it a bit further than some of the public
would like'.

'He sold out in a way', says Ray Jackson. 'There wasn't much originality around. There were pretty good players, but the guys were just sort

of emulating what had gone before'. Pete Sears: 'All that "Da Ya Think I'm Sexy?" stuff, he suffered a bit when he got into that'. Those comments have the smack of old colleagues straining not to be too cruel. Music critics didn't quite have the same compunction. Paul Nelson, for instance.

Nelson had kept the faith with Stewart at a point when his fellow writers were becoming increasingly uninterested in his work. Even someone as devoted as Nelson, however, turned out to have his breaking point. He felt he had no option but to dismiss *Blondes Have More Fun* as an album 'where absolutely everything fell flat'. In a 1981 *Rolling Stone* review, Nelson was writing, 'As a young man in his twenties, Rod Stewart seemed to possess an age-old wisdom: some of the things he told us we could have learned from our grandfathers. In his thirties, however, he suddenly metamorphosed into Jayne Mansfield'. For those not *au fait* with the 1950s/1960s celebrity concerned, Mansfield was a blonde movie star and singer of minimal talent but notorious for a tangled and tumultuous love life and endless hunger for publicity. The aforementioned book that Nelson published in 1981 with Lester Bangs positively demolished Stewart. Issued by Delilah Communications, it—perhaps deliberately—gave no exterior appearance of the vitriol inside. From its functional title, to its licensed cover shot of Stewart in a head-cocked, winsome pose, to its précis-less back cover adorned with a colour photo of a sparkly-vested Stewart in full stage flight, it had the appearance of fan fodder. For the attentive, there was a clue to be discerned in the two slyly subversive plate sections. These lavish colour spreads featured no captions, but were noticeably pointedly different to one another. The first one contained a variety of pictures of Stewart from the Mercury/Faces days, him looking every inch both an exciting artist and likeable, feet-on-the-ground ordinary bloke; the second displayed him in all his Jayne Mansfield glory: garish outfits, coquettish poses and a complete absence of subtlety or taste, as well as a complete lack of self-knowledge about how pitiful he looked. The book's second chapter was a rap between the two authors. 'I just sort of feel sad', said Nelson of the modern-day Stewart. 'It's really too bad that it's come to this'. 'I guess the question is, do they perceive the patheticness?' said Bangs of Stewart's present-day fans. 'And obviously they don't'.

This doesn't even begin to compare, though, to the disenchantment of Greil Marcus. When *Rolling Stone* decided to issue a 1980 update to their *Illustrated History of Rock & Roll* book, Nelson didn't have the heart to revise the hagiographic Stewart chapter he'd contributed to the 1975 edition. Marcus took the assignment, and—in one of the greatest pieces of music journalism ever published—went to town. 'Rarely has a singer had as full and unique a talent as Rod Stewart; rarely has anyone betrayed his talent so completely', he wrote. 'Once the most compassionate presence in music, he has become a bilious self-parody—and sells more records than ever. . . . He had an unmatched eye for the tiny details around which lives turn, shatter, and reform . . . and a voice to make those details indelible. . . . Full of the rewards he received for his work, and seemingly without noticing, he exchanged passion for sentiment, the romance of sex for a tease, a reach for mysteries with tawdry posturing, and was last seen parading his riches, his fame and his smugness, a sort of hip Engelbert Humperdinck'. Of the Mercury albums' musicians, Marcus said, 'Playing around Stewart more than behind him, and never named as a group, they would become one of the finest rock and roll bands of all time'. He said of Stewart's first three albums, 'If ever any rocker chose the role of Everyman and lived up to it, it was Rod Stewart'. He stated that *Every Picture Tells a Story* could 'hold its ground with any rock and roll record ever made'.

When it came to *Never a Dull Moment*, although conceding that it was a strong record, he said, 'There was much missing: mainly that sense that life itself had been crammed onto a 12-inch piece of plastic'. *Smiler* he dismissed as 'just rock-star flimsy: accidental genius turned to formula'. From all the product of Stewart's post-Mercury/Faces career so far, he had time only for 'Tonight's the Night' ('a seduction song so transparent, helpless, and forthright that not even a cynic—which is what Stewart has made this fan—can resist it'). Of his new band (those aforementioned 'hacks' whose every note had allegedly already been bled dry), Marcus said, 'They couldn't push him, because they wouldn't understand the idea'. Pointing out that punks viewed him as 'the epitome of the corrupt star living off the gullibility of his audience, blowing his fans a kiss while his heart held only contempt', Marcus stated, 'He provided no reason to make one think the punks were wrong'.

PEOPLE LIKE NELSON, MARSH AND MARCUS might have felt a glimmer of hope in their hearts if they heard the news that, for his putative follow-up to *Blondes Have More Fun*, Stewart brought in Micky Waller to play drums.

There were evidently no hard feelings about the legal case Waller had brought against Stewart in 1978 for £6,000 worth of unpaid royalties from *Smiler*. (The claim was settled out of court.) 'They were good', says Waller of the Rod Stewart Band/Group compared to the unnamed Mercury ensemble. 'Different, but good'. Waller noticed an alteration in Stewart's modus operandi. 'For those sessions he did rehearse, and I remember thinking, "Rod's changed a lot—he's getting much more professional"'. Ultimately, Stewart scrapped the tracks he'd recorded with Waller (the two remained friends) and the album featured the drumming of Appice, Colin Allen and Roger Bethelmy. Perhaps dispensing with his tracks was a symptom of the professionalism to which Waller refers.

'Micky had gone off to law school or something and didn't have what it takes anymore, or we'd become more discerning', says Cregan. 'His kick drum was not quite in the pocket. Skills have improved a lot. People don't really like things to speed up and slow down very much. Writers and producers and record makers, we're not forgiving as we used to be'. Cregan is not unaware of the fact that this change may not be a good thing. 'It was always about the vibe as much as anything back in the day when there was no ProTools'. Some veteran Stewart fans might go further and suggest that, in finally dispensing with Waller, Stewart was closing the door on ever recapturing his old brilliance. No click track could have accommodated Waller's panoramic drum rolls on *Every Picture Tells a Story*.

Cregan isn't sure that trying out Waller was due to not wishing to use Appice anymore. 'It might have been we were just in England', he suggests. However, the Vanilla Fudge man would only be minimally represented on this and the next Stewart long player, and thereafter not at all. 'There was a kind of power struggle', claims Cregan. 'I think he thought he should have been the musical director or the band leader. He tried to push me out the door and was not successful and it backfired on him'.

Dowd produced one track on the new album before bailing. It would seem to have been his decision rather than Stewart's. Dowd explained to

John Tobler and Stuart Grundy, 'I have to feel that I can contribute or give some input to the people I'm working with, otherwise I'm not helping them. It's almost like you become a member of the family for a while, but I've never made a career out of an artist. . . . We got in a bind, to the point where all the song concepts were the same, or sounded the same, because we were using the same people'. Cregan: 'I loved Tom Dowd, I loved working with him, I learnt so much, but I think he'd come to the end of his particular run. He said he only expected to make a couple of records with each artist, that he would always want to move on'. He adds, 'I took over from Tom. Because I'd been a producer before I joined the band, I was always in the control room, checking on what was going on, so I took on the role of being co-producer when Tom was there. Rod said to me, "Do you think we could make the record without Tom?" I said, "Well, does he do anything that I don't know about? Do you have meetings with him where you discuss this and that?" He said, "No, not at all. I only see him when you see him, when we're in the studio". So I said, "Okay then, I'll do it with you'. Production of the LP—which would be released in November 1980 under the title *Foolish Behaviour*—was credited to Harry the Hook (i.e. Stewart, the *nom de guerre* being a reference to his proboscis) in collaboration with Andy Johns (here unusually credited as Jeremy Andrew Johns) and the Rod Stewart Group. The latter was now augmented by keyboardist Kenny Savigar. Almost all tracks are credited as written by Stewart/Chen/Savigar/Cregan/Grainger, a democratic split Cregan instituted, albeit for one album only, to cut down on arguments.

An explosive opening is attempted in the shape of 'Better Off Dead' (a track attributed to Stewart/Chen/Savigar/Appice). However, Stewart makes the mistake of thinking that plugging into rock's uptempo rockabilly roots is the same thing as generating excitement. At best, the track only achieves a state of toe-tapping cacophony.

In complete contrast, 'Passion' is classy and atmospheric. Across five and a half minutes, Stewart makes the vicissitudes of love seem like a political thriller, complete with a post-Watergate aura of paranoia. However, the fact of the sultry soundscape being intruded upon by the synthetic sound of synthesizer is a sign of horrors to come in future years.

On the album's title track, for the first time ever on a recording, Stewart is heard to use his own accent. As is usually the case for a British artist of his generation—a cohort that equated Americanisms with stylishness and Britishisms with almost the very opposite—it's used in a laddish, self-mocking way, which is just as well because it helps take the edge off a song that deals with grisly stuff: the narrator's homicidal fantasies about his wife ('I have a duty to take her life'). The narrator goes through the various methods of murder in detail before waking up and finding it was all a dream. 'So Soon We Change' sees Stewart and co having another crack at reggae. This time they get it right, with a nimble 'riddim', a mellow tune and a reflective lyric about the depredations wrought by time on life and friendship.

The side closes with the well-thought-of 'Oh God, I Wish I Was Home Tonight', a track cited by multiple people at this general point in time as proof that Stewart was still at least a little in touch with his Mercury-era muse. Although it's true that it boasts the quality of thoughtfulness so often lately lacking in Stewart's art and personal life—as well as those Pavlovian tones of fiddle and claims of poverty that were bound to make some old fans misty-eyed—it's in truth overrated, being monotonous, overlong and possessed of a cringe-makingly unsubtle rhythm track. That it fades out arbitrarily in the middle of a vocal line adds to the impression of it being more of a loop than a song. Moreover, Stewart's request to the lover from whom he's separated to keep her 'legs closed tight' is a reminder of precisely the kind of tone he didn't stoop to in the early 1970s.

Side two opens with 'Gi' Me Wings', a piece of uptempo synth-rock that tackles the subject of depression in a blandly anthemic manner. 'My Girl' (Stewart/Chen/Savigar/Cregan/Grainger/Appice) is a bright, poppy tribute to Stewart's young daughter, Kimberley, which is sweet enough but has a chorus uncomfortably similar to that of the Four Tops' song of the same name.

'She Won't Dance with Me' is a collaboration between Stewart and Jorge Ben, the composer of 'Taj Mahal', the song that provided melodic inspiration for 'Da Ya Think I'm Sexy?' Which leads one to wonder whether this song was Stewart's recompense in the absence of 'Sexy?'s unchanged writing credits. If so, Ben got more out of it than the listener. That Stewart is getting a bit old to be writing resentful songs about the anxieties of getting snubbed on the dance floor is brought home by the knowledge that these days he has the responsibilities of adulthood, his marriage to Alana Hamilton in 1979 having already produced two children.

The album closes on a poor note with 'Somebody Special' (a collaboration by the Stewart/Chen/Savigar/Cregan/Grainger axis together with Cregan's old boss Steve Harley) and 'Say It Ain't True'. Both are suffocating plastic pop of the type that would typify the 1980s, complete with light but metronomic drumming, sickly glistening keyboards, soporific backing harmonies and utterly un-majestic strings.

Foolish Behaviour marks the milestone of being the first album on which Stewart has had a hand in the composition of all songs. Another nominal sign of progress is the modernistic production and musical techniques. Both steps forward are illusory. Back in the 1970s, in filling half of his albums with covers, Stewart redefined the concept of a credible artist that the Beatles had apparently set in stone in around 1964. As for the contemporary stylings, new doesn't mean superior: popular music was about to enter a horrifying period wherein artists who should have known better swamped their work in methods that were modish but ruinous. Not that, here, there is all that much to ruin. There are flashes of skill, both lyrical and musical, but—the title track aside—no real displays of inspiration or insight.

'In the last few years, the superb singer and (sometimes) songwriter of *Every Picture Tells a Story, Gasoline Alley* et al. has been eclipsed by the schoolboy in disgrace', wrote Laura Fissinger of the album in *Trouser Press*. 'Stewart's balance between locker room and confessional has shifted insidiously toward the ambience of snapping towels. Whether his credibility has worn away is a rhetorical question; it has, and *Foolish Behaviour*'s plusses are moot points'. While she acknowledged that Stewart could still sing, she summarised, 'Keeping up with Rod and his pals no longer seems worthwhile. Stewart's a competent cartoon now, and not much of a laugh either'.

Fissinger's review summed up the feeling of many towards Stewart these days: having passed through anger and sadness at his artistic and spiritual decline, critics were generally now resigned to his loss as a musical heavyweight. This time, though, Stewart wasn't even pleasing his undiscriminating, Manilow-nexus fanbase. The chart positions superficially tell a tale of reasonable success. The 'Passion' single was a US number 5, albeit only a number 17 in the UK, where 'My Girl' additionally made number 32. *Foolish Behaviour* itself made number 12 in the US and number 4 in the UK. However, within weeks of the LP's release, the public were treated to the actually quite shocking sight of rows of Rod Stewart's latest adorned with the discount stickers that are the tell-tale sign of storemanager anxiety to offload.

Whether it be the critics or the public, though, Stewart was about to give those who'd written him off pause for thought.

.

11

THE FINAL ACCLAIM

THAT SUCH A FORMER FRIEND, FAN AND ALLY as Paul Nelson had a major hand in a denunciation like the Delilah Communications book may have had an effect on Stewart. Something certainly did. In March 1982, *Rolling Stone* printed an extraordinary *mea culpa* of an interview conducted by Robert Palmer that was headed 'Rod Stewart Says He's Sorry'.

'I deserved a lot of the knocking that I got', Stewart stated. 'I had it coming. I went through a period when I lost all contact with rock & roll. I was completely wound up in self-image . . . I can't stand to listen to "Da Ya Think I'm Sexy?" anymore; that knocking I got did me a lot of good. I realised I'd let a bit of credibility go right down the toilet, and I think I've finally returned to what I do best, to shoutin' rock & roll'.

Of course, the punk rockers who had been responsible for so much of the knocking he'd experienced were very much practitioners of 'shoutin' rock & roll'. Although Stewart opined that punks 'just haven't matured' and that 'you can't keep whining and moaning about the state of the bloody world for the rest of your life', he did finally have positive things to say about that movement's figureheads. 'The Sex Pistols were a bloody marvelous thing', he said. 'They were everything that period was supposed to be, and they broke up and didn't give a shit'. He also offered, 'I really like the Clash—"The Magnificent Seven" is wonderful, one of the best tracks of last year'.

The interview hadn't, of course, been arranged for the purpose of Stewart unburdening himself of his sins. He was promoting new product, specifically an album titled *Tonight I'm Yours*. 'I hope the album's as good as I think it is', he anxiously offered, 'cause I've taken so much of a bashing over the last three or four years'. Well, leaving aside the technicality that it was impossible for a third party to fully know precisely how good Stewart imagined the LP to be, *Tonight I'm Yours* was, upon its November 1981 release, greeted with more critical enthusiasm than any of his long-playing efforts in a decade. Not least of the good reviews was one by Paul Nelson, who was given the job of assessing it by *Rolling Stone*. Nelson spent the first paragraph bringing people up to speed on Stewart's career trajectory, an absolutely essential move because many current music consumers who were in their teens during the late 1970s had no knowledge of Stewart beyond a ridiculous butt-waggling apparition they had seen their parents watching on the TV.

Older consumers yet to hear the album would have been heartened by some of Nelson's comments, not least because they knew it would not be easy to please someone of the opinion that Stewart was less Jack the Lad than Jayne Mansfield. Nelson adjudged *Tonight I'm Yours* 'surprisingly fine', stating that 'the main reason for its excellence is precisely that Stewart has examined his recent history and decided to apologise for it'. It was probably more coincidence than design that the album's first words saw a narrator tell a third party that he could tell by the look in their eyes that they'd been bored for a long, long time and that he wanted to turn it all around. The lyric belonged to the album's title track, which was a 'Stay with Me'–style one-night-stand anthem. Nelson, though, chose to see meaning in it.

With this outing, the Rod Stewart Band/Group—synonymous with a large chunk of what we might term Stewart's era of disrepute—was gone, the sole exception being Jim Cregan (although Appice appears on a brace of tracks). 'There was a weird something happened, and I'm not quite sure what it was', says Cregan. 'I got offered a trip to cross the Atlantic in Mike Batt's yacht. We were at sea with no communication for thirteen or fourteen days. During this time, the American Music Awards came up and we had the opportunity to go and do it. We were on holiday. We'd finished a long tour, we had six weeks off, and this came up in the middle of it and it was going to take place in Hollywood. I think there was a bit of, "Oh, fuck 'em, have we really got to come back to do this?" and Rod was grumpy about that. I wasn't involved in any of this because nobody could get hold of me. So I got into Antigua in the Caribbean and there's a telephone call or telex or something: "Call the house — Rod wants to talk to you". He said, "Are you in or are you out?" I said, "I've no idea what you're talking about". He said, "Get your arse over here now because we're gonna do the American Music Awards". And that was it — Phil Chen and Gary were gone. To this day, I'm not sure what happened other than I think they might have pouted about coming back'. So could Stewart be ruthless when he felt it was needed? 'Yeah, I guess he can. . . . Every so often, Rod gets up in the morning and he thinks he's "Rod Stewart" and then you don't want to be around him'.

The main new additions are Robin Le Mesurier on guitar, Jimmy Zavala on harmonica and saxophone, Jay Davis on bass and Tony Brock on drums. Nelson thought this change 'a terrific idea' and asserted 'Rod Stewart's current crew . . . can really play'. He also approved of Stewart producing again (Cregan gets a co-producer credit). He said of Stewart, 'The feeling has returned. When the singer throws in a laugh or a whoop now (as in "Only a Boy"), it's no longer the cocky superstar's nasty snigger of the last several LPs but something genuine and touching'. Yet Nelson included some odd caveats and ended proceedings on a strangely ambivalent note, making his appraisal in retrospect seem as self-deluding as all those old positive reviews of Faces albums or the straining-to-say-something-nice write-ups of *Smiler* and *Atlantic Crossing*, not to mention a way-paver to a reassessment that many made of *Tonight I'm Yours* — and Stewart's career — after the initial rapture had worn off.

The album certainly gets out of the blocks with alacrity. 'Tonight I'm Yours (Don't Hurt Me)' (written by Stewart, Cregan and Savigar) positively hurtles along. It also confirms that Stewart has embraced new technology wholeheartedly, seamlessly integrating galloping synthesizers and sequencers into his music, which still retains a grit and gravitas beyond the likes of voguish plastic-pop merchants like Depeche Mode and Heaven 17. 'The drum machines were a whole big thing going on', says Cregan. 'Rod does keep his ear to the ground'.

'How Long' was written by Paul Carrack for Ace, the British band for whom he acted as vocalist. A classy midtempo demand to know the precise extent of a partner's infidelity, it was a UK top-20 single in 1974 and a US number 3 the following year. Stewart lunges for a greater passion than Carrack's understated but seething template and comes up short. Despite the trying-too-hard feeling, it's still a good listen, and an *a cappella* end section is an interesting touch.

Tora! Tora! Tora! was a 1970 motion picture about the Axis strike on Pearl Harbor. Stewart appropriates the Japanese codeword for 'lightning attack' for a song about, er, the joys of going out drinking with his mates and leaving a hail of destruction in his wake. The instrumentation is as one-dimensional and undeveloped as the mindset behind the lyric. No doubt Stewart would respond to such cavils with a line from the song, which itself is hardly Confucian in its philosophising: 'If you can't take a joke, then there ain't no point in living'.

In 1956, 'Tear It Up' by Johnny Burnette and the Rock 'n' Roll Trio (written by Johnny and Dorsey Burnette and David Burlinson) was one of the first iconic rock recordings. By covering it, Stewart seems self-consciously determined to assert his raw rock roots. Unfortunately, it feels slightly fraudulent: Stewart has always been more soul-, blues- and folk-oriented. Having said that, he and his band come up with a good rendition, broadening out what was an almost generic piece of rockabilly with adroit piano work and replacing that style's staccato rhythm with something more smooth-rolling.

'Only a Boy' (Stewart/Cregan/Savigar) closed side one with a song that seemed deliberately designed by Stewart to convince the lost fans that he could still, if he so chose, do for them what he'd once done so consistently. He carefully assembles several of the old ingredients from his Mercury days, including a rapscallion attitude, invocation of a working-class hinterland, a winning acknowledgement of his own ridiculousness and the strains of fiddle. The glossy sound of his current band and their slick harmonies makes the concoction noticeably distinct from the scruffy tones of yore, and the lyric's reference to his privileged recording artist career underlines the fact that we've come a long way since then, but it mostly achieves the desired effect. When in the opening seconds an artfully muffled Stewart imitates his old disapproving schoolteachers, it's absurdly moving, as is his later references to council houses, unemployment exchanges and packets of three, even if they're probably barely comprehensible to non-Britons.

One can't help noticing, though, that 'Only a Boy' is the first original on the album to communicate that the artist is a mature character, or even a grown man.

The opening track of side two plays host to another maneuver apparently designed to provoke Pavlovian responses in the old guard, this one in the form of Stewart's return for the first time since *Smiler* to Bob Dylan covers. However, with Paul Nelson no longer an ally or a fan (at least until the point where he heard the album), the days were over when Stewart could rely on him to recommend obscure byways of Dylan's oeuvre to tackle. In lieu of that, Stewart opts for a version of 'Just Like a Woman', a well-known Dylan song from his 1966 *Blonde on Blonde* album which had been a UK hit single for Manfred Mann and a minor US hit for Dylan himself. It's a song of a different stripe to the early, naturalistic Dylan creations Stewart had previously covered, with Dylan at the time of composition now well into his switch to more allusive and poetical songwords. Contradictorily, though, the pretty melody and conventional structure makes it one of the closest things to a pure pop number ever to emerge from Dylan's pen. Stewart turns the song into an example of what the world would come to term 'power ballad'. It's slightly laughable the way that he invests great passion—including a trademark 'Whoo!'—into songwords that he, just like the rest of us, doesn't quite understand. However, it broadly works, evoking a late-night, loved-up vibe.

'Jealous' (Stewart/Appice/Davis/Johnson) is another foray into disco, and one that sounds even more like 'Miss You' than did 'Da Ya Think I'm Sexy?', with Jimmy Zavala's harmonica resembling Sugar Blue's celebrated harp work on that Stones hit. It doesn't rely on resemblance to antecedents for its power, however, being pleasingly funky musically and utterly convincing lyric-wise in its sweaty unease at the prospect of losing a lover to a third party.

It's slightly depressing that such vibrant grooves give way to the smug, soporific tones of 'Sonny'. Everything about this slab of 1980s synth-pop is irritating, from the distractingly masculine name for the female object of worship to the compressed, echoing drums, to the antiseptic keyboards, to the fact that an outside party—Elton John's long-term lyricist Bernie Taupin—was drafted in to assist Stewart, Cregan and Savigar to perfect a song that never surpasses the status of banal.

It being the case that punks had consigned Stewart to old-fart status half a decade before, some might find it ironic that 'Young Turks'
(Stewart/Appice/Hitchings/Savigar) is an anthemic celebration of youth.
Nonetheless, it's both exciting (its tempo is positively breakneck) and
moving (when Stewart asserts that the couple around whom the song
revolves had to take their chance at happiness because life is brief and
'time is a thief', it brings a lump to the throat). Cregan rachets up the
emotion by peeling off an utterly simpatico guitar solo.

'Never Give Up on a Dream' is Stewart, Cregan and Taupin's tribute
to cancer victim Terrance Stanley Fox, who ran 3,339 miles on an artifi-
cial leg before the disease took his life. Although ostensibly poignant, the
song is so melodramatic and self-conscious that it puts a barrier between
the listener and his emotions. The emotiveness of the subject is further
undermined by the fact that Stewart assumes that his ostentatious compassion means that he can abandon the lyrical meticulousness that has
latterly, despite his other failings, become a strength of his writing: how,
for instance, can someone's heart 'burst like the sun'?

With regards to those odd notes of ambiguity in Paul Nelson's sometimes euphoric review of *Tonight I'm Yours* . . . On the possibility of the
first verse of the title track being interpretable as a promise that Stewart
will make good his recent artistic malaise: 'Easier said than done, but
Stewart tries. Oh, how he tries'. On the astute move of breaking up the
Rod Stewart Band/Group: 'As good as the new group is, however, it has
yet to develop much of a personality. The singer still has to supply that'.
On the Mercury-era band: 'You won't find that kind of willful instrumental primitivism on *Tonight I'm Yours*, and I, for one, miss it. But then, this
is the '80s, and you're not supposed to rock the boat'. On Stewart's compositional skills: 'Stewart seems to be struggling a bit as a lyricist (why
else include three cover versions?)'. Nelson's final paragraph, in fact, was
almost a crescendo of opacity and truth-avoidance: 'That's the comeback
record, make of it what you will', he said before wandering into a solilo-
quy about the very nature of rock, whose instantaneous, combustible and
life-affirming/life-threatening nature he compared to the fast-changing
qualities of first love: 'You don't know what to make of it. Hoping you're
not a total fool, you close your eyes, kiss the girl and she shows you the
door. But is it an entrance or an exit? Small wonder we're all scarred and
scared'.

A sense of spoke-too-soon attended the reaction to the album by another disillusioned ex-fan, Robert Christgau. He described *Tonight I'm Yours* as a 'comeback', yet ultimately felt that the record deserved only a B grade, which his Consumer Guide key almost wryly defines as 'an admirable effort that aficionados of the style or artist will probably find quite listenable'. (The four-rungs-higher A+ grade—with which he garlanded *Every Picture Tells a Story*—is 'an organically conceived masterpiece that repays prolonged listening with new excitement and insight. It is unlikely to be marred by more than one merely ordinary cut'.)

Tonight I'm Yours has several fine moments and much energy and heart but it soon becomes apparent that there is less to it than first meets the ear. The instrumentation undoes much of the good work. Here we have something far worse than the relentlessly smooth sounds of the Rod Stewart Band/Group: soundscapes that are cloying and unbending. Highly competent and fashionable though they might be, one can never love them. All of Stewart's original music—good or bad—would now be inflected with this plasticky timbre, one that is so anathema to fans of classic, warm, analog rock. There was also the fact that, for all his attempts to remain sonically in step with the times, Stewart was in other ways being embarrassingly left behind by them. When it comes to the title track, the listener's smile fades and his toe stops tapping when it becomes fully clear what the song is about. The narrator is telling a woman to grab her coat and tell her friends that she's spending the night with him but makes it clear that he's not looking for something everlasting. 'Stay with Me' articulated such thoughts with a certain impishness and did so at a point where the writers' ages made the sentiment slightly less undignified, but the venom with which a (married) man of thirty-six spits out the line 'I don't care if I see you again' is almost disturbing. When the track was released on single, its promotional film (or 'video' as the world was just learning to call such things) only emphasised the track's shortcomings, a crass parade of soft-porn imagery that revealed Stewart as a man embarrassingly tone-deaf to changing times.

For the record, the 'Tonight I'm Yours' single was a British top 10 and US number 20. The album also spawned two other hits, 'Young Turks' making number 11 in the UK and number 5 Stateside and 'How Long' grazing the UK top 40. The album itself was a UK top tenner and just missed the US top 10. That, though, wasn't the point. Stewart's career trajectory had already confirmed that he could rack up ever higher sales levels in almost inverse proportion to the dismay of people lamenting that his records weren't as good as they once were. For that minority of the planet who felt he'd lost his gifts, *Tonight I'm Yours*—after enthusiastic first impressions had faded—confirmed that they were never coming back, and that this was because the person who Rod Stewart had once been no longer existed.

The interviews Stewart granted to promote the album may have contained *mea culpas* for the 1974 to 1980 period, but what followed made one wonder whether the contrition was motivated less by embarrassment at his product and performances during that time than the fact that *Foolish Behaviour* had been the first Stewart album to hit the remainder racks. Witness the first track on *Body Wishes*, Stewart's 1983 follow-up to 'Tonight I'm Yours'. Written by Stewart and Robin Le Mesurier, the execrable 'Dancin' Alone' finds the thirty-eight-year-old Stewart obtaining spiritual satisfaction from dancefloor back flips and somersaults.

A Peter Pan complex is one thing, but bottomless self-regard is another. Stewart's interview with BBC's Radio One to promote *Body Wishes* was cringe-making. He at all times projected to DJ Janice Long an absurd narcissism crossed bizarrely with insecurity. When praising Elvis Costello as a great lyricist, he hastily appended, 'But I don't care, 'cos I'm a better singer than him'; when discussing writing about sexual inexperience, he felt compelled to point out that that sort of gaucheness was in the past—''cos I'm pretty cool'.

Tonight I'm Yours turned out to be even more of a false dawn than the Rolling Stones' *Some Girls*. Like that 1978 long-playing apologia, it was an implicit acknowledgement of recent underachievement whose promise of rehabilitation all too quickly turned to dust. Like the Stones, Stewart never made a great album again—with the difference that *Some Girls* continues to fizz whereas *Tonight I'm Yours* went flat when left out in the open air. The runes could now be read and they stated that *Tonight I'm Yours*—intermittently great, more often good-to-mediocre and sometimes plain awful—was the best Stewart could ever muster. In that sense, the story of what one might call the original Rod Stewart—the one that is the subject of this book—ends there.

MORE THAN THREE DECADES AFTER THEIR SPLIT, the esteem in which the Faces were once held is now receding into history, their evaporating (as opposed to declining) reputation the inevitable consequence of the fact that they left almost nothing truly top-drawer for posterity. Although those who saw them in the flesh testify that they were almost without peer, such hymns of praise are meaningless to young people who do not have a catalogue of recordings with which to corroborate them. Stewart's work of the same period, on the other hand, remains largely undimmed by time—unless you count the fact that a smaller number of people are inclined to investigate it because of the distaste his subsequent image (particularly that of the late 1970s) provokes in them.

'I look at it like all good footballers should—I want to retire at the top', Stewart told the *NME*'s James Johnson in June 1973. 'It doesn't tend to happen in this business and it's sad'. Of course, Stewart turned out to be no more immune to that syndrome than any other recording artist (Bobbie Gentry excepted). He soldiered on, leaving behind an aesthetic bar graph that—as with everyone else—peaked before his early thirties and then described a long decline.

Body Wishes was, incredibly, a small commercial renaissance for Stewart, bequeathing his first UK number 1 for five years in the shape of 'Baby Jane', which also reached number 14 in the States. Said hit had its qualities in its honest depiction of the sort of semi-spiteful, semi-fond feelings provoked by a dying relationship, but follow-up 'What Am I Gonna Do' was an utterly banal piece of synth-pop that still made a UK number 3 (no. 35 in the States).

Other albums naturally span off big hits. Meanwhile, *Unplugged . . . and Seated*, his 1993 entrée in MTV's Unplugged series, reminded people of his rootsy past and shifted millions in the process. However, diminishing inspiration was confirmed by the fact that, as Stewart entered the twenty-first century, it was purely as a covers artist. 'He didn't like the process, hadn't enjoyed it', says Cregan of Stewart's songwriting. Increasingly unable to compose, Stewart gave up on his muse ever returning, but Cregan says this caused him no torment. 'He said, "There's plenty of good songs out there for me to sing"'.

Remarkably, Stewart parlayed his drying up into a commercial tool by recording *It Had to Be You*, a collection of old-time pop standards.

The phenomenon of Stewart wrapping his tonsils around the creations of the likes of the Gershwins, Hoagy Carmichael, Cole Porter et al., turned out to be so much to the public's liking that the album's subtitle, *The Great American Songbook*, appeared on four further such collections. In line with his new unoriginal but lucrative career arc, there also came from Stewart covers albums of soul standards, rock classics and Christmas anthems, everything but a collection of self-written or partly self-written songs. He brought individuality to his output only via his distinctive rasp, which remained intact despite a brush with throat cancer.

This all changed at the beginning of the second decade of the twenty-first century. The way that Stewart wrote about it in his autobiography, Cregan reactivated his dormant interest in songwriting by practically forcing him into a composing session after unexpectedly bringing a guitar round. 'He thought that would read better than the actual truth', says Cregan. 'The reason I had a guitar in my car was because he said, "Bring a twelve-string". I normally wouldn't bother bringing a guitar over there, because a. there's a couple of guitars laying around in the first place and b. I go there for the social part of it and I'm not going to try and turn it into work. I also try very hard not to take advantage of our friendship and try and use it to further my career'.

Stewart may have been already primed to prod his dormant muse, but the upshot was that it was woken from its long slumber. Cregan: 'We sat in the living room and we knocked up a song called "Brighton Beach" and that was the start of it. He enjoyed writing that song'. What changed? 'He says it was writing the book. He realised that he could put a sentence together and that he quite enjoyed it'. Songs began flowing, with Stewart realising he now had an entire lifetime of experience to draw upon, much of it detailed in that aforementioned autobiography, *Rod*. The result was the 2013 album *Time*, a reminiscence-soaked collection with the artist's name featuring in almost all of the publishing credits. (The exception was a cover of a song by Tom Waits, who has in the latter part of Stewart's career replaced Dylan as his favourite artist to cover.) Apart from the single example of 'Brighton Beach', Cregan surprisingly wasn't his collaborator. 'I was in Britain and he was in LA', Cregan explains. 'And Kevin Savigar was right there on his doorstep. He's a fine writer, and he's a lot quicker than me'.

It was a strong album, albeit one that cynically took to the max Stewart's propensity to invoke his Mercury days with confessionals and lashings of fiddle without actually going back to the unkempt sound that he had long abandoned for something more technically accomplished but less soulful. Having said that, it displayed a self-knowledge that the Mercury-era Stewart lacked. He may have come across as humble, humane and wise on those first four or five solo albums, but we know—from both his own testimony and that of others—that that was dismayingly often not the case.

If *Time* hadn't happened, it probably wouldn't have mattered much to Stewart's ultimate standing. He has moved into a territory whereby he has been around so long and had such a presence in the culture that people simply accept him as he is and any misgivings about his perceived shortcomings as either a person or an artist are subsumed within the status of something even more elevated than superstar: national institution. It's understood and comfortably accepted that such people (also called 'heritage artists') did all their really worthwhile work decades ago. On top of that, the culture has now dispensed with concepts like guilty pleasures. People can be liked ironically and artists can be venerated simply because they are survivors. Certainly, nobody is going to any longer muster resentment or anger that Rod Stewart's music is no longer as good or his image as down-to-earth and likeable as they respectively were from 1969 to 1972, even if they are old enough to remember just how vital and admirable he was during that period. They also aren't going to be bothered by the fact that Stewart is the type of celebrity about whom fatuous West-End stage shows are written (Ben Elton's jukebox musical *Tonight's the Night*) and whose anti-conventionalism is so far in the past that he is prepared to dip the knee (he was knighted in 2016).

Now that the dust has settled and betrayed emotions cooled, it's clear that Stewart has no more to be ashamed of than any other musical luminary, and has more to be proud of than most. The highlights of Stewart's catalogue can stand scrutiny alongside those of the Beatles, the Rolling Stones, Bob Dylan, Jimi Hendrix or any other popular-music titan. Moreover, more than half a century after its release, *Every Picture Tells a Story* remains one of the greatest albums ever released by any artist.

With regards to Stewart the man, Cregan says, 'Ninety-nine per cent of the time, he's this lovely bloke who's interested in football and wine and going to the pub and going to the match and sitting around having dinner and laughing and joking. When you see Rod being interviewed, that's really what he's like. He's very funny, he's great company and as far as I'm concerned, he deserves all the success he's got. He's got a God-given gift of a voice which he uses brilliantly: timing, phrasing. He's a great singer, and he's a great bloke'.

Such an assessment is, of course, partial, and completely contradicts the testimony of others, such as Keith Altham. However, when it comes to his domestic arrangements, Stewart can be unequivocally said to have achieved maturity. In a 2015 *Uncut* interview, he apologised to all of womankind for the commitment-averse nastiness of tracks like 'Stay with Me'. He has been apparently faithful to Penny Lancaster since their marriage in 2007. (It would perhaps be politic to gloss over the fact that Lancaster was only born in 1971, i.e. the year that twenty-six-year-old Stewart made a commercial breakthrough not long after wondering whether he was too old to do so.) Cregan, who was best man at the pair's nuptials, says, 'Penny Lancaster is one of the loveliest human beings you could bump into. She's given him a bit of grounding'.

'Like it took him ages to become a bit mad from all his success, I think it's taken him a lifetime to recognise that he should have done things differently', says Dee Harrington about her ex-fiancé. 'He carries a lot of guilt about the kids, and never being there for them, because he did a lot of that. He's being himself again now. . . . There's something he said the other day which I was so pleased to hear. He said, "I'm on my last hits tour. I will never do this tour again. I will never play these big hits, because I don't want to be playing and singing 'Hot Legs' when I'm eighty". He has managed to see the reality of who he is'.

ACKNOWLEDGEMENTS

THE AUTHOR WOULD LIKE TO EXTEND HIS THANKS to the people listed below for granting interviews. Some interviews were conducted specifically for this book. Others were for a 2006 magazine feature on *Every Picture Tells a Story*, although much of the latter material is itself seeing print for the first time here.

Keith Altham	Dee Harrington
Ted Anderson	Ray Jackson
Mike Bobak	Kenney Jones
Michael Brewer	Ian McLagan
John Craig	Pete Sears
Jim Cregan	Jerry Shirley
Billy Gaff	Micky Waller

SELECTED BIBLIOGRAPHY

BOOKS

Bangs, Lester, and Paul Nelson. *Rod Stewart*. London: Sidgwick and Jackson, 1982.

Burton, Peter. *Rod Stewart: A Life on the Town*. London: New English Library, 1977.

Ewbank, Tim, and Stafford Hildred. *Rod Stewart: The New Biography*. London: Portrait, 2003.

Gambaccini, Paul (ed). *Critic's Choice: Top 200 Albums*. London: Omnibus Press, 1978.

Miller, Jim (ed). *The* Rolling Stone *Illustrated History of Rock & Roll*. Revised and updated. London: Pan Books, 1981.

Neill, Andy. *Had Me a Real Good Time: Faces, Before, During and After*. Updated edition. London: Omnibus Press, 2016.

Pidgeon, John. *Rod Stewart and the Changing Faces*. Electronic edition. London: Backpages Ltd, 2011.

Stewart, Rod. *Rod: The Autobiography*. London: Century, 2012.

Tremlett, George. *The Rod Stewart Story*. London: Futura, 1976.

WEBSITES

https://www.billboard.com

https://www.officialcharts.com

https://www.robertchristgau .com

https://www.rocksbackpages.com

https://www.rodstewartfanclub.com

https://secondhandsongs.com

INDEX

ALSO BY THE AUTHOR

In *The Clash: The Only Band That Mattered*, Sean Egan examines The Clash's career and art through the prism of the uniquely interesting and fractious UK politics of the Seventies and Eighties, without which they simply would not have existed. Tackling subjects such as The Clash's self-conscious tussles with their record label, the accusations of sell-out that dogged their footsteps, their rivalry with the similarly leaning but less purist Jam, the paradoxical quality of their achieving platinum success and even whether their denunciations of Thatcherism were proven wrong, Egan has come up with new insights into a much-discussed group.

New Waves, Old Hands, and Unknown Pleasures: The Music Of 1979 tells the varied, vibrant, and often unexamined story of popular music in the seismic last year of the Seventies. It reveals the stories behind key recordings, traces the trajectories of commercial and artistic successes, and explains the musical and socio-political context behind the sounds of the day.

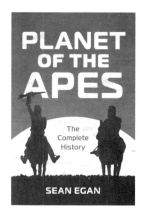

With the help of new and exclusive interviews, *Planet of the Apes: The Complete History* examines the contributions of producers, directors, writers, actors, and makeup artists in an attempt to gain an understanding of how a media property changed the world.